Contributions of the Committee on Desert and
Arid Zones Research
of the Southwestern and Rocky Mountain Division of the
American Association for the Advancement of Science

## Previous Symposia of the Series

1. *Climate and Man in the Southwest.* University of Arizona, Tucson, Arizona. Terah L. Smiley, editor. 1957
2. *Bioecology of the Arid and Semiarid Lands of the Southwest.* New Mexico Highlands University, Las Vegas, New Mexico. Lora M. Shields and J. Linton Gardner, editors. 1958
3. *Agricultural Problems in Arid and Semiarid Environments.* University of Wyoming, Laramie, Wyoming. Alan A. Bettle, editor. 1959
4. *Water Yield in Relation to Environment in the Southwestern United States.* Sul Ross College, Alpine, Texas. Barton H. Warnock and J. Linton Gardner, editors. 1960
5. *Ecology of Groundwater in the Southwestern United States.* Arizona State University, Tempe, Arizona. Joel E. Fletcher, editor. 1961
6. *Water Improvement.* American Association for the Advancement of Science, Denver, Colorado, J. A. Schufle and Joel E. Fletcher, editors. 1961
7. *Indian and Spanish-American Adjustments to Arid and Semiarid Environments.* Texas Technological College, Lubbock, Texas. Clark S. Knowlton, editor. 1964
8. *Native Plants and Animals as Resources in Arid Land of the Southwestern United States.* Arizona State College, Flagstaff, Arizona. Gordon L. Bender, editor. 1965
9. *Social Research in North American Moisture-Deficient Regions.* New Mexico State University, Las Cruces, New Mexico. John W. Bennett, editor. 1966
10. *Water Supplies for Arid Regions.* University of Arizona, Tucson, Arizona. J. Linton Gardner and Lloyd E. Myers, editors. 1967
11. *International Water Law Along the Mexican-American Border.* University of Texas at El Paso, Texas. Clark S. Knowlton, editor. 1968
12. *Future Environments of Arid Regions of the Southwest.* Colorado College, Colorado Springs, Colorado. Gordon L. Bender, editor. 1969
13. *Saline Water.* American Association for the Advancement of Science, New Mexico Highlands University, Las Vegas, New Mexico, Richard B. Mattox, editor. 1970
14. *Health Related Problems in Arid Lands.* Arizona State University, Tempe, Arizona, M. L. Riedesel, editor. 1971
15. *The High Plains: Problems in a Semiarid Environment.* Colorado State University, Fort Collins, Colorado. Donald D. MacPhail, editor. 1972
16. *Responses to the Dilemma: Environmental Quality vs. Economic Development.* Texas Tech University, Lubbock, Texas, William A. Dick-Peddie, editor. 1973
17. *The Reclamation of Disturbed Arid Lands.* American Association for the Advancement of Science, Denver, Colorado, Robert A. Wright, editor. 1978
18. *Energy Resource Recovery in Arid Lands.* Fort Lewis College, Durango, Colorado. K. D. Timmerhaus, editor. 1979
19. *Arid Land Plant Resources.* Texas Tech University, Lubbock, Texas. J. R. Goodin and D. Northington, editors. 1979

# Origin and Evolution
of Deserts

# The Committee on Desert and Arid Zones Research of the Southwestern and Rocky Mountain Division of the American Association for the Advancement of Science Statement of Purpose

The objective of the Committee on Desert and Arid Zones Research is to encourage the study of phenomena relating to and affected by human occupation of arid and semiarid regions, primarily within the areas represented by the Southwestern and Rocky Mountain Division of the A.A.A.S. This goal involves educational and research activities, both fundamental and applied, that may further understanding and efficient use of our arid lands.

COMMITTEE (1980 and 1981)

Chairman:
 Robert A. Wright, West Texas State University, Canyon
Secretary:
 John A. Ludwig, New Mexico State University, Las Cruces
 Gordon V. Johnson, University of New Mexico, Albuquerque
Members:
 Joseph R. Goodin, Texas Tech University, Lubbock
 David K. Northington, Texas Tech University, Lubbock
 James W. O'Leary, University of Arizona, Tucson
 Marvin L. Riedesel, University of New Mexico, Albuquerque
 Klaus D. Timmerhaus, University of Colorado, Boulder
 Stephen G. Wells, University of New Mexico, Albuquerque
 Bruce A. Buchanan, New Mexico State University, Las Cruces
 Donald R. Haragan, Texas Technical University, Lubbock
 Walter G. Whitford, New Mexico State University, Las Cruces

Mailing Address

Dr. M. Michelle Balcomb, Executive Officer
SWARM/AAAS
Colorado Mountain College
300 County Road 114
Glenwood Springs, CO 81601-9990

# Origin
# and Evolution
# of Deserts

Edited by
**Stephen G. Wells**
and
**Donald R. Haragan**

University of New Mexico Press
Albuquerque

Library of Congress Cataloging in Publication Data
Main entry under title:

Origin and evolution of deserts.

(Contributions of the Committee on Desert and Arid Zones Research of the Southwestern and Rocky Mountain Division of the American Association for the Advancement of Science)
 Papers presented at two symposia (1980 and 1981) dealing with the origin and evolution of deserts.
 Includes bibliographies.
 1. Deserts—Congresses.   I. Wells, Stephen G.
II. Haragan, Donald R.   III. Series.
GB611.074        1983        551.4        83-1340

ISBN 0-8263-0605-5
ISBN 0-8263-0582-2 (pbk.)

© 1983 by the University of New Mexico Press.
All rights reserved.
Manufactured in the United States of America.
Library of Congress Catalog Card Number 83-1340.
International Standard Book Number 0-8263-0605-5 (cloth)
                                    0-8263-0582-2 (paper)

First edition.

# Contents

Foreword
*Walter G. Whitford* .................................................. ix

## PART I: 1980 Symposium

Preface
*Stephen G. Wells* ................................................. 3

### Physiographic Settings and Geologic Evolution

1 Physiographic Overview of Our Arid Lands in the Western U.S.
*Charles B. Hunt* ................................................. 7

2 Some Land Management Problems in Our Western U.S. Arid Lands
*Charles B. Hunt* ................................................. 65

3 The Plate Tectonic Setting of Cordilleran Deserts
*Peter J. Coney* .................................................. 81

### Landscape Evolution

4 Effect of Caliche on Desert Processes
*Laurence H. Lattman* ........................................ 101

### Development of Vegetation and Climatic History

5 Paleobotanical History of the Western Deserts
*Daniel I. Axelrod* ............................................. 113

6 Development of Vegetation and Climate in the Southwestern United States
*Thomas R. Van Devender* and *W. Geoffrey Spaulding* ....... 131

# PART II: 1981 Symposium

Preface
*Donald R. Haragan* .............................................. 159

## Deserts and Desertification:
### Geological and Climatological Perspectives

7 A Geological Perspective of the Desert
  *Farouk El-Baz* .................................................. 163
8 Desertification: A Climatological Perspective
  *Derek Winstanley* ............................................... 185
9 Another Look at the Concept of Desertification
  *Michael M. Verstraete* .......................................... 213

# FOREWORD

## HISTORICAL PERSPECTIVES AND TODAY'S DESERTS

### Walter G. Whitford
New Mexico State University
Las Cruces, New Mexico

If we are to understand the present, we must develop an understanding of the past; if we do, then, understand the present, we are apt to make reasonable decisions for the future. This is true whether the topic be political, social, economic, or scientific. Today the human community living in, working, and utilizing the resources of arid and semiarid regions of the world operate in relative ignorance about the interrelationship of abiotic and biotic features of such regions. Recent attempts at synthesis have largely failed to provide a historical or evolutionary perspective to deserts (Goodall and Perry, 1979). Data in that volume on climatic features and effects are considered with little attempt to link past and present climates with a view toward identifying future trends in climate. In another recent review, Bull (1981) addresses soils, geology, and hydrology of deserts with some references to past climates, but little integration occurred between a historical perspective and the work on present-day landforms.

This volume contains papers presented at two recent symposia dealing with the origin and evolution of deserts: first in North America and then in North Africa. The historical perspectives offered in these essays should provide some important insights into desert processes. By utilizing the historical perspective, readers have an opportunity to consider the future of North American and North African arid regions (or other of the world's arid regions) and to suggest topics for research that can provide alternatives to potentially disastrous trends.

The inseparability of geological processes, climatic change, and changes in organisms that can survive or thrive in a region are reinforced by the essays in this book. Among the primary causes of aridity on the earth's continents are the building of mountains that intercept moisture-laden air moving from the oceans over the continental land masses. The mountains produce rain shadows and local orographic climatic differences. The tectonic origins of mountains thus contribute directly to the aridity that characterize large areas of the earth's surface. The historical drying of formerly moist regions due to plate tectonic results in natural selection of biota for characteristics that allowed exploitation of these "new," elevated, dry regions. Superimposed on this general trend are the climatic cycles induced by changing air-flow patterns and ice sheets at the higher latitudes. These "shorter-term" climatic fluctuations shaped the present-day arid regions. The changes in degree of aridity—alternating drier and wetter periods—provided the water and wind power that have engineered present-day landscapes: the dunes, mesas, desert pavements, canyons, buttes, and basins that characterize arid landscapes.

Given the dynamics of arid regions in the historical and geological past, can we avoid wondering where we now are in terms of climate and landscape formation? Are we in the midst of a gradual drying period and, if so, will our activities degrade or improve the arid landscapes for human use and habitation? Is desertification or degradation of lands at the edges of the severely dry deserts a process that would occur without human perturbation? Is that perturbation merely an acceleration of the inexorable change that would occur any way or is the reduction in productivity of marginal semiarid lands solely attributable to human activity? It should be obvious that these questions cannot be resolved within the pages of this volume, but the reader will be presented with evidence and argument for both points of view.

This volume addresses two general questions: (1) How did the North American desert landforms and vegetation originate? (2) How have deserts changed in the recent past and what are the influences of shifting climate and human perturbation on the present and future boundaries of the world's deserts? These are particularly important questions to be addressed at this time.

Arid and semiarid regions of the world are receiving increasing pressure from rapidly expanding human populations, in migration of peoples seeking to exploit mineral and other resources of these regions, or because people simply want to enjoy the more salubrious climate characteristic of many such areas when compared to normally colder and wetter regions. Human pressures on the arid and semiarid regions increase despite our relative ignorance about such regions. We think of arid regions as being limited for human use by lack of critical resources, especially water, but as is pointed out by Hunt in this volume, even the surficial geology is fragile to say nothing of the living components of such systems. Human-use patterns can markedly affect hydrology, change landforms, and result in degradation of the environment.

The papers in this volume provide the basis for a global view of processes shaping deserts both in the distant past and present, and implications from that historic material are made for the future. Taking Coney's description of the formation of the Cordilleran and subsequent development of rain-shadow deserts suggested, to me at least, the processes that formed the basin deserts of Oinghai and Kinjiang provinces in China (Walker, 1982). The overriding importance of physical climatic features such as wind in structuring landforms in deserts is forcefully brought home by El Baz using data not only from ground studies in North Africa but also from the NASA space probes to Mars.

The importance of geological processes in shaping present-day deserts is not limited to mesas, sand dunes, desert pavements, and so forth, but also affect the biota. Lattman describes the importance of landscape features and parent rock in caliche formation. The positioning of caliche has a marked effect on vegetation (Burk and Dick-Peddie, 1973), and therefore on many other kinds of organisms.

The paper by Axelrod combined with those by Coney, Lattman, and Hunt provide some important and interesting perspectives concerning arid regions of the world today. Some arid regions are relatively young geologically—for example, North American and South American deserts, and deserts of the Middle East and Asia—while others are apparently much older and have probably had an arid or semiarid climate for many millions of years—Australia and South Africa, for example. However, it is clear from the discussion by Axelrod that dry areas existed even during geological eras when present-day deserts were shallow seas. The scheme presented by Axelrod for the origin of present-day desert floras is probably as applicable to the other deserts in the world as to North American deserts; that is, desert species derived from tropical savanna, dry tropical forests, selerophyll woodland, and grassland from the late Cretaceous through the Pliocene. Here again the interaction of geological processes and global climate influenced the adaptations of desert floras providing the fascinating convergence in adaptations seen today in floras of the world's deserts. Axelrod's kaleidoscopic view of changing vegetation over millions of years is nicely complemented by that of Van Devender and Spaulding who view the shifts in climate and vegetation in the Quaternary which relate to present-day climates and vegetation. The paper by Winstanley, in which climatic trajectories of the recent past and immediate future are discussed, gains from the Quaternary geological and vegetation perspectives of Van Devender and Spaulding and El Baz.

The reader of this volume should look for and be struck by the impact of seemingly rather slight shifts of climate on the structures of arid and semiarid systems. Because so many desert organisms live so close to their tolerance limits and ability to exploit the minimal resources provided by desert environments, even slight changes in climate or resources can push many such species over the brink to local extinction. Indeed even Darwin (1859) commented that in absolute deserts the struggle for life is almost exclusively with the elements. However, Darwin did not anticipate the changes that could potentially be wrought by man and his technology. When climatic changes are exacerbated by human perturbation through harvesting of vegetation, increased animal or vehicular traffic, and diversion of such resources as water, the natural pattern of change is accelerated and in some cases compounded. The essay by Verstraete is an important contribution to the volume because it brings together various concerns researchers and policy makers need to consider when they use and interpret the concept *desertification*.

It is worth repeating that we cannot understand the present nor modify our actions to avoid mistakes in the future without a solid historical perspective. This volume provides both a historical and a future perspective.

## REFERENCES

Bull, W. B. 1981. "Soils, a Geology and hydrology of deserts," Evans, D. D., and J. L. Thames (eds.). *Water in Desert Ecosystems.* US/IBP Synthesis Series 11, Dowden, Hutchinson and Ross, Inc. Stroudsburg, NY.

Burk, J., and W. A. Dick-Peddie. 1973. "Comparative production of *Larrea divaricata* Cov. on three geomorphic surfaces in southern New Mexico," *Ecology* 54:1094–1102.

Darwin, C. R. 1859. *On the origin of species by means of natural selection.* J. Murray. London.

Goodall, D. W., and R. A. Perry (eds.). 1979. *Arid land ecosystems: structure functioning and management.* Vol. 1. Cambridge University Press, Cambridge, Great Britain.

Walker, A. S. 1982. "Deserts of China." *American Scientist* 70:366–376.

# Part I

## 1980 Symposium

# PREFACE

Stephen G. Wells

University of New Mexico
Albuquerque, New Mexico

Large portions of western North America share one common hydrologic condition, a paucity of water. Within these areas, mean annual precipitation is typically less than 250 mm, mean annual runoff is less than 25 mm, and general ground-water availability is sparse. Such areas are characterized by desert landscapes. Unraveling the origins and evolution of these desert landscapes began in the late 1800s with geologic expeditions of J. W. Powell and biologic investigations of C. H. Merriam, both of whom worked in the Grand Canyon area. At that time little was known about the history or antiquity of geologic, biologic, and climatic processes and features of the North American deserts. Approximately 100 years later, scientists have demonstrated that these desert landscapes are a complex composite of large-scale geologic processes, such as plate tectonics, and long-term climatic alteration to arid conditions, both of which have occurred over millions of years. Few publications, though, emphasize the time and sequence of the processes or emphasize the interdependence of these processes in creating desert landscapes. Consequently, the Committee on Desert and Arid Zones Research of the Southwestern and Rocky Mountain Division of the American Association for the Advancement of Science sponsored a symposium in Las Vegas, Nevada, April 9 to 12, 1980. That symposium focused on the history and interdependence of geologic, biologic, and climatic components of today's North American deserts.

The title of the volume, "Origin and Evolution of Deserts," is not intended to imply an exhaustive review of this topic for North America, but rather it is intended to illustrate the long-term evolution of selected regional features and processes. These desert features and processes are summarized in the three sections of this part of the volume. Section 1 provides an overview of the regional geologic setting and its evolution through geologic time (that is, over millions of years); section 2 includes studies concerning the development of landscapes over the geologic framework; and section 3 includes research related to the long-term development of vegetation and climate which affected the landscape evolution. It is hoped that these six essays will provide a clearer understanding of the time required for the creation of the desert landscapes and will demonstrate that desert landscapes are the product of the interaction of long-term, complex, geologic processes and a widespread change in climatic conditions toward aridity, which culminated during the past 10,000 years in North America.

# Physiographic Settings and Geological Evolution

# 1

# PHYSIOGRAPHIC OVERVIEW OF OUR ARID LANDS IN THE WESTERN U.S.

Charles B. Hunt

University of Utah
Salt Lake City, Utah

## INTRODUCTION

Powell's (1879) report on the lands of the arid region of the U.S. covered the lands west of the 100th meridian, which approximately coincides with the 20 inches (508 mm) rainfall line. Others before him had referred to these western areas as "The Great American Desert." In this quantitative age it might be fashionable to define the terms *arid lands* and *deserts* with a number of coefficients that balance such factors as precipitation, evaporation, transpiration, and, from personal experience, I add perspiration. But even if an exact definition could be agreed upon, the facts of life outdoors are such that it would have to be applied in a general way. We might as well be general and use the terms to refer to lands that are barren or sparsely vegetated because water is scarce.

Lustig (1974) uses a three-fold classification: semiarid, arid, and extremely arid, the latter being characterized as having experienced twelve months or more of no precipitation. I use those terms but define them loosely as averaging 10 to 20 inches (254 to 508 mm), 5 to 10 inches (127 to 254 mm), and less than 5 inches (127 mm) annual precipitation (Fig. 1.1). Even this simplified terminology can not be used consistently. For example, surfaces of some alluvial fans in the Great Basin of the western U.S. and some shale deserts on the Colorado Plateau are in fact extremely arid because runoff is excessive, even where annual precipitation averages several inches. No flowering plants grow in these areas. Conversely, other tracts of ground receive more than their share of water because of runoff from neighboring tracts.

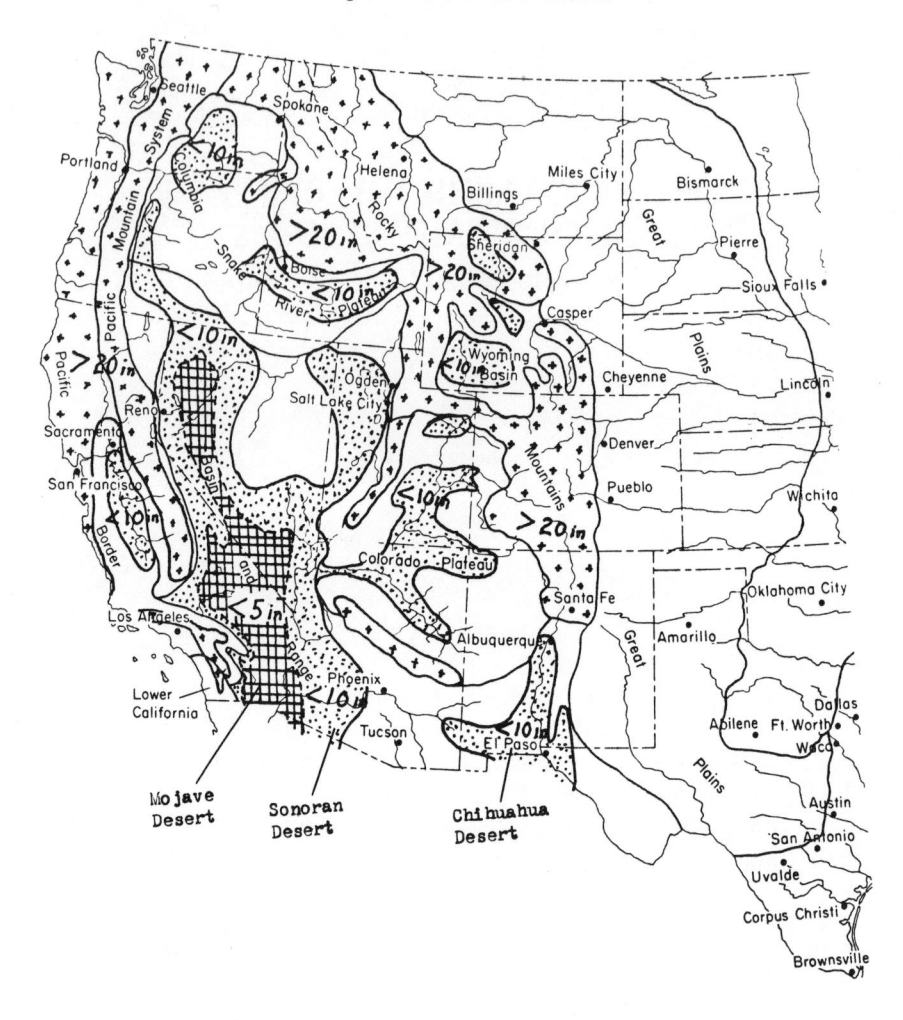

Figure 1.1. Our arid lands, like those on other continents, center in the Horse Latitudes, but our arid lands extend northward because of rain shadows cast by mountains and high plateaus. A northward extension of the Mojave Desert lies east of the Sierra Nevada. The Colorado Plateau desert is a northward extension of the Sonoran Desert and lies east of Utah's High Plateaus (see Fig. 1.4). A northward extension of the Chihuahua Desert forms the semiarid Great Plains which are east of and in the rain shadow of the Rocky Mountains. The westernmost deserts are characterized by maximum precipitation during the winter. The central deserts have biseasonal (winter and summer) precipitation. The eastern deserts receive their precipitation mostly during the summer, that is, the growing season.

Other climatic processes of arid lands include strong wind and dry electric storms. Eolian features include sand dunes, ventifacts, frosted windshields, and overturned trailers. A highway sign reads "Warning: strong cross winds. Trailer house gulch." Dry electric storms cause forest or brush fires. These are a particularly serious problem on the high mountains even where the average annual precipitation approximates 20 inches (508 mm).

In speaking about the southwestern U.S. deserts, we must include mountains and plateaus receiving more than 20 inches (508 mm) annual precipitation for two reasons. The main reason is that such highlands are source areas of the major rivers that traverse the deserts. And, secondly, they create rain shadows that localize and accentuate the deserts. Four major rain shadows occur: immediately east of the Sierra Nevada and Cascade Range, which extends almost to the border with Canada; on the Colorado Plateau leeward of the High Plateaus of central Utah; in the Wyoming Basin east of the Middle Rocky Mountains; and on the Great Plains, extending eastward from the Colorado Rockies.

These deserts occur in physiographic provinces that basically are structural members of the continental crust. Each province has its unique geologic history, related of course to its neighbors, yet distinct from them. Each has its own climate, hydrology, ecology, and other environments. It is a big country, but as will be brought out in Chapter 2, it is becoming crowded.

## STRUCTURAL MEMBERS—PHYSIOGRAPHIC PROVINCES

Figure 1.2 shows the physiographic subdivisions of the southwestern U.S. that fit into larger units of the continental structure. North America, like the other continents, is a slab of comparatively light crustal rock floating on a denser substrate referred to as the mantle. Each continental slab, including North America, is composed of three major geologic parts: a shield, a surrounding stable platform, and mobile belts marginal to this platform. The shield portion of North America is called the Canadian Shield, a mass of very ancient rocks including the oldest known on the continent. Surrounding this is a broad stable platform of similar rocks approximately 30 miles (48 km) thick, covered by a few thousand feet of Paleozoic and Mesozoic sedimentary rocks. These formations are mostly flat-lying but are warped into broad, more or less circular upwarps and basins. These gentle structures are interrupted by the uplifts at the Colorado Rockies but reappear to the west and southwest in the Colorado Plateau, which also is part of the stable platform (Fig. 1.2B).

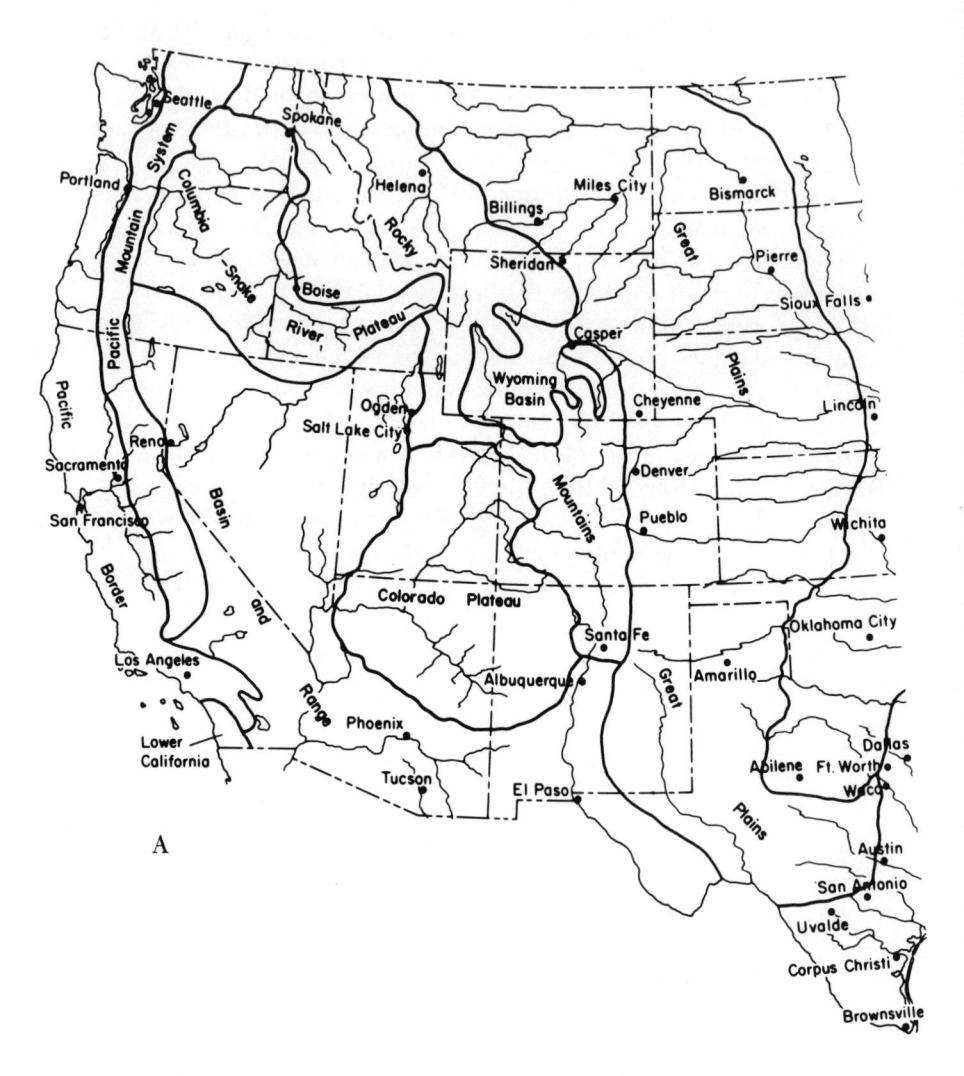

Figure 1.2. Physiographic provinces (A) and their landforms (B) in the arid regions (compare Fig. 1.1); Hunt 1974.[1]

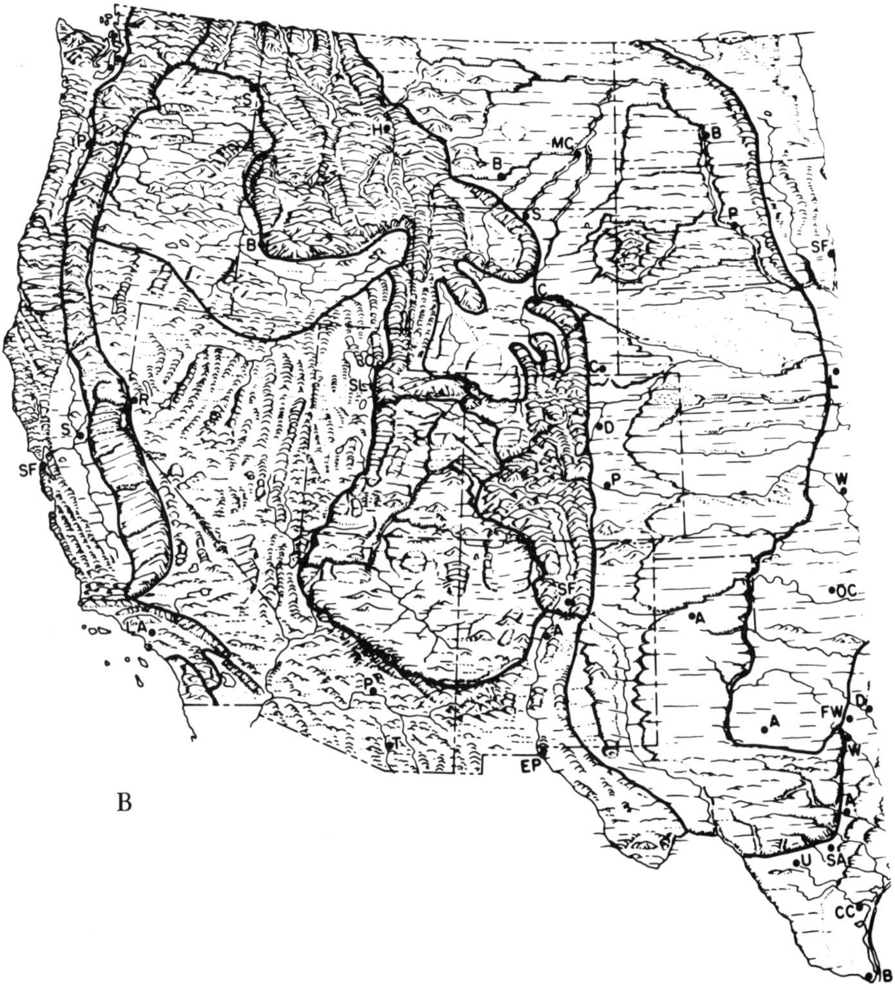


B

Along the west edge of the Colorado Plateau, the stable platform plunges downward into a belt that was mobile during the late Precambrian, Paleozoic, and Mesozoic (Fig. 1.3). In this mobile belt developed great troughs, geosynclines, trending approximately north, and in them were deposited immense thicknesses of marine sediments. The important contrast between the stable platform and the geosynclinal mobile belt is well illustrated by the differences between the formations and structures at Grand Canyon and those just 75 miles (121 km) west at Death Valley, California. At Grand Canyon the Paleozoic formations aggregate 4,000 feet (1,219 m) thick and are only slightly deformed (Fig. 1.4). In the geosynclinal belt to the west the late Precambrian, Paleozoic, and early Mesozoic formation aggregate almost 100,000 feet (30,480 m) thick and are severely folded and faulted. The difference in the accumulated sediments amounts to a 10 percent slope westward of the ancient Precambrian floor that forms the stable platform and basement under the geosynclines.

## COLORADO PLATEAU—CENTERPIECE OF THE SOUTHWEST[5]

The Colorado Plateau (Fig. 1.5, 1.6), covering about 130,000 square miles (336,700 km$^2$) between the Rocky Mountains and Great Basin, is by far the most colorful part of the U.S. This area is not just desert, it is Painted Desert with brightly colored canyons, high plateaus, volcanic mountains, sand deserts, shale deserts, and grotesque badlands, plus alcoves, arches, and natural bridges. Only a small part of the Plateau experiences less than 10 inches (254 mm) annual precipitation (Fig. 1.1); yet, parts of the shale deserts must be classified as extremely arid because the ground is nearly impermeable adobe, and virtually all precipitation quickly runs off. By comparison the sand deserts, including those with active dunes, are verdant pastures because the loose sand overlies old weathered sand that perches moisture seeping through the active sand layers. In wet years sunflowers may grow 6 feet (2 m) tall on the hot dry sand.

Two dozen or so parks and monuments illustrate why the Colorado Plateau is our centerpiece. In addition there are national recreational areas along the Colorado River at Lake Powell, in the heart of the canyon country, and at Lake Mead at the foot of Grand Canyon. Two national monuments of historic interest are El Morro (Inscription Rock), New Mexico, and Pipe Springs, Arizona. The Navajo and Hopi Indian Reservations are of considerable interest as well.

Outstanding physiographic features of the Colorado Plateau are its:
- Structural geology, which consists of extensive areas of nearly hori-

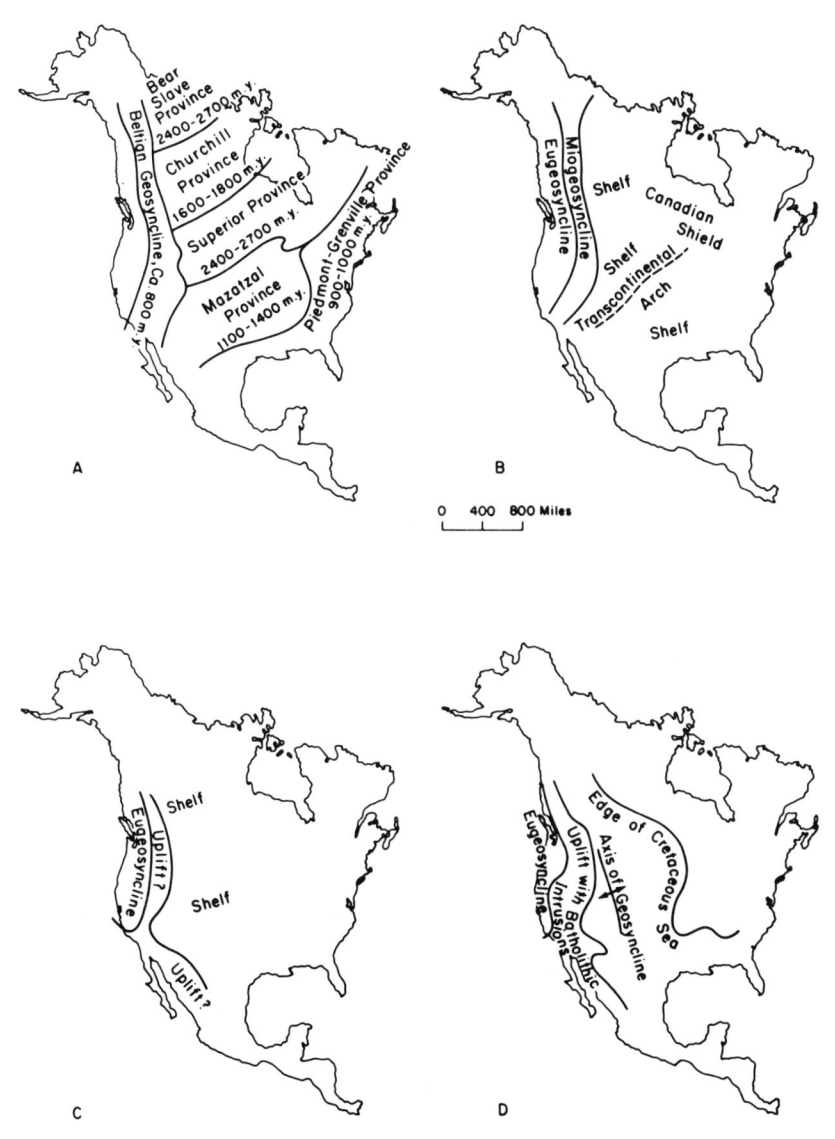

Figure 1.3. Structural setting and evolution of western United States during the late Precambrian (A), Paleozoic (B), early Mesozoic (C), and Cretaceous (D). The stable platform was a shelf intermittently flooded by shallow marine seas. The mobile belt along the west edge of the shelf was site of geosynclines, the western parts of which collected marine muds and volcanic-derived sediments (eugeosynclines); whereas, the eastern parts collected marine carbonate and related deposits (miogeosynclines). The pre-Cretaceous geosynclines are each offset westward from earlier ones; Hunt 1974.[1]

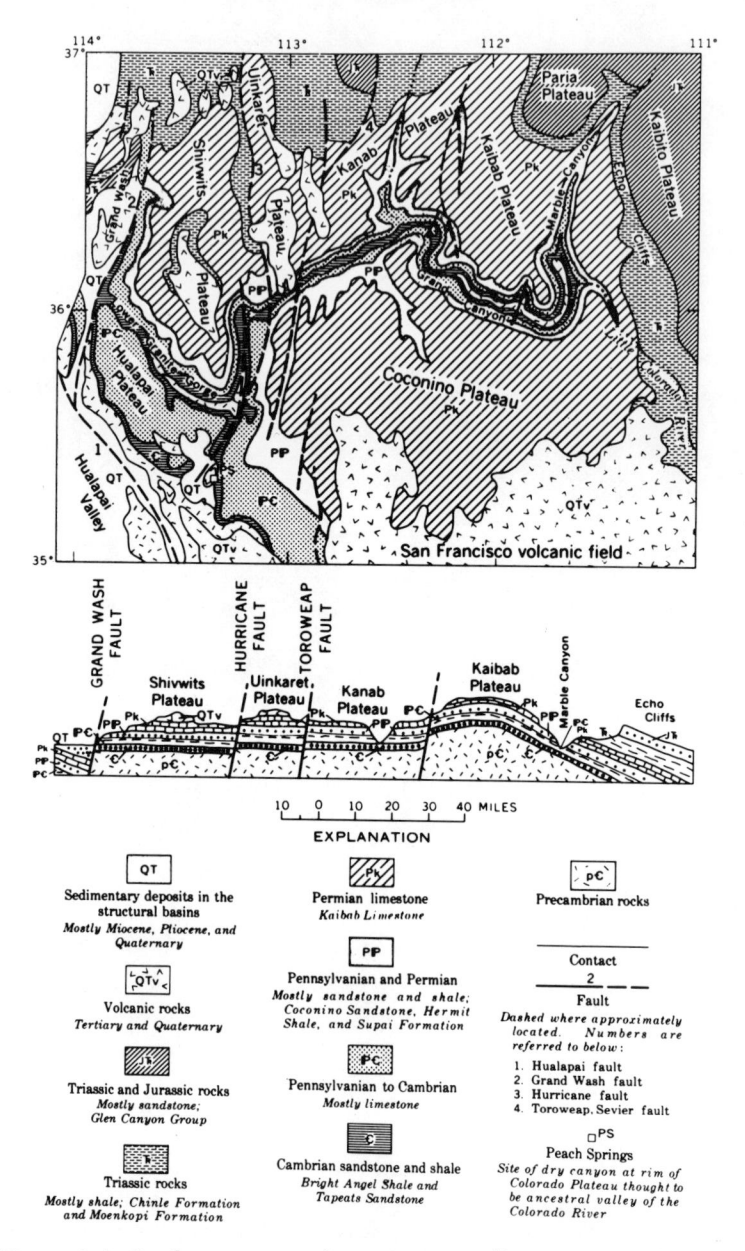

Figure 1.4. Geologic map and cross section illustrating geologic structure at Grand Canyon which is at the west edge of the stable platform; Hunt 1969b.[2] The Basin and Range province is downfaulted from the Plateau along the Grand Wash fault. To the west is the mobile belt where the rocks are geosynclinal in origin and about twenty times thicker than at Grand Canyon.

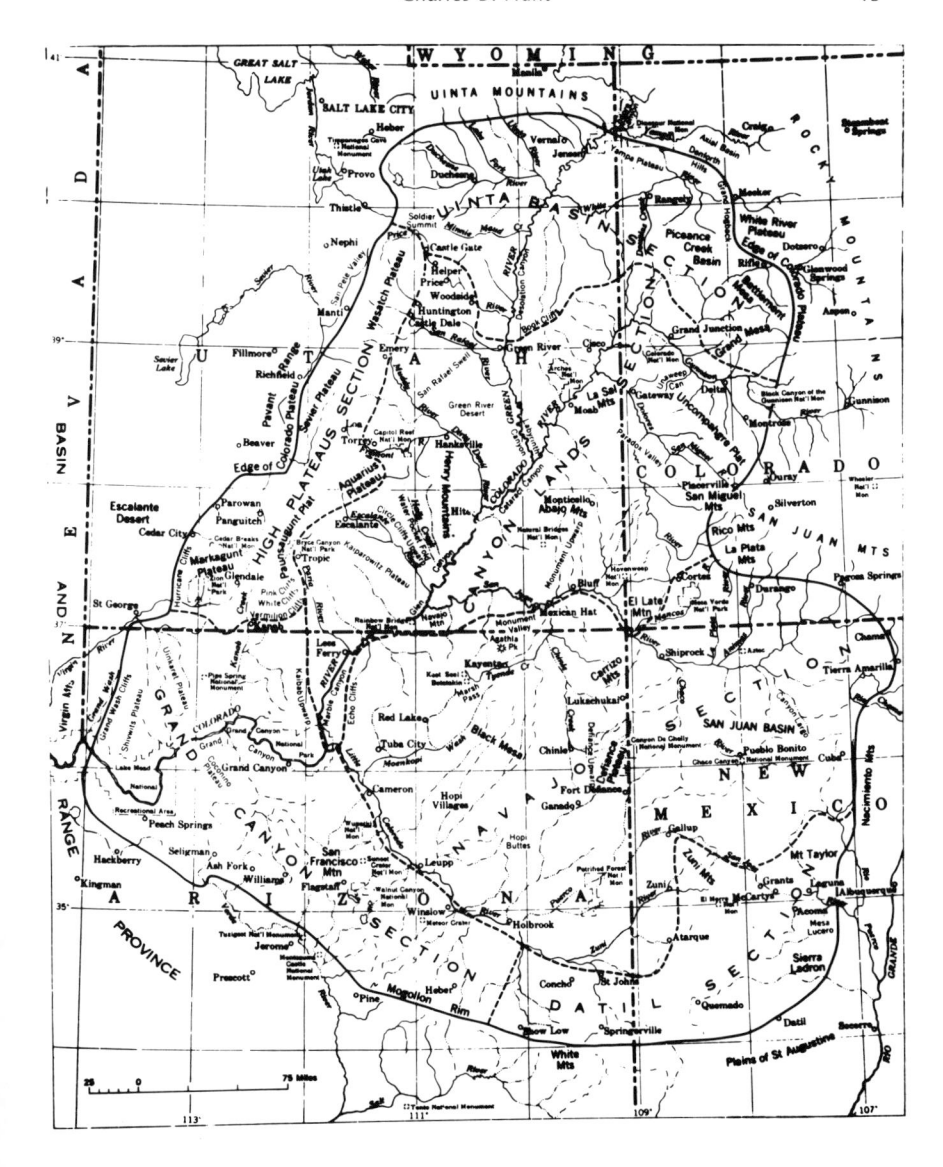

Figure 1.5. Index map of the Colorado Plateau; Hunt 1972. Lake Powell, on the Colorado River, extends down Glen Canyon to the Utah–Arizona state line; Canyonlands National Park includes the canyons upstream. Topographically, the Plateau is saucer-like with altitudes averaging about 5,000 ft (1,524 m) in the Navajo and Canyon Lands sections. The Datil, Grand Canyon, and Uinta Basin sections average around 7,000 ft (2,134 m) altitude. The High Plateaus are as high as 10,000 ft (3,048 m).

16      *Origin and Evolution of Deserts*

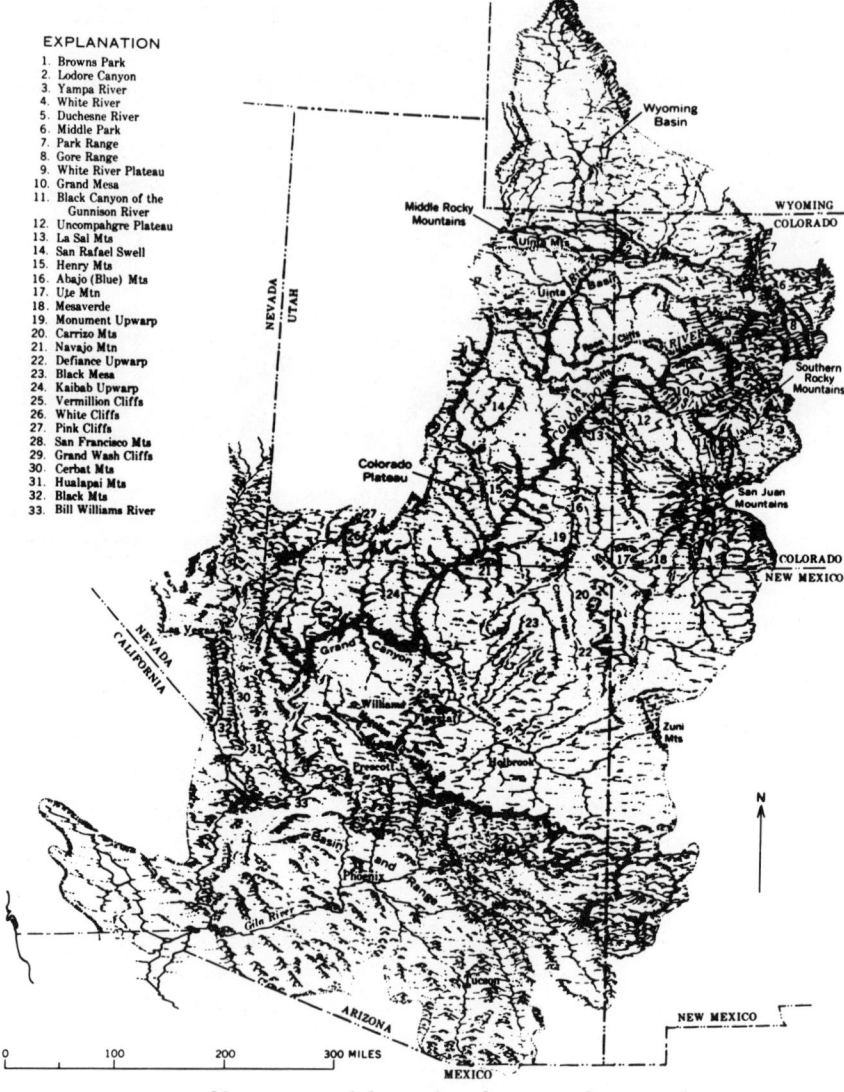

EXPLANATION
1. Browns Park
2. Lodore Canyon
3. Yampa River
4. White River
5. Duchesne River
6. Middle Park
7. Park Range
8. Gore Range
9. White River Plateau
10. Grand Mesa
11. Black Canyon of the Gunnison River
12. Uncompahgre Plateau
13. La Sal Mts
14. San Rafael Swell
15. Henry Mts
16. Abajo (Blue) Mts
17. Ute Mtn
18. Mesaverde
19. Monument Upwarp
20. Carrizo Mts
21. Navajo Mtn
22. Defiance Upwarp
23. Black Mesa
24. Kaibab Upwarp
25. Vermillion Cliffs
26. White Cliffs
27. Pink Cliffs
28. San Francisco Mts
29. Grand Wash Cliffs
30. Cerbat Mts
31. Hualapai Mts
32. Black Mts
33. Bill Williams River

Figure 1.6. Landform map of the Colorado River drainage basin; Hunt 1969b.[2] The Colorado Plateau is mostly in this drainage basin; the southeast corner drains to the Rio Grande, and the western edge drains to the Great Basin. Landforms on the Plateau are those characteristic of generally horizontal sedimentary rock, such as plateaus and mesas with cuestas and hogbacks interrupted by isolated mountains. Landforms in the Basin and Range part of the drainage basin are those characteristic of faulted basins and ranges. The Rocky Mountains, including those around the Wyoming Basin, are structural uplifts.

zontal sedimentary formations (Fig. 1.4); structural upwarps that form striking topographic features (Fig. 1.6); igneous structures which include some large central-type volcanoes (Fig. 1.7), numerous cinder cones and volcanic necks, high lava-capped plateaus and mesas, and dome mountains (Fig. 1.8) caused by intrusion of stocks and laccoliths (Fig. 1.9); and the whole plateau uplifted as much as 3 miles (5 km) since the Cretaceous;
- Great altitude, reflecting recency of the uplift. The general plateau surface is higher than 5,000 feet (1,524 m), and some plateaus and peaks are as high as 11,000 feet (3,353 m);
- The Colorado River which is deeply incised in steep-walled canyons (Fig. 1.6), most of which have brilliantly colored walls;
- Aridity with resulting water shortage, extensive areas of bare rocks, sparse vegetation, and sparse population;
- Brilliantly colored and highly varied desert scenery.

The Colorado Plateau comprises that part of the continent's stable platform lying west and southwest of the Colorado Rockies. Its western edge coincides with the ancient flexure where the platform ended and the basement rocks plunge downward under the late Precambrian, Paleozoic, and early Mesozoic geosynclines from which the Great Basin evolved. The Plateau marks the western edge of the Late Cretaceous trough (geosyncline) whose axis was along the site of the Colorado Rockies. The western shore of the Late Cretaceous sea was at or near the western edge of what now is the Plateau (Fig. 1.3).

The major break in the continental structure represented by the boundary between the stable platform and mobile geosynclinal belt of the Great Basin to the west is not difficult to see. Grand Canyon, for example, exposes the entire section, only 4,000 feet (1,219 m) thick, of Cambrian to Permian epicontinental marine formations that were deposited on the platform while it was submerged (Fig. 1.4). To a considerable degree, the thickness of this section is typical of the platform all the way eastward to the Appalachians. Yet, westward of the Plateau, in the Great Basin, these formations are considerably thicker (so are the late Precambrian and the early Mesozoic formations).

The Colorado Plateau has the general structure of a stack of saucers, tilted towards the northeast (Fig. 1.10). The Plateau adjoins the Rocky Mountains along the low northeastern part of the structure. As a consequence of the saucer structure, younger rocks (Tertiary) crop out on the north and east sides of the Plateau and older rocks (Paleozoic and Precambrian) crop out along the southwestern rim overlooking the much lower Basin and Range province in southwestern Arizona.

Although the major structural elements defining the Colorado Plateau are inherited from Cretaceous and older continental structures, the Pla-

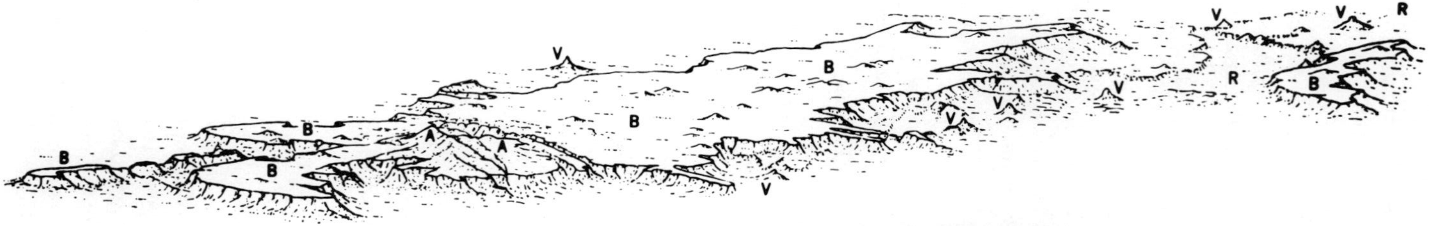

A, Mount Taylor; B, basalt-capped mesas; V, volcanic necks; R, valley of Rio Puerco

Width of view about 70 miles

After Hunt, 1938

Figure 1.7. Diagrammatic view of the Mount Taylor volcanic field, New Mexico. Mount Taylor (A) is a large, central-type volcano built of rhyolitic tuffs and latitic and andesitic lavas. It is geologically similar to the San Francisco Mountain in the Grand Canyon area. The lava caps and cinder cones on the mesas (B) are basaltic. These features are younger than the Mount Taylor cone and apparently spread on pediments eroded around the base of the larger cone (A). Since the basaltic eruptions, erosion has lowered this southeast edge of the Colorado Plateau by 1,500 to 2,000 ft (457 to 610 m).

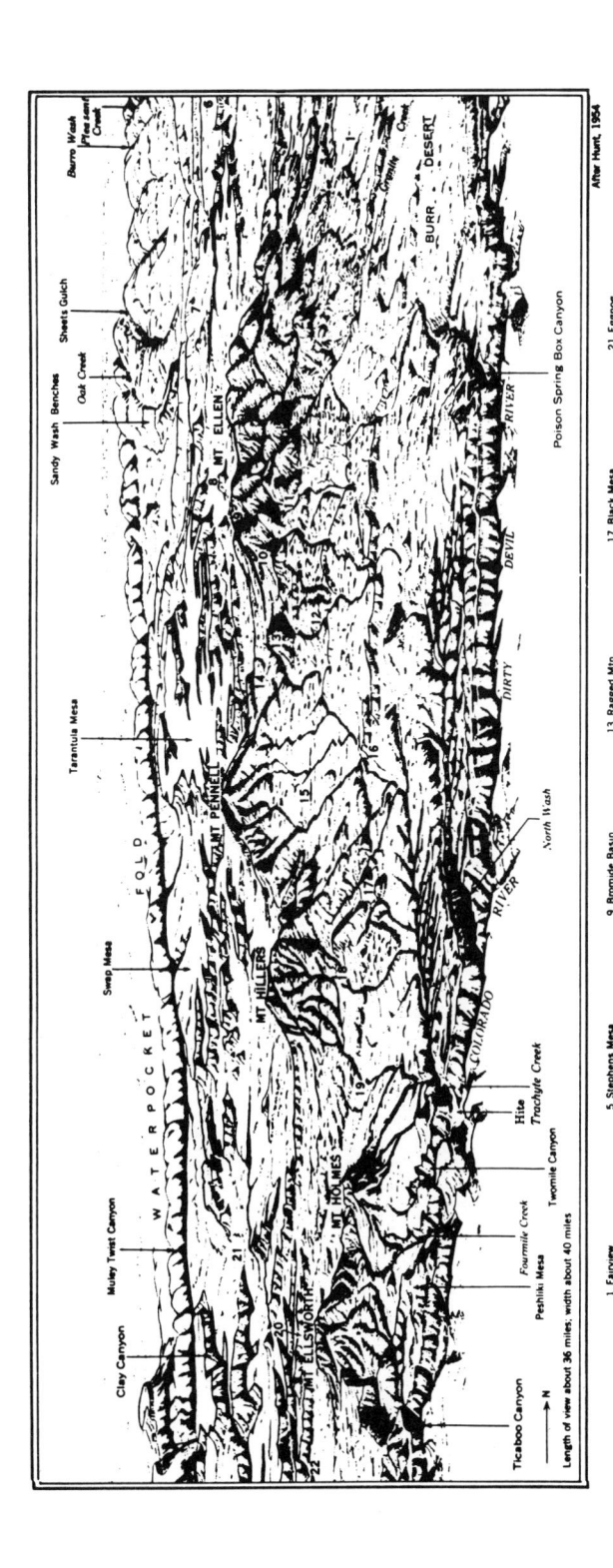

Figure 1.8. Diagrammatic view of the Henry Mountains region, Utah, a view that is typical of the Canyon Lands section of the Colorado Plateau. The mountains are structural domes produced by the intrusion of stocks and laccoliths. The intrusions occurred during the Miocene and at that time this was a Cretaceous-shale landscape. The canyons incised into the Jurassic and older rocks are no older than late Pliocene, as is indicated by rimrock gravels derived from basaltic lavas on the High Plateaus. The Waterpocket Fold is the steep east flank of the Circle Cliffs upwarp.[3]

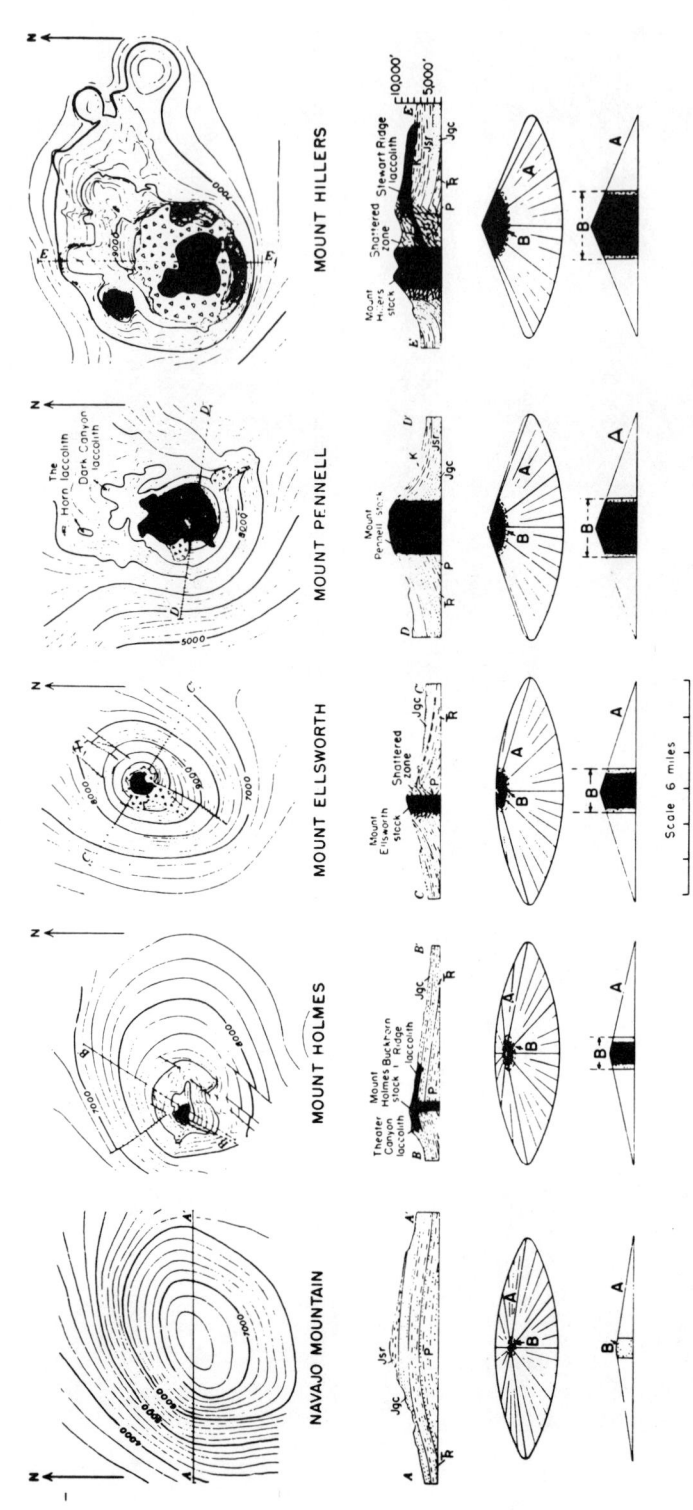

Figure 1.9. Diagrams illustrating relationships between the stocks and domes at the laccolithic mountains on the Colorado Plateau. The basal areas of these domes are about the same, but the heights of the domes are different and are proportional to the volumes of the stocks at their centers. The space occupied by the domes would be closed if the domes were flattened. Aeromagnetic surveys confirm the geologic interpretation that the stocks are steep-sided, roughly cylindrical intrusions. The laccoliths are tongue-shaped satellites of the stocks and form anticlinal ridges radiating from the stocks.[3]

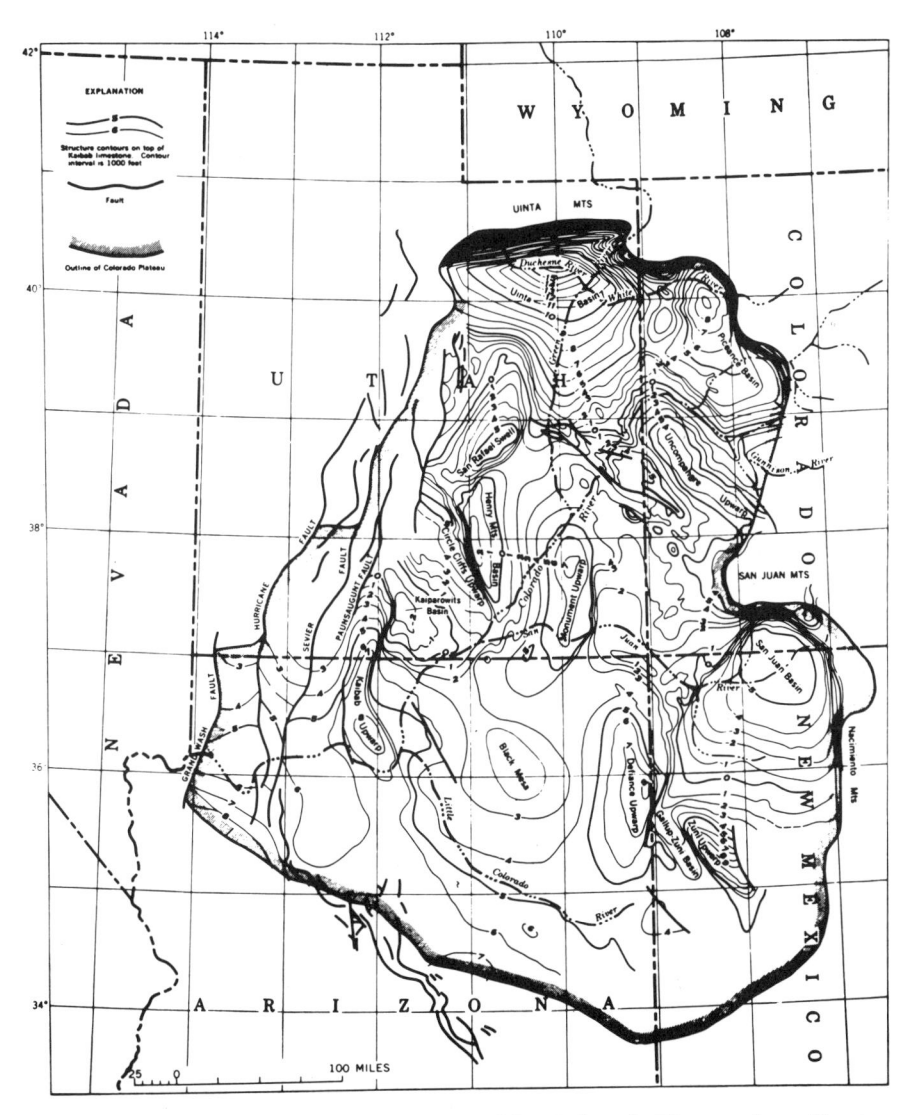

Figure 1.10. Structure contour map of the Colorado Plateau; from Hunt 1969b.[2] The Plateau is part of the continent's stable platform and has the structure analogous to that of a series of stacked saucers tilted northeastward. The structural height of the Plateau is 4 mi (6 km) higher at its southwest rim than it is at the north. The Colorado River has eroded its course against that regional dip since latest Miocene time.

teau itself as a topographic feature is the product of Cenozoic earth movements and igneous activity. The Plateau and the Colorado Rockies are the structurally high part of a tremendous Cenozoic arch—a geanticline that extended from central United States westward nearly to the Pacific Coast. The Great Basin, a block-faulted area, is the collapsed western flank of the arch. The Colorado Plateau is a segment of the eastern flank that still is attached to the Rocky Mountain geanticline.

## THE GREAT BASIN[6]

The Great Basin, lying west of the Colorado Plateau, is not ". . . as the title might suggest, a single cupshaped depression gathering its waters at a common center, but a broad area of varied surface, naturally divided into a number of independent drainage districts" (Gilbert 1890, p. 5). The Great Basin is a section of the Basin and Range province (Fig. 1.11), first referred to as "Basin Ranges" by Powell but renamed and redefined Basin and Range province by Fenneman (1928).

The average elevations of the Mojave Desert and Salton Trough are much lower than the Great Basin as defined by Fenneman (1928); the mountains are of smaller size and of lower relief. The desert basins of these areas are more extensive than those of the Great Basin. Also, they are hotter and drier than the Great Basin and have very different vegetation. Physiographically, the southern sections differ from the Great Basin, but structurally they are more closely related to it than to the parts of the Basin and Range province in Arizona east of the Colorado River. The late Precambrian and Paleozoic rocks include geosynclinal deposits like those in the southern part of the Great Basin; whereas, east of the Colorado River the formations are thin and related to those on the stable platform.

Southern reaches of the Colorado River receive no tributaries from the western Great Basin (Fig. 1.12), because the drainage is thoroughly disintegrated by late Cenozoic deformation. East of the Colorado River, tributaries are well developed with through-flowing streams like the Bill Williams and Gila rivers. The physiographic contrast assuredly is due to differences in structural deformation, but why do the earthquake epicenters (Fig. 1.13), clustered on the California side of the River, end so abruptly on the Arizona side? And why did the Colorado River choose that straight, narrow southerly course? The course is along a late Cenozoic estuary of the Gulf of California, but why the estuary?

The topography of the Great Basin consists typically of linear, north-south mountains separated by broad desert valleys. Many of them are closed basins. Altitudes range from below sea level at Death Valley to

more than 13,000 feet (3,692 m) at White Mountains Boundary Peak, but relief between valleys and adjoining mountains generally is less than 5,000 feet (1,524 m). Subdivisions of the Great Basin are (Fig. 1.14):
- Central area of elevated basins and ranges
- Bonneville basin east of the Central area
- Lahontan basin west of the Central area
- Lava and Lake area at the northwest corner of the section
- Southern area.

The Central area is characterized by valleys that are mostly 5,000 feet (1,524 m) altitude. Some are closed but none contains perennial lakes. Dry lake beds (playas) and alluvial flats make up about 10 percent of the Central area. The remainder is about equally divided between mountains and gravel fans sloping from them. A large part of the Central area drains west to the Lahontan basin by way of the Humboldt River.

Altitudes in the Bonneville basin east of the Central area average lower; most of the basins there are below 5,000 feet (1,524 m). Great Salt Lake, in the lowest basin, is about 4,200 feet (1,280 m) in altitude. Lakes, playas, and alluvial flats comprise about 40 percent of this subsection; mountains constitute about 25 percent, and the gravel fans cover the remainder. These proportions are very different from those in the Central area and undoubtedly record important differences in their structural histories.

The Bonneville basin also differs from the Central area in its lack of transverse drainage like the Humboldt River. The Bonneville basin includes three lakes: Great Salt, Utah, and Sevier lakes (Fig. 1.14). The latter is dry most of the time because the water is consumed for irrigation. A small area at the northeast corner of the Bonneville basin drains to the Snake River.

The Lahontan basin, between the Central area and the Sierra Nevada, resembles the Bonneville basin. The greater part is playa and alluvial flat. It too contains lakes, such as Pyramid, Winnemucca, and Walker lakes (Fig. 1.14). Carson Sink is a huge playa at the mouth of the Humboldt River (Fig. 1.14).

The Lava and Lake area northwest of the Lahontan basin is topographically higher, mostly a block-faulted lava plateau with numerous volcanic cones and irregular depressions. Because of the lava flows and cones, the topographic grain has less linearity than the other parts of the Great Basin. Part of the Lava and Lake area, including Goose Lake on the Oregon–California boundary (Fig. 1.11), drains outward via Pit River, a tributary of the Sacramento River.

Topography in the Southern area resembles that in the Central area, but the altitude averages very much lower. Towards the southern part of this area, the ranges are aligned north but are separated from those of the Central area by a northwest-trending belt of mountains and hills

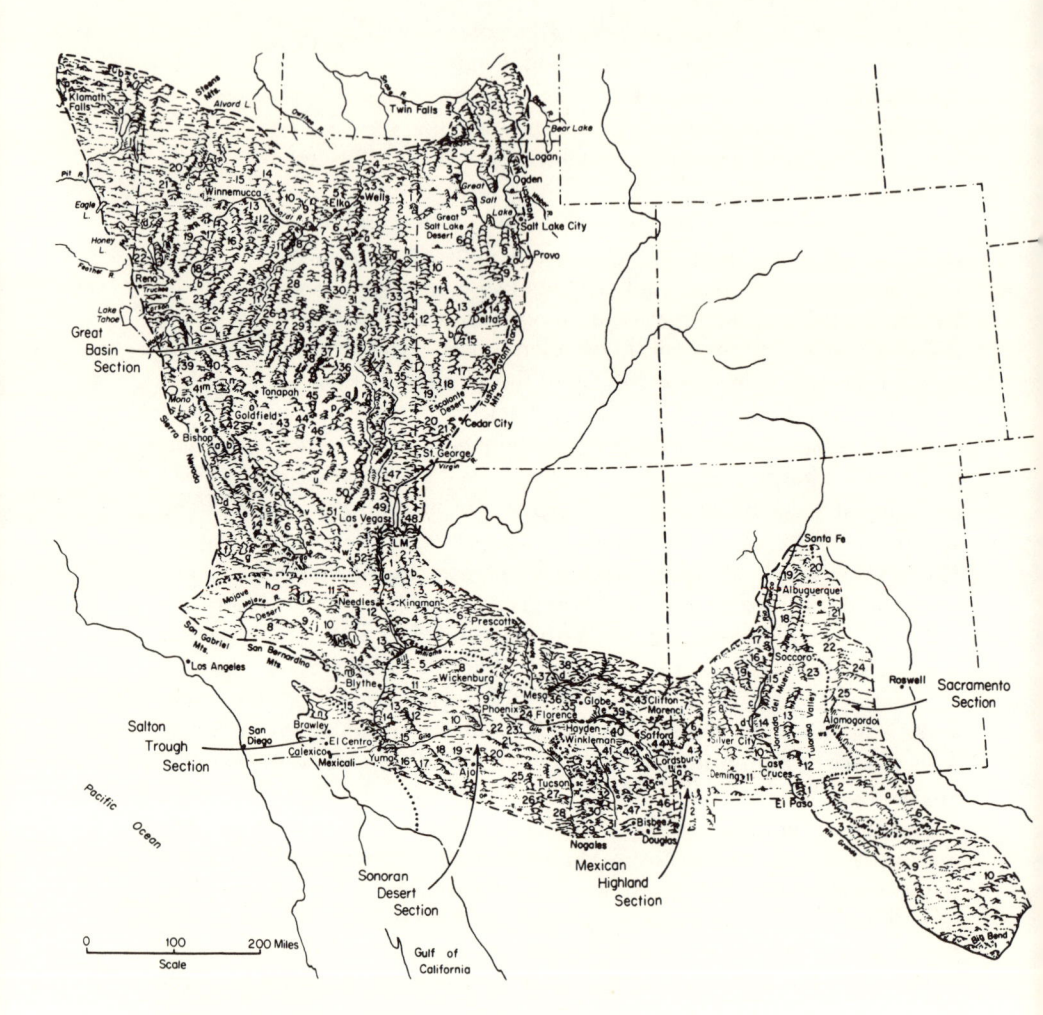

Figure 1.11. Physiographic map of the Basin and Range province; from Hunt 1974.[1]

**KEY TO MOUNTAINS**

*Idaho*
1. Portneuf Range
2. Bannock Range
3. Deep Creek Mts.
4. Sublett Range
5. Cotterell Range

*Utah*
1. Promontory Mts.
2. Raft River Mts.
3. Hogup Mts.
4. Newfoundland Mts.
5. Lakeside Mts.
6. Cedar Mts.
7. Stansbury Mts.
8. Oquirrh Mts.
9. Tintic Mts.
10. Deep Creek Range
11. Fish Springs Range
12. Confusion Range
13. House Range
14. Canyon Mts.
15. Cricket Mts.
16. Mineral Mts.
17. San Francisco Mts.
18. Wah Wah Mts.
19. Needle Range
20. Bull Valley Mts.
21. Pine Valley Mts.

*Nevada*
1. Pilot Range
2. Toana Range
3. Pequop Mts.
4. Blanchard Mtn.
5. Independence Mts.
6. Ruby Mts.
7. Sulphur Springs Range
8. Cortez Mts.
9. Tuscarora Mts.
10. Shoshone Mesa
11. Shoshone Range
12. Battle Mt.
13. Sonoma Range
14. Osgood Range
15. Santa Rosa Range
16. East Humboldt Range
17. Humboldt Range
18. West Humboldt Range
19. Trinity Range
20. Calico Mts.
21. Granite Range
22. Virginia Mts.
23. Stillwater Range
24. Clan Alpine Mts.
25. Desatoya Mts.
26. Toiyabe Range
27. Toquima Range
28. Simpson Park Mts.
29. Monito Range
30. Diamond Mts.
31. White Pine Range
32. Egan Range
33. Schell Creek Range
34. Snake Range
35. Wilson Creek Range
36. Grant Range
37. Pancake Range
38. Hot Creek Range
39. Wassuk Range
40. Gillis Range
41. Excelsior Mts.
42. Silver Peak Range
43. Cactus Range
44. Kawick Range
45. Reveille Range
46. Belted Range
47. Mormon Mts.
48. Virgin Mts.
49. Muddy Mts.
50. Sheep Range
51. Spring Mts.
52. McCollough Range

*California*
1. Warner Range
2. White Mts.
3. Inyo Mts.
4. Panamint Range
5. Funeral Mts.
6. Black Mts.
7. Avawatz Mts.
8. Ord Mts.
9. Bullion Mts.
10. Bristol Mts.
11. Providence Mts.
12. Chemehuevi Mts.
13. Whipple Mts.
14. Turtle Mts.
15. Chocolate Mts.

*Arizona*
1. Black Mts.
2. Cerbat Mts.
3. Hualpai Mts.
4. Chemehuevi Mts.
5. Harcuvar Mts.
6. Santa Maria Mts.
7. Bradshaw Mts.
8. Harquahala Mts.
9. White Tank Mts.
10. Gila Bend Mts.
11. SH Mts.
12. Kofa Mts.
13. Dome Rock Mts.
14. Trigo Mts.
15. Castle Dome Mts.
16. Gila Mts.
17. Cabeza Prieta Mts.
18. Mohawk Mts.
19. Grover Mts.
20. Sanceda Mts.
21. Sand Tank Mts.
22. Maricopa Mts.
23. Sierra Estrella
24. Salt River Mts.
25. Comobabi Mts.
26. Baboquivari Mts.
27. Sierrita Mts.
28. Tumacacori Mts.
29. Patagonia Mts.
30. Santa Rita Mts.
31. Huachuca Mts.
32. Whetstone Mts.
33. Rincon Mts.
34. Santa Catalina Mts.
35. Pinal Mts.
36. Superstition Mts.
37. Mazatal Mts.
38. Sierra Ancha
39. Gila Mts.
40. Santa Teresa Mts.
41. Galiuro Mts.
42. Pinaleno Mts.
43. Natanes Mts.
44. Peloncillo Mts.
45. Dos Cabezas Mts.
46. Chiricahua Mts.
47. Mule Mts.

*New Mexico*
1. Peloncillo Mts.
2. Animas Mts.
3. Big Hatchet Mts.
4. Big Burro Mts.
5. Summit Mts.
6. Pinos Altos Range
7. Mogollon Mts.
8. Black Range (Mimbres Mts.)
9. San Mateo Mts.
10. Sierra de las Uvas
11. Florida Mts.
12. Organ Mts.
13. San Andres Mts.
14. Caballo Mts.
15. Fra Cristobal Mts.
16. Magdalena Mts.
17. Sierra Ladron
18. Manzano Mts.
19. Sandia Mts.
20. Ortiz Mts.
21. Pedernal Hills
22. Gallinas Peak
23. Sierra Oscura
24. Capitan Mts.
25. Sacramento Mts.

*Texas*
1. Franklin Mts.
2. Hueco Mts.
3. Quitman Mts.
4. Sierra Diablo
5. Guadalupe Mts.
6. Delaware Mts.
7. Apache Mts.
8. Davis Mts.
9. Sierra Vieja
10. Glass Mts.

**KEY TO LAKES AND PLAYAS**

*Utah*
a. Utah L.
b. Sevier L.

*Nevada*
a. Franklin L.
b. Carson Sink
c. Black Rock Desert
d. Smoke Creek Desert
e. Pyramid L.
f. Winnemucca L.
g. Goshute Valley
h. Antelope Valley
i. Cave Valley
j. Railroad Valley
k. Gabbs Valley
l. Walker L.
m. Teels Marsh
n. Columbus Marsh
o. Clayton Valley
p. Penoyer Valley
q. Garden Valley
r. Coal Valley
s. Desert Valley
t. Dry Lake Valley
u. Indian Spring Valley
v. Pahrump Valley
w. Ivanpah Valley
x. Lake Mead

*Oregon*
a. Klamath Lakes
b. Summer L.
c. Abert L.
d. Goose L.

*California*
a. Deep Springs Valley
b. Eureka Valley
c. Saline Valley
d. Owens L.
e. Panamint Valley
f. China L.
g. Searles L.
h. Coyote L.
i. Soda L.
j. Bristol L.
k. Cadiz L.
l. Danby L.
m. Palen Dry L.
n. Salton Sea

*Arizona*
a. Lake Mohave
b. Red L.
c. Havasu L. (Parker Dam. Res.)
d. Theo. Roosevelt L.
e. San Carlos Res.
f. Wilcox Playa (Sulphur Springs Valley)

*New Mexico*
a. Alkali Flat
b. Plains of San Augustin
c. Elephant Butte Res.
d. Caballo Res.
e. Estancia Basin

*Texas*
a. Salt Basin

**KEY TO NATIONAL PARKS AND MONUMENTS**

LC, Lehman Cave Nat. Mon., Nev.
Death Valley Nat. Mon., Death Valley, Calif.
JT, Joshua Tree Nat. Mon., Calif.
LM, Lake Mead Recreational Area, Ariz.-Nev.
SC, Saguaro Cactus Nat. Mon., Ariz.
OP, Organpipe Cactus Nat. Mon., Ariz.
CH, Chiricahua Nat. Mon., Ariz.
WS, White Sands Nat. Mon., N. Mex.
Big Bend Nat. Park, Big Bend, Texas

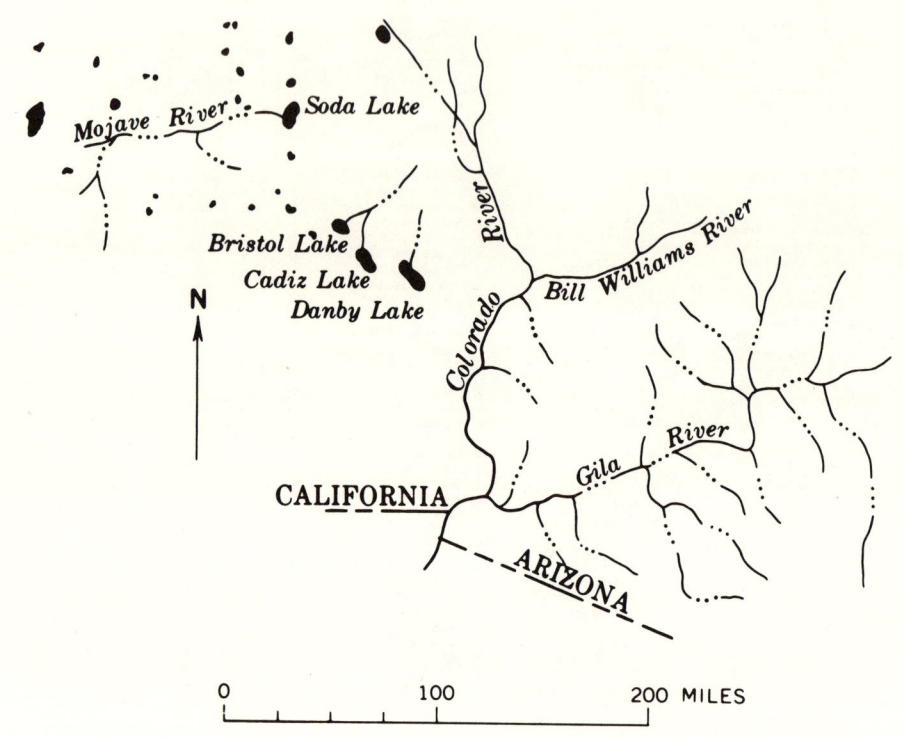

Figure 1.12. Contrast in drainage east and west of the Colorado River where it flows south between Arizona and California. On the east is an integrated system of tributaries. On the west, the tributaries have been interrupted by late Tertiary and Quaternary earth movements, and the western drainage that formerly was tributary to the Colorado River is now ponded in a series of playas; from Hunt 1969b.[2]

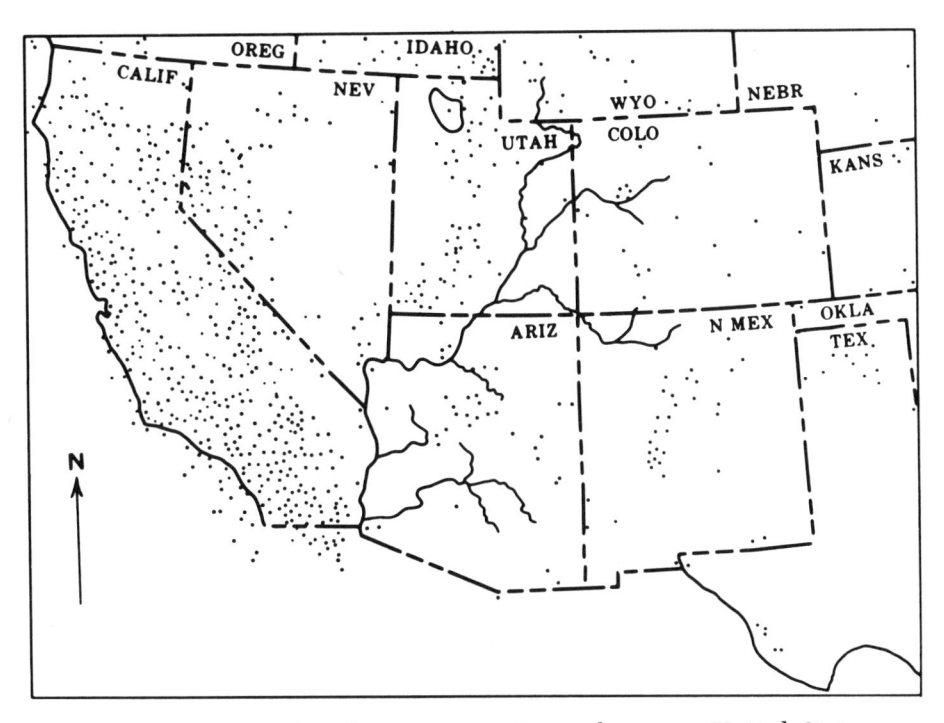

Figure 1.13. Earthquake epicenters in southwestern United States; from Childs and Beebe 1963. The southerly course of the Colorado River between Arizona and California separates a structurally stable area on the east, that has dendritic drainage, from a structurally unstable area on the west that has interrupted drainage. Structural instability of the area west of the River is also indicated by Holocene fault scarps and measurable earth tilt as well as by the numerous earthquake epicenters.

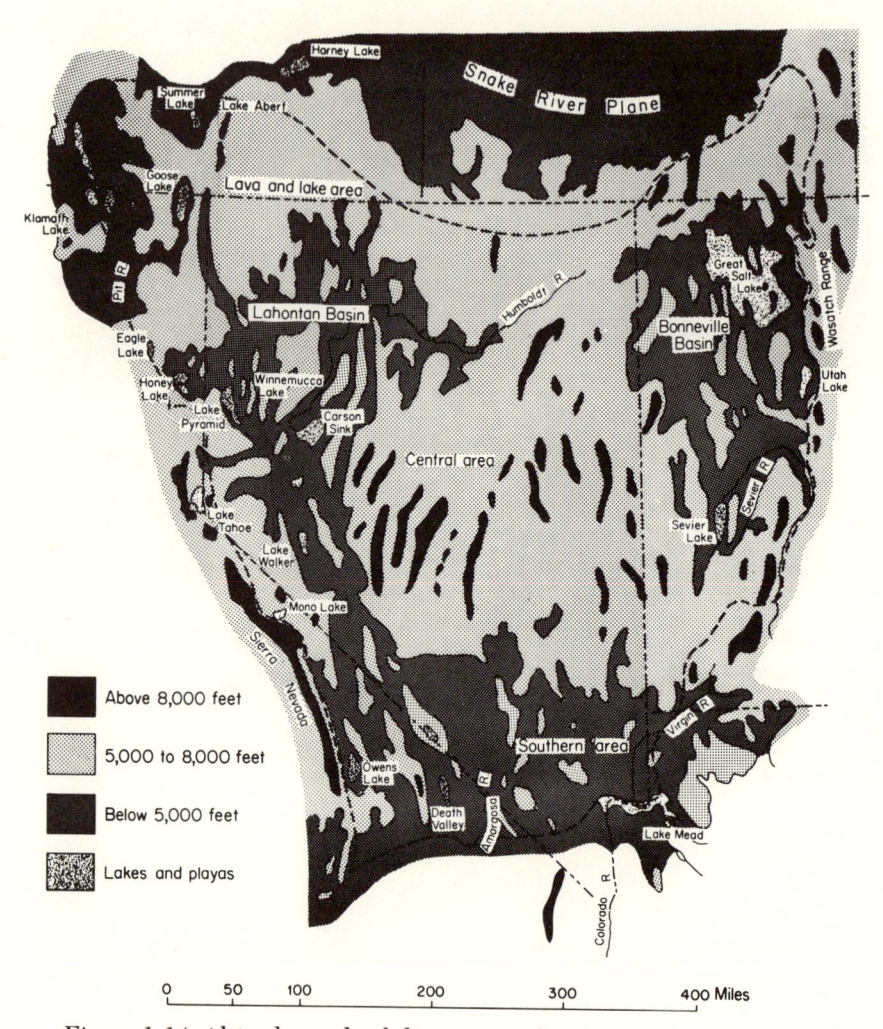

Figure 1.14. Altitudes and subdivisions in the Great Basin. The central area is topographically high; the Lake Bonneville and Lahontan basins are topographically low. The Great Basin appears to be arched. Several peaks above 8,000 ft (2,438 m) are not shown on the map; they are mostly in the central area and are of small extent; from Hunt 1974.[1]

paralleling the southwestern border of Nevada. In the western part of the Southern area, at the foot of the Sierra Nevada, are Mono and Owens lakes. Death Valley, with more than 200 square miles (518 km$^2$) about 250 feet (75 m) below sea level, collects runoff from 9,000 square miles (23,310 km$^2$) but is rarely flooded. Most of the time it is a salt-crusted playa.

The southeastern part of the Southern area drains to the Colorado River via the Virgin River. Small minnow-like fish, isolated at springs in the Southern area, are related to Colorado River species and indicate that much or all the Southern area formerly drained to the Colorado River (Hubbs and Miller 1948).

The structural history of the Great Basin is even less well understood than is that of the Colorado Plateau. Figure 1.13 summarizes the late Precambrian, Paleozoic, and Mesozoic structural history. Early and middle Precambrian history is completely lost in obscurity and even the late Precambrian of the Great Basin is little known except in the southern and along the eastern edge of the province. At least 30,000 feet (9,144 m) of sediments accumulated in the late Precambrian geosyncline (Fig. 1.3) which was oriented 45 degrees to the major structures of the stable platform and Shield. During the Paleozoic a second geosyncline occupied much of what is now the Great Basin. In the Central area and to the east, Paleozoic sedimentary rocks, 30,000 feet (9,144 m) thick, include considerable thicknesses of carbonate rocks. To the west the rocks include considerable thicknesses of black shale. During the Triassic and Jurassic these relationships continued but farther west where another 30,000 feet (9,144 m) of sediments were deposited. The thicknesses aggregate nearly 100,000 feet (30,480 m). However, the basinal axes are offset westward as if the axis of the Paleozoic geosyncline was west of the Precambrian one, and the axis of the early Mesozoic geosyncline was still farther west.

The continent probably was drifting across the mantle during these early stages of Great Basin history, but the early Mesozoic and older structural elements are best explained by the classical geosynclinal hypotheses of Hall and Dana. Plate tectonics does explain the late Mesozoic and Cenozoic structural history (see Coney, this volume). During the geosynclinal episodes deposits that became sedimentary rocks in the Great Basin were derived from the west at uplifts like that of the Antler orogeny (Roberts 1968), and were transported towards the Canadian Shield, overlapping its edge at the stable platform. Since the Cretaceous, sediment transport has been in the opposite direction.

Folding and thrust faulting also were directed towards the Shield, as they were along the opposite side of the continent in the Appalachian Mountains. One of the thrust faults that developed during the Paleozoic, the Roberts Mountain thrust (Merriam and Anderson 1942; Gilluly 1965; Roberts 1965), has been interpreted as having scores of miles of displacement because formations representing the black-shale facies are thrust into rocks of the carbonate facies far east of the western-most carbonate formations. The inferred displacement, though, seems excessive and implies that the boundary between the facies was linear with a northward trend (see for example Gilluly 1965b, Figs. 4–7). However, the boundary may have been irregular with limestone banks trending northwestward and separated by troughs containing black shale. By this hypothesis there would have been several thrusts, each with little displacement as the troughs were squeezed between resistant areas. A different mechanism involving multiple thrusts with small displacements postulates an uplift progressing eastward (Ketner 1977).

## BASIN AND RANGE PROVINCE IN SOUTHERN ARIZONA, NEW MEXICO, AND WESTERN TEXAS

Reference has already been made to the curious structural and physiographic contrast in the two parts of the Basin and Range province east and west of the Arizona–California boundary. The anomalously straight course of the Colorado River southward from Hoover Dam is matched by the equally anomalous course of the Rio Grande across New Mexico. The valley of the latter is referred to as the Rio Grande rift, but naming the feature does not explain why it is there or how it developed. In fact, the block faulting that characterizes the Rio Grande rift in New Mexico continues northward along the Colorado Rockies to Wyoming.

The rectangular portion of the Basin and Range province between the Colorado River and Rio Grande (Fig. 1.11) was part of the stable platform during the Paleozoic and early Mesozoic, and as such was more related to the Great Plains and Colorado Plateau than it was to the Basin and Range province of which it now is part. During the Early Cretaceous, parts of southern Arizona and southwestern New Mexico were downfolded into a geosyncline that extended southeastward to the Gulf of Mexico. The area represented by the present Colorado Plateau was elevated. Then the relative positions became reversed during the Late Cretaceous; the southern area became elevated and shed sediments northeastward into the Late Cretaceous geosyncline that spread across what now are the Great Plains, Colorado Rockies, and Colorado Plateau (Fig. 1.3). Relative elevations again became reversed in middle and late Tertiary when structural movements again dropped the southern area, which then became part of the Basin and Range province and lower than the Colorado Plateau.

In middle and late Mesozoic the Sierra Nevada batholith formed. How and why it formed is still a mystery so it seems convenient simply to requisition the Devil for the necessary materials and heat. Whatever caused it, Mesozoic and Paleozoic rocks in the Great Basin were folded, thrust faulted, and uplifted to form the mountains that shed sediments eastward into the Cretaceous geosyncline (Fig. 1.15). The igneous activity seems to have spread eastward during the Cretaceous and Tertiary, forming stocks and laccoliths in the deformed rocks of the Great Basin. The Cretaceous historical record in the Great Basin is generally negative, one of erosion, but the volume of Cretaceous sediments eroded there and deposited to the east indicates an average of a few cubic miles of material removed from each square mile of the Great Basin (Roberts 1968). Figure 1.15 illustrates Spieker's (1946) interpretation of the mountainous, eastern part of the Great Basin during the Late Cretaceous (also, see Misch 1960).

In the Southern area the curious Amargosa thrust fault (Noble 1941) may have begun developing as early as the Cretaceous. This is a gravity fault with younger rocks having moved westward onto older ones. Westward gravity sliding may have been aided by the 10 percent or so of slope westward of the basement rocks under the geosynclines. Because the upper plate of the Amargosa thrust consists of 40,000 feet (12,192 m) of concordant late Precambrian and Paleozoic rocks (Hunt and Mabey 1966), including representatives of all the periods, it must have moved as a unit at the beginning. It is broken by gravity faults branching from the main fault, and subsequently, during the Tertiary, it was folded and faulted in the course of which gravity displacement was renewed in individual segments as late as the Quaternary. I have attributed the fault as being started by gravity sliding into the potential void created by development of the Sierra Nevada batholith (Hunt 1975, p. 144).

There has been recent interest in trying to decipher structures that trend westward across the grain of the Great Basin (Stewart et al. 1977). Might these be continental expressions of deformed beds in the subduction zone connected with the fractures extending westward from the coast into the Pacific?

Block-faulted basins began forming in the Great Basin at least as early as the Oligocene, as indicated by the Titus Canyon Formation in the Death Valley area (Stock and Bode 1935). To what degree the ancestral structural basins were due to early Tertiary folding is unclear. There was plenty of block faulting during the middle and late Cenozoic, and this deformation is continuing, as indicated by the seismically active belts (Fig. 1.13), tilting at Lake Mead, tilting in Death Valley, young fault scarps, and displacement of benchmarks (Hunt and Mabey 1966). One of the late chapters in the structural history of the Great Basin concerns the isostatic doming of the Lake Bonneville basin as a result of unloading in that region by desiccation of Lake Bonneville (Gilbert 1890, Crittenden 1963).

Part of the evidence for the late Tertiary displacements is found on the Colorado Plateau (Fig. 1.16). Gravels there, distributed along tributaries

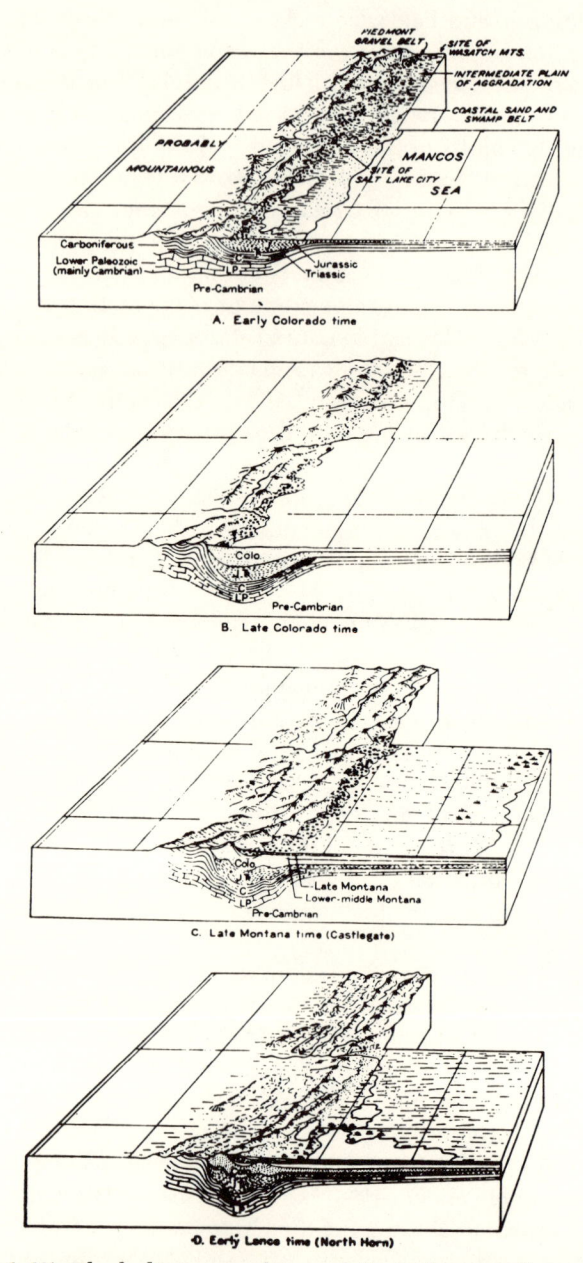

Figure 1.15. Block diagrams of central Utah showing four stages of the structural development during Late Cretaceous time; from Spieker 1946.

to the Little Colorado River, were derived from mountains that now are south of and below the rim of the Colorado Plateau. Those gravels are part of a drainage system that must have discharged from the Plateau at the abandoned canyon crossing the rim of the Plateau at Peach Springs, Arizona. Deposits in the abandoned canyon have been dated at 18.2 m.y. (million years) (Young 1966), and they show that the canyons in that rim of the Plateau already were 3,000 feet (914 m) deep and that the Plateau was within 2,500 feet (762 m) of its present topographic and structural height when those deposits were laid down. As will be discussed later in this paper, the ancestral Grand Canyon was eroded by the Little Colorado River; the main stem of the Colorado River did not drain southward until late Miocene or Pliocene, several million years after the deposits formed in the abandoned canyon at Peach Springs.

One of the curious features of this southern part of the Basin and Range province is the tremendous closed basin athwart the continental divide in southwestern New Mexico. Road maps of the State of New Mexico, the New Mexico State Geologic Map, and even the 1970 edition of the National Map Atlas shows a continental divide winding southward across that part of this State. A road sign by Interstate I-10 announces "Continental Divide"; not so. The western limit of drainage to the Atlantic Ocean is near the top of the bluff along the west side of the Rio Grande at Las Cruces, New Mexico. The eastern limit of drainage to the Pacific Ocean is at the Gila River and the western slope of the Peloncillo Mountains at the New Mexico–Arizona boundary. The 125-mile-wide (201-km-wide) Southwest Divide basin (my name for this feature) between these rims drains neither to the Atlantic nor to the Pacific; it is a vast closed basin having interior drainage and extending across the so-called continental divide.

The Southwest Divide basin is the sump into which the Mimbres River drains, the only important river entering it. This basin is the former sump of the Rio Grande which originally drained southward across its present position near Las Cruces and on southwestward across what now is La Mesa to a playa in Chihuahua. Additionally, the basin is the former sump of the New Mexico portion of the Gila River which formerly drained south across the plain at Lordsburg to the Animas Valley.

Like the Great Basin, the Southwest Divide basin is not a single cup-shaped depression, but a broad area of varied surface divided into a number of independent drainage districts. Among the mountains that break its surface are the fault blocks at the East Potrillo Range and the Florida Mountains. Most of the surface is loose sand, much of it mantling basaltic lavas. Between the highland areas are playas. Volcanic features

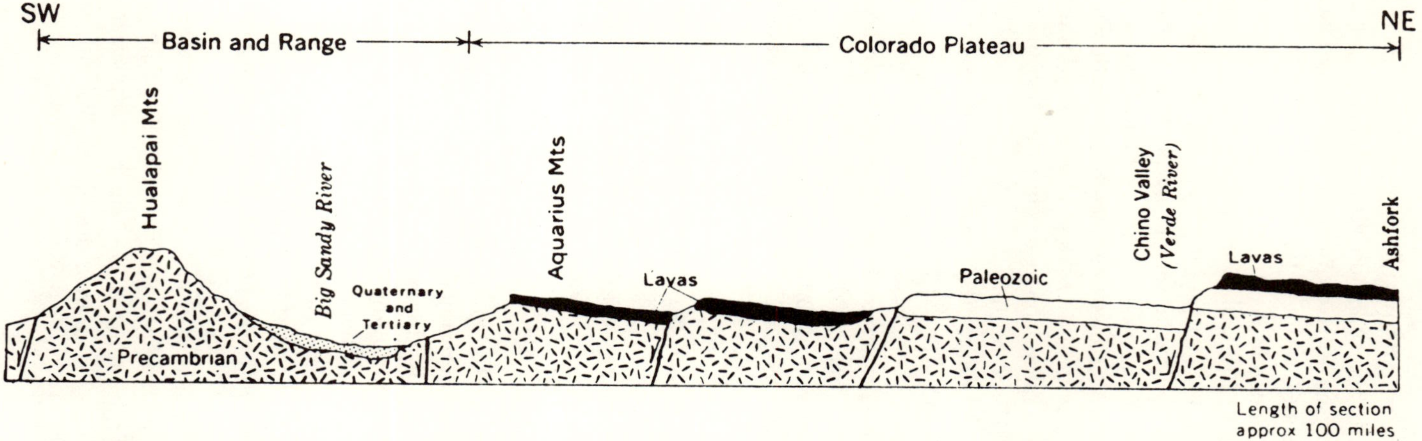

Figure 1.16. Cross sections across the southwest (A) and south (B) rims of the Colorado Plateau illustrate the structural rise towards the rim. A. Diagrammatic section northeast from the Hualapai Mountains. The more southwesterly faults have the greater displacements and probably are the older faults. In early Miocene time the strike valley at Big Sandy River was probably just beginning to form and very likely was similar to the present strike valley at Chino Valley. Under the lavas, at many places on the Colorado Plateau, are stream gravels derived from mountains of Precambrian rocks that have been separated by faulting from the Colorado Plateau, such as the Hualapai Mountains which formerly were much higher than the rim of the Plateau.

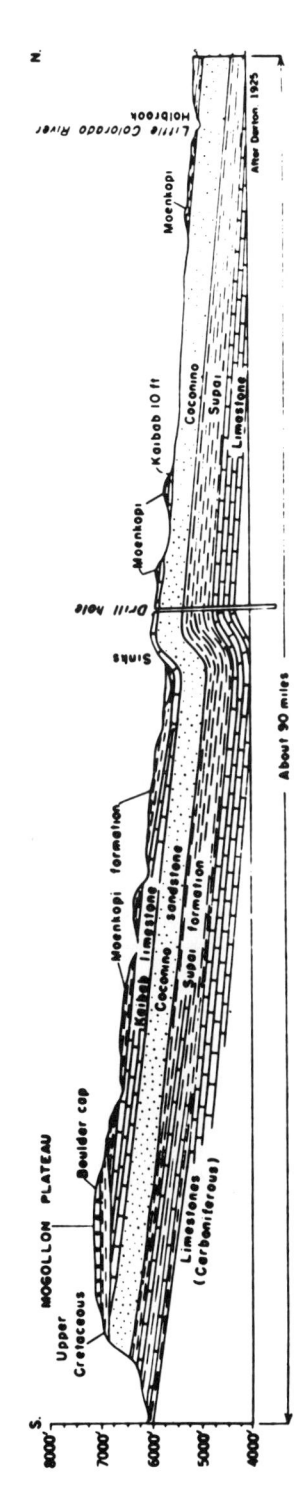

B. Cross section of Mogollon Rim. The boulder cap overlying the Cretaceous formations includes Precambrian rocks derived from mountains of those rocks south of the rim and now faulted below it, as in (A). Note also the angular unconformity under the Cretaceous rocks indicating uplift and erosion in the Triassic-Cretaceous interval; Darton, 1925.

of interest include the well-developed cone at Aden Crater and the maar-type craters at Kilbourne Hole, Hunts Hole, and a third near the border with Mexico.

## SEISMICITY AND PRESENT-DAY STRUCTURAL DEFORMATION

At least three different lines of evidence show that the southwestern U.S. deserts are undergoing varying degrees of earth movement at the present time. These are: (1) numerous earthquake epicenters, especially along the eastern and western edges of the Great Basin, epicenters south of the Colorado Plateau, and along the Rio Grande rift (Fig. 1.13); (2) numerous Holocene fault scarps in the areas where the epicenters are clustered, tilted alluvial fans, warped or faulted Pleistocene and Holocene shorelines and glacial moraines; and (3) measurable displacement of benchmarks and instrumental measurements at numerous places.

The distribution of earthquake epicenters in and around the Basin and Range province suggests that the province as a whole may be moving relative to its neighbors, but that the interior of the province either is relatively stable or is being arched without the kind of displacements that produce earthquakes. Figure 1.13 shows few epicenters in the interior of the Great Basin. Also, there are few in the Basin and Range province south of the Colorado Plateau, despite the long history (Fig. 1.16B) of reversals of displacement between those two provinces. In general, the frequency of Holocene fault scarps and other displaced late Pleistocene features accords with the frequency of earthquake epicenters.

Three kinds of surveys record present-day earth movements. Precise level surveys at Lake Mead show that the lake basin has sunk a few millimeters, presumably because of the weight of water. And at Las Vegas, Nevada, the surveys show more than 2 feet (0.6 m) of lowering attributable to withdrawal of ground water under that basin. The surveys also show that the entire area around Lake Mead has been tilted a few millimeters southwestward since the surveys were begun in 1935.

In Death Valley, tiltmeters show that tilting of the fault blocks is continuing. The rates of tilting are variable, and when earthquakes occur nearby the direction of tilting may reverse, as if the fault blocks were settling back. Vertical and horizontal displacements have not been measured in Death Valley. However, level-line surveys reveal differences in altitude when the lines are resurveyed. Topographic engineers and geodosists generally have attributed these differences to errors in the surveying, but geologists point out that the indicated changes in altitude all too often are in the direction that the crustal blocks have been moving.

I have argued that the engineers are more competent than they have supposed themselves to be, and that it is the crust that is unreliable, not the surveys.

## DRAINAGE SYSTEMS AND SOME PRINCIPLES FROM JOHN WESLEY POWELL'S STUDIES

It seems curious, at first, that our deserts, the land of little water, should have contributed so greatly as a field laboratory for understanding fluvial processes. In part, this is because of the recency of the structural displacements, the rather conspicuous relationship of stream courses to the structural features, and the dry beds of streams which can be studied before and after floods of various magnitudes.

The morphologic relationships between streams and folds as Powell (1875) observed them are shown in Figure 1.17A and B. He noted that the valleys formed by streams are modified by the amount of bedrock dip, by their resistance to erosion, and by diversions such as those caused by lava flows. Powell (1876) also contributed a morphologic classification of mountain forms and their relation to geologic structure, and later he broadened this classification to include many kinds of landforms, such as plains, plateaus, lakes, and marshes, as well as mountains (Powell 1896).

Of much greater infuence on geologic thought, however, is Powell's analysis of the dynamic relationship between rivers and the structural features they traverse. A drainage might be older than one fold that is crossed and younger than another. Geologists still debate the age relationships between the Colorado River and the folds it traverses (to be discussed later in this paper). In considering this problem, Powell distinguished three types of age relationshps.

In one type of drainage, which he termed consequent, the stream course is directly inherited from a bedrock surface formed by folding, tilting, or other earth movement that is more rapid than the downcutting by the river. The axis of a newly formed syncline contains a consequent stream course; the axis of a newly formed anticline becomes a drainage divide with consequent drainage off the flanks.

However, most the Colorado River drainage (Powell's principal laboratory) is not consequent, and he distinguished two types of nonconsequent valleys. One type, which he called antecedent, persists on a land surface where folds or other displacements develop after a stream course has been established. In this type the folds or other displacements are produced slowly such that the drainage lines are not diverted, and the streams cut downward vertically as the folds are uplifted across the stream course. An analogy is that of pushing a block of wood into a chain saw.

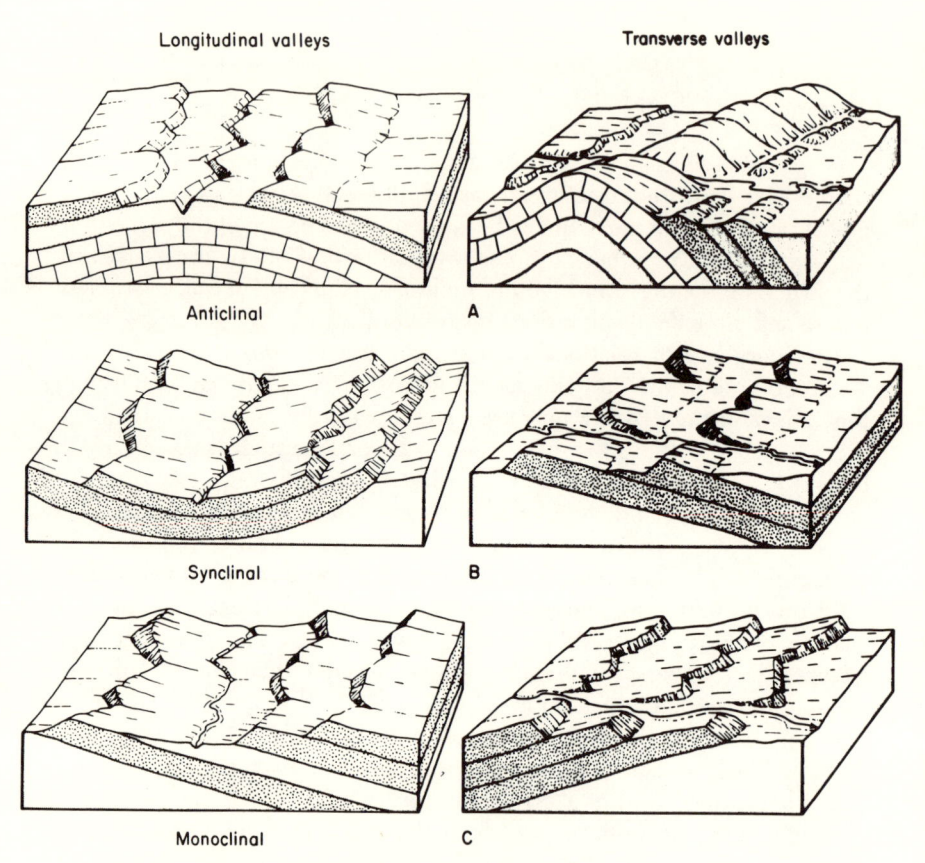

Figure 1.17. A classification of parallel (A) and traverse (B) valleys according to Powell (1876, 1896). In the traverse valleys, A = diaclinal, B = cataclinal, and C = anaclinal valleys.

A second kind of nonconsequent drainage he called superimposed. This involves burial of an old structure such that younger sediments unconformably rest on the structure. Drainage that develops on the younger sediments cuts vertically into the buried structures, as they are exhumed, and becomes incised into the structures.

Powell concluded that the canyon of the Green River across the Uinta Mountains and the canyons of the Colorado River across the Colorado Plateau, including Grand Canyon, were due to antecedence. He was vague about the age of the rivers, but about the Uinta uplift Powell (1876) wrote that ". . . the Uinta upheaval began at the close of Mesozoic time, and has continued intermittently near to the present. . . ." But his interpretation of antecedence requires a too ancient drainage system, and later workers correctly pointed out that many of the drainage anomalies on the Colorado Plateau are better explained by superposition than by antecedence. So it became fashionable to dismiss Powell's hypothesis.

Now it appears that Powell's hypothesis was partially viable. The course of the Green River across the Uinta Mountains was established after the Miocene–Pliocene Browns Park formation was deposited (Hansen 1969) which is much too late for the canyon to be due solely to antecedence. But the canyon through the mountains cannot be due solely to superposition either. The altitude of the canyon rim is about the same as the altitude of the terminal moraines where the headwaters of the Green River discharge into the Wyoming Basin from the Wind River Mountains, and there is not enough Pliocene and Quaternary sediment in the delta of the Colorado River to restore the surface to the height that would be necessary for the Green River to be superimposed across the Uinta Mountains. Thus, part of the topographic relief there must be due to Pliocene or Quaternary deformation, or both, and part of the canyon deepening must be due to antecedence (as Powell indicated).

Powell explicitly stated that folds develop slowly over long periods of time, the rate averaging little or no faster than downcutting by the streams. Geologists profess not to be catastrophists yet geologic literature is replete with great upheavals, called orogenies. At heart, geologists still seem to be revolutionaries, but the amount of earth movement in the Colorado River basin seems to have been roughly proportional to the times that were involved and, considering the basin as a whole, so has the rate of erosion. It is doubtful that during the Cenozoic there has been any period as long as the Quaternary (approximately 2.5–3 m.y.) without major earth movements somewhere in the river basin.

The concept of superposition requires tht the uplifts crossed by the Colorado River be completed too anciently. Some of the barriers are old; others are demonstrably young. Neither the hypothesis of superposition nor the hypothesis of antecedence is adequate alone to explain most of the drainage anomalies. Both processes are needed, a concept of duality I have referred to as anteposition (Hunt 1956). By this interpretation the river course across a particular structural barrier may have been established by superposition, and because of continued uplift of the barrier, at later times the canyon across it became deepened by antecedence.

Powell observed that rates of erosion and the capacity of streams to transport sediment were dependent on the discharge and velocity of the stream. The discharge depends on rainfall and catchment area; the velocity depends on the declivity. The greater the declivity, the greater the velocity and turbulence and the greater the transporting capacity of the stream. Steep headwaters move coarse debris; the flatter and quieter lower stretches move muds. Thus, Powell provided an explanation for the concavity of stream profiles. Powell also gave us the concept of base level. In 1875 he wrote that "We may consider the level of the sea to be a grand base level, below which the dry land cannot be eroded; but we may also have, for local and temporary purposes, other base levels of erosion, which are the levels of the principal streams . . . Where . . . a stream crosses a series of rocks . . . some of which are hard, and others soft, the harder rocks form a series of temporary dams, above which the corrasion of the channel through the softer beds is checked, and thus we may have a series of base levels of erosion, below which the rocks, . . . though exceedingly friable, cannot be degraded."

## CASE HISTORIES OF SOME RIVERS IN THE SOUTHWEST DESERTS

### Pecos River and Rio Grande

The Pecos River and Rio Grande illustrate additional processes by which river systems have evolved. Originally, the Pecos River was part of a consequent drainage system discharging eastward onto the Great Plains at the Llano Estacado (Fig. 1.18), where the streams laid down fan deposits of sand and gravel (Ogallala Formation) unconformably on tilted Permian and Triassic rocks. In the Pliocene a tributary of the ancestral Rio Grande eroded headward in a strike valley near the western edge of the fan deposits. This erosion probably was hastened by solution of the Permian salt beds. When the strike valley had been extended headward to a position approximately west of Portales, New Mexico, it captured the ancestral Pecos River which drained southeastward from the Sangre de Cristo Mountains and drained eastward with the other consequent streams crossing the Llano. On the Ogallala Formation, the ancestral Pecos River occupied a broad, shallow, and sand-covered valley at Portales. The capture and diversion occurred when the ancestral river was about 300 feet

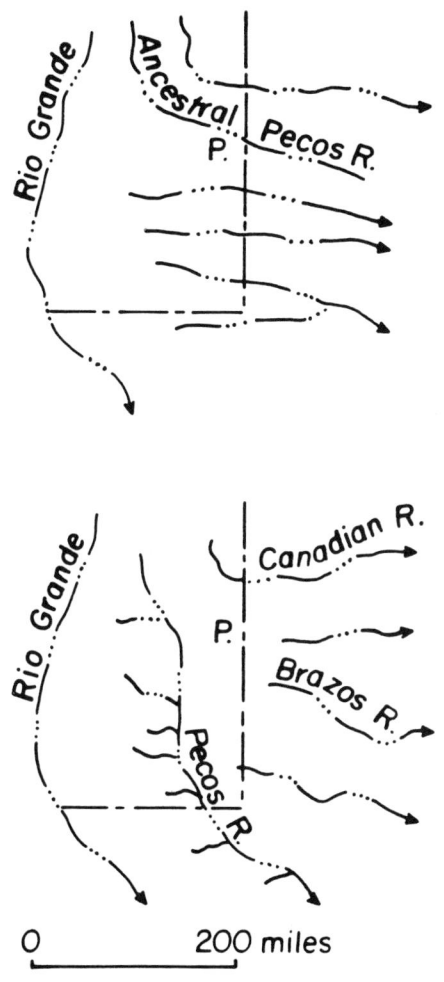

Figure 1.18. Change in drainage in eastern New Mexico as result of capture by headward erosion by the Pecos River. The ancestral, Pliocene drainage (upper diagrams) flowed eastward across the Great Plains along a sandy, now dry valley known as the Portales Sag (P). Present drainage (below) is southward; adapted from Plummer 1966.

(91 m) higher than the present Pecos River, probably during the early Pleistocene.

The history of the Rio Grande (Fig. 1.11) is very different from that of the Pecos and that of the streams on the Colorado Plateau as described by Powell. During the Miocene and possibly as early as Oligocene, block faulting began, and structural valleys developed along the Rio Grande and some of the neighboring valleys such as Estancia basin, Jornada del Muerto, and Tularosa valley. The ancestral Rio Grande, heading in the San Juan Mountains of southern Colorado, may originally have discharged eastward onto the Great Plains. With onset of the block faulting the drainage was diverted southward, and the debris overflowed from one basin to the next filling the structural basins with debris.

Details of the ancestral path of the Rio Grande as it drained southward are obscure because the river gravels are intertongued with valley fill locally derived from the newly uplifted mountains. One course may have been south along the Jornada del Muerto, then diagonally southwestward across the present river course in the vicinity of Las Cruces, New Mexico, and ending in the Southwest Divide basin in Chihuahua. Another possible route was southward from the Jornada to Mason Draw and thence south into the Southwest Divide basin. Still a third possible route may have been south from Las Palomas Valley to the present sump of the Mimbres River, northeast of the Florida Mountains. At one time or another the Rio Grande probably occupied each of these possible routes to its sump in Chihuahua.

When the ancestral Rio Grande had developed its course to a position about 200 feet (61 m) higher than its present position above El Paso, Texas, it was diverted southward through the gap at El Paso, either by capture by a tributary of the Rio Conchos or by overflow at a meander located against the El Paso gap. When this division happened, probably during the early Pleistocene, the river joined the Rio Conchos and discharged to the Gulf of Mexico.

## Gila River and disintegrated drainage of the Mojave Desert

The contrast has been made in this paper between the through-flowing drainage systems of the Gila and Bill Williams rivers in southern Arizona east of the Colorado River and the completely disintegrated drainage to the west in the Mojave Desert (Fig. 1.12). The Arizona rivers probably evolved by a combination of processes that included some cases of anteposition, some diversions by piracies like that along the Pecos River, and basin filling and overflow like that along the Rio Grande.

The ancestral drainage on the Mojave Desert is a "fish" story. Fishes now isolated at springs in areas north to Death Valley, in the incomparably dry Amargosa River and along the Owens River are related to Colorado River species. This condition indicates that the drainage originally was tributary to the Colorado River, presumably via the depressions marked by Bristol, Cadiz, and Danby Dry Lakes. Just how and when that area was deformed enough to disintegrate the ancestral drainage is not at all clear. This deformation occurred recently enough for the fishes to have maintained specific characters, yet evidence in Death Valley suggests that it occurred as long ago as middle Pleistocene (Hunt and Mabey 1966).

## Humboldt River

The Humboldt River (Fig. 1.11) is not a mighty stream, but it is and has served as an important route for providing water to travelers across the Nevada deserts. Bancroft (1890, p. 15) wrote:

> In the course of westward-marching empire few streams on the North American continent have played a more important part than the Humboldt River of Nevada. Among the water courses of the world it can lay claim neither to great beauty nor to remarkable utility. Its great work was to open a way, first for the cattle train and then for the steam train, through a wilderness of mountains, through ranges which otherwise would run straight across its course. It is the largest river of this region, and the only one hereabout running from east to west. Most of the others are with the mountains, north and south.

The Humboldt River crosses one important structural barrier, about 30 miles (48 km) below Elko, Nevada, where the river flows through a gorge which traverses a fault block of late Tertiary volcanic and sedimentary rocks. The remainder of the river flows around the major uplifts rather than crossing them. The ancestral Humboldt may have drained to the Pacific, by way of a windgap at the head of the Feather River. It now discharges into and becomes dissipated in the huge sump at Carson Sink.

How and why the Humboldt River developed its course across the topographic and structural grain of the Great Basin (Fig. 1.11) is not known. The history probably involved various combinations of the processes already described.

## Colorado River

There have been two principal theories about the age of Grand Canyon and of the Colorado River. One interpretation is that they are young, no older than middle or late Pliocene (say less than 5 m.y.). The other interpretation is they are old, early Miocene or even late Oligocene (say 25 m.y. old). In this article and in previous attempts to develop an hypothesis (Hunt, 1956, 1969b, 1974), I have favored the interpretation that the canyon and the river are old. My thinking about particular parts of the hypothesis has evolved considerably since that first effort, but the main thrust has continued. The question, in my view, is not whether the Colorado River is developed before the Pliocene, but how much earlier?

The theory that the canyon and river are young stems from Blackwelder (1934) and Longwell (1936, 1946) who pointed out, quite correctly, that the Colorado River could not have discharged out of the mouth of Grand Canyon until after the Muddy Creek Formation and Hualapai Limestone (considered a member of the Muddy Creek Formation by Blair and Armstrong 1979) had been deposited in Grand Wash. Blackwelder and Longwell inferred, quite incorrectly, that the whole river system must be young. The fact is that some parts of the river system are young, as young as Quaternary, but other parts are demonstrably old, as old as Oligocene.

The question about the origin of the Colorado River was posed by G. K. Gilbert (1876, p. 101) who wrote: "What is the relation of the drainage system . . . to the displacements?" Also, how much is due to that combination of those processes referred to as anteposition (Hunt 1956), how much is due to piracy and capture (for example, see Bradley 1936, p. 189; McKee and others 1967), and how much is due to ponding and overflow of basins as they became filled (Fig. 1.19)?

The question "how old is the Colorado River," is oversimplified to the point of being misleading and self-defeating. The structural barriers crossed by the river and its tributaries (Fig. 1.5) are of different ages, and most of them involve late Tertiary and Quaternary as well as early Tertiary deformation. The questions about age and process need to be asked about each reach separately, and the parts then fitted together to reconstruct the whole history. Any acceptable theory must accommodate all the facts, not just some of them.

## Grand Canyon and the canyons upstream from it

By my interpretation Grand Canyon began as an antecedent canyon eroded by the Little Colorado River during the early Miocene. It did not discharge from the Colorado Plateau at Grand Wash but via an abandoned canyon that breaches the rim of the Plateau at Peach Springs, Arizona (Fig. 1.20). The fill in that canyon has been dated at 18.2 m.y. (Young 1966). The canyon therefore must be as old as early Miocene. This abandoned canyon is not a unique feature in the Colorado River system; another example is Unaweep Canyon where the Gunnison, and probably the Colorado River, once traversed the Uncompaghre uplifts. The de-

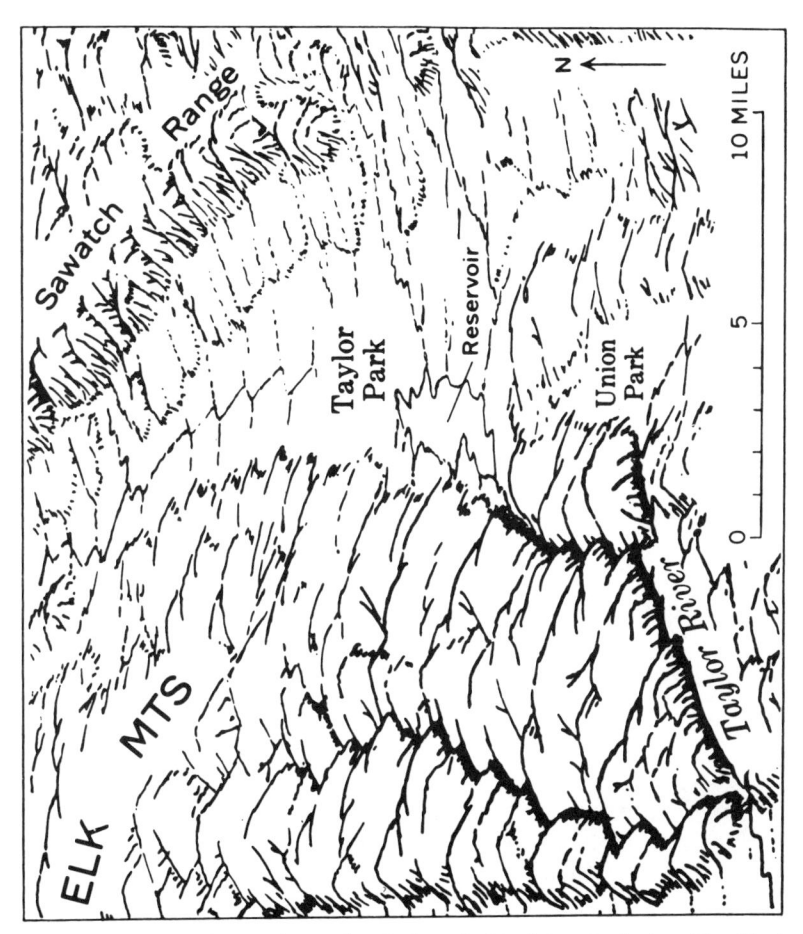

Figure 1.19. Taylor Park, in the Colorado Rockies, is drained by Taylor River Canyon, which has been eroded through a fault block of Precambrian and Paleozoic rocks; from Hunt 1969b. How and when did Taylor River erode that canyon? The question exemplifies the problem of age and origin of almost every stretch of the Colorado River. Antecedence? Superposition? Anteposition? Piracy? Basin filling and overflow?

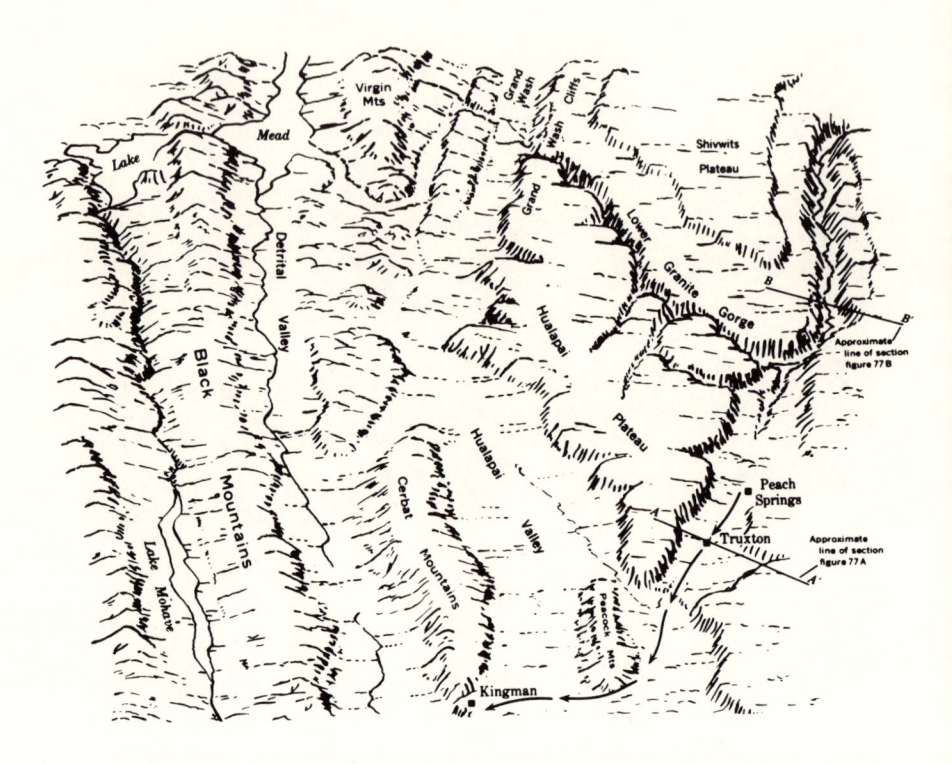

Figure 1.20. Upper diagram illustrates the abandoned, dry canyon breaching the southwest rim of the Colorado Plateau at Peach Springs, Arizona. The dry canyon is partly filled with deposits (see cross section at right of Early Miocene age). The Lower Granite Gorge of Grand Canyon approximately coincides with a synclinal axis that plunges northwestward about 2,000 ft (610 m) from near the upper end of the dry canyon to the Grand Wash fault, where the fold is truncated. Paleozoic limestones overlying the granite is cavernous and would have drained any water ponded by the fill in the dry canyon. The lower diagrams show cross-sectional relationships of the dry canyon and its fill to the present canyon. The formations dip northeastward from the edge of the Plateau to the bend at the head of the Lower Granite Gorge; from Hunt 1969b.[2]

Charles B. Hunt

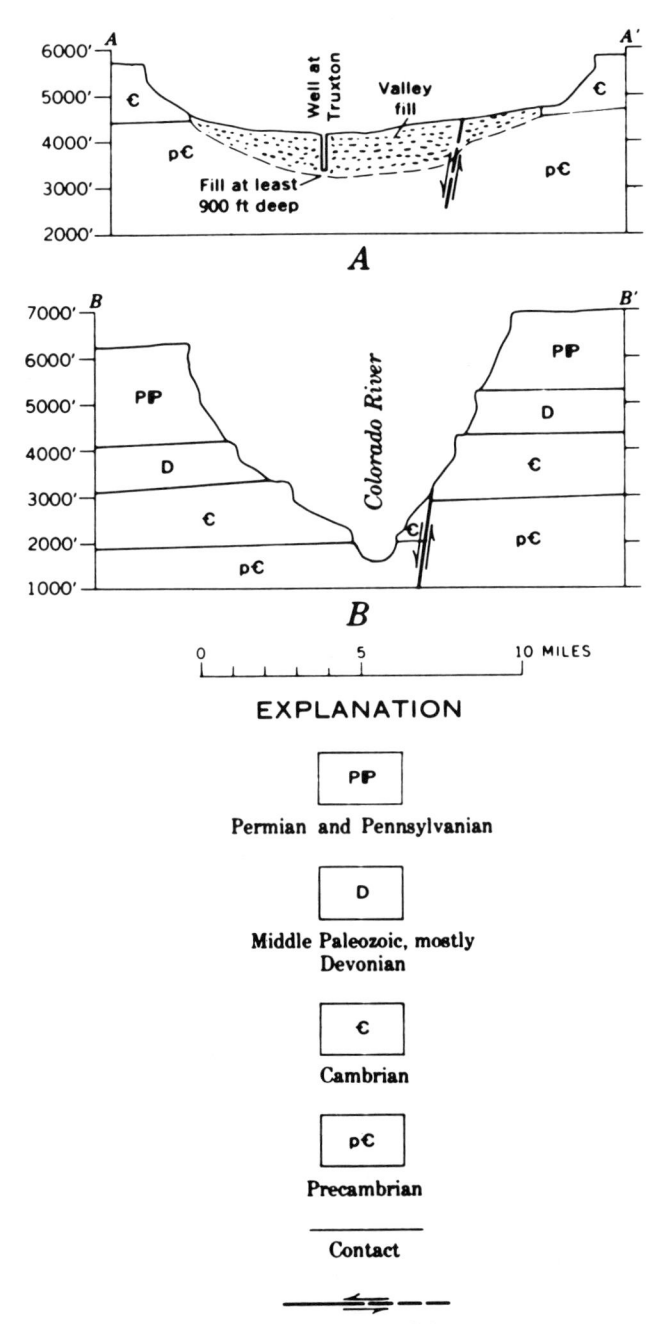

A

B

0    5    10 MILES

EXPLANATION

PP

Permian and Pennsylvanian

D

Middle Paleozoic, mostly Devonian

Ȼ

Cambrian

pȻ

Precambrian

———
Contact

⇄ – –
Fault, showing direction of movement
*Dashed where approximately located*

positional fill of the Peach Springs Canyon has been judged to be part of the Muddy Creek Formation (Hunt 1956) and therefore had a source area toward the southwest. The deposit was transported northeastward into the Canyon. Those arguing for a relatively young Grand Canyon have interpreted these features of the Peach Springs area to indicate that the canyon was eroded by a stream draining northeastward (Luchitta 1972, Young and Brennan 1974). Such supposed drainage would have flowed against the slope of the bedrock floor of the canyon, and it would have drained upstream into the Grand Canyon, a proposition I cannot take seriously. Moreover, 18 m.y. ago the Grand Canyon probably had younger formations on the rim than it has now. Perhaps even the Vermillion Cliffs (Figs. 1.4, 1.5) extended that far south.

Materials sufficient to partly fill the abandoned canyon could have been provided by the volcanism that occurred about that time in the nearby parts of the Basin and Range province. Volcanic rocks could have ponded the ancestral Little Colorado River. In middle and late Miocene time, the Little Colorado River lost its headwaters when the mountains in southern Arizona, that had been a major source area, were faulted off the Colorado Plateau (McKee and McKee 1972, Hunt 1956). Whatever the details of that drainage history, the abandoned canyon at Peach Springs provides incontrovertible evidence that the Grand Canyon region was within 2,500 feet (762 m) of its present structural height by the early Miocene and that there already was a canyon at least 3,000 feet (914 m) deep upstream from it. If the Chocolate and Vermillion cliffs extended to the present day rim of the canyon, the Grand Canyon at that time was as deep as it is today.

Any theory must also account for the Hualapai Limestone which was deposited in Grand Wash just south of the mouth of present Grand Canyon (Fig. 1.21). The limestone is more than 600 feet (183 m) thick and was deposited at the head of an estuary where marine water from the Gulf of California was diluted by fresh water about 8.7 m.y. ago (Blair and Armstrong 1979). South of these limestone outcrops is a buried salt deposit dated at 10 m.y. (Peirce 1976, cited by Blair and Armstrong 1979). There is no clastic delta. Blair and Armstrong (1979) infer that the fresh water probably was supplied by the ancestral Colorado River "from an unknown source." I agree and interpret the water as having been supplied by springs issuing from the cavernous limestones folded into the synclinal axis that is near and parallel to the lower reach of Grand Canyon. Any ponding of the ancestral river by the fill in the canyon at Peach Springs would have produced a lake with a 2,000 foot (607 m) head and would have leaked like a sieve. This is piping on a grand scale (some say on an outrageous scale). But this hypothesis would account for both the Hualapai Limestone

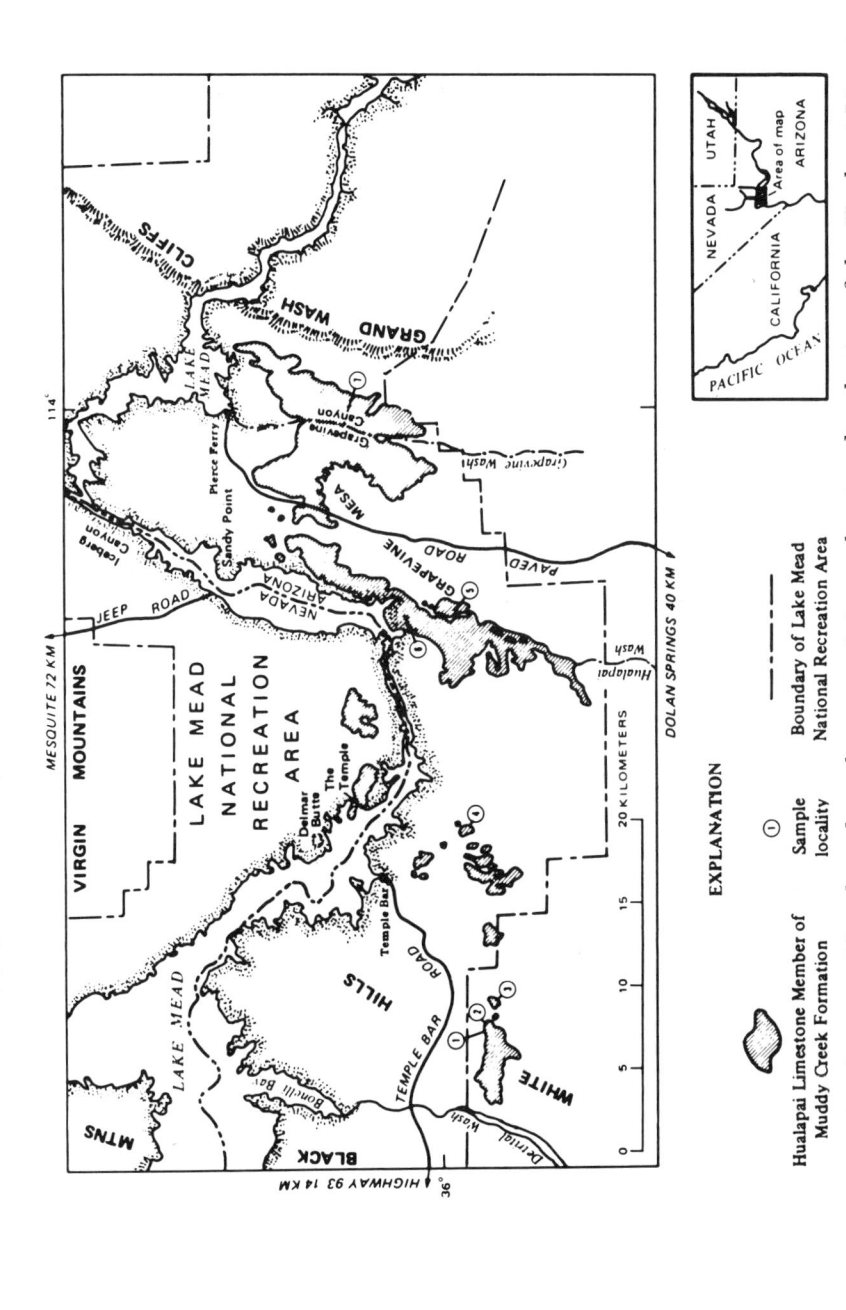

Figure 1.21. Southeastern Nevada and northwestern Arizona showing distribution of the Hualapai Limestone; from Blair and Armstrong 1979.

and the absence of a clastic delta. When I first proposed the interpretation, an editor commented, "After reading your explanation of the Lower Granite Gorge, I just felt flushed."

## Little Colorado and San Juan Rivers

The Little Colorado River has a trellis drainage pattern that is unique in the Colorado River system (Fig. 1.4, 1.5). By my interpretation this trellis pattern evolved while the Little Colorado River was developing its course along a strike valley and was cutting downward at the Grand Canyon. Evidence that the Little Colorado's tributaries drained from mountains, which are no longer attached to the Colorado Plateau, is recorded by gravels from Precambrian rocks that now are faulted below the rim of the Plateau (Hunt 1956).

The main, northern stem of the Colorado River was not involved in this early history of Grand Canyon. Green River did not join the system until after the Browns Park Formation had been deposited in latest Miocene or earliest Pliocene time. It appears to have discharged to the Great Plains, probably via Shirley Basin, and possibly, it was joined by the ancestral Colorado River when it had its course north of the White River Plateau (Fig. 1.4, 1.5) (Hunt 1969, Larson et al. 1975).

## SURFICIAL DEPOSITS

Surficial deposits are of three basic types: (1) residuum, which is formed more or less in place by weathering of bedrock, and organic deposits like peat; (2) a transition category of deposits moved chiefly by gravity down hillsides and known as colluvium, including talus, debris avalanches, and landslides; and (3) transported deposits which are those derived by weathering at one site and transported by any of several means and deposited at a second site. Transportation may be by glaciers, streams, wind, or currents in ancient or modern lakes. In addition there are other miscellaneous deposits including young basaltic lavas, scoriae, or ash and spring deposits of travertine.

Perhaps the most important residual deposit in the desert is caliche (Gile et al. 1966) the subject of a chapter in this volume (see Lattman, this volume). Caliche is particularly well developed and extensive in the hot, southern parts of the Basin and Range province. Caliche is less well developed in the northern part of the Great Basin and Colorado Plateau. On the Colorado Plateau, the most extensive residual deposit is a fluffy, weathered layer on shale deserts. This is a highly ephemeral deposit that is easily washed away during storm events. Another kind of residual deposit, consisting of organic matter and muds, accumulates in marshes along springs at the edges of playas. Finally, on mountain tops that are or have been subject to considerable frost heaving one finds patterned ground.

Gravity deposits are mostly in the mountains but are widely distributed along cliffs and on the back side of hogbacks on the Colorado Plateau deserts. The most extensive deposits are colluvial, that is, the mantle of loose material moving slowly by creep down steep hillsides. Commonly, two and rarely three ages of colluvium can be distinguished: (1) modern colluvium that is accumulating today mostly in the hillside washes; (2) early Holocene colluvium blackened with desert varnish and bordered by gullies eroded into the hillside on each side of the deposit; and (3) protruding mounds of older colluvium that are erosional remnants of probable late Pleistocene age. The early Holocene deposits can be dated by archeological remains on them.

Rock falls, talus, debris avalanches, and landslides are important features of most desert mountains whose height extends them into the semi-arid zone. Most of these deposits were first formed during past, wet climatic periods, notably during the late Pleistocene and middle Holocene, but most are readily reactivated when local conditions are optimum such as water seeping into the sole of an old slide or a severe winter causing renewed freeze and thaw.

Stream deposits include alluvial floodplains and terraces along stream and alluvial fans around the base of the mountains. The floodplain deposits may be of several ages, and there may or may not be terraces (Fig. 1.22). In some localities, remains of Pleistocene animals occur in the oldest deposits along a stream. Middle Holocene deposits may be identified by the associated occurrence of preceramic artifacts and modern fauna. Late Holocene deposits contain artifacts of the pottery occupations. Floodplains generally have been favored for agriculture because the ground is easily tilled and productive. In many valleys it can be irrigated.

Other stream deposits include the gravel fans that are such a conspicuous feature of the Basin and Range province, but those fans have their analog on the Colorado Plateau in thin deposits washed onto pediments. Figure 1.23 illustrates the typical history of pediment gravels on the Plateau. The surfaces of the pediment gravels resemble those on the fans in the Basin and Range, but the deposits are thin, generally less than 20 feet (6 m) thick. The fans in the Basin and Range province are hundreds or even a few thousand feet thick. Ground water is deep under the Basin and Range fans but there is a shallow, perched water table under the pediment gravels on the Colorado Plateau.

Figure 1.24 illustrates several features of the fans in Death Valley which are typically found in many of the desert basins. The gravels grade into

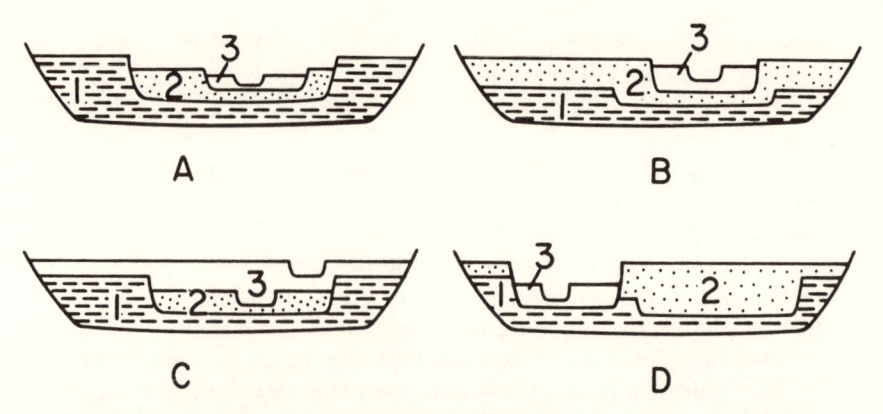

Figure 1.22. Diagrammatic sections illustrating some common stratigraphic relationships in the alluvial deposits on the Colorado Plateau; from Hunt 1956. The number of alluvial terraces may or may not be the same as the number of episodes of cut and fill recorded by the alluvial deposits; deposit 1 = late Wisconsin alluvium, deposit 2 = pre-pottery Recent alluvium, and deposit 3 = Historic alluvium.

silts of the floodplain or playa in the middle of the valley. The fans are long and high on the side of the basin that has been recently uplifted but are short and steep on the side that has been tilted downward. Uplifted parts of the fans are characterized by elevated benches of old gravels whose surfaces slope more steeply than the present washes. The younger gravels overlap and bury the lower ends of the old gravel deposits. Figure 1.25 illustrates different patterns of mountain fronts depending on kind and recency of structural movements along the high parts of the fans.

Eolian features are most conspicuous at the sand deserts. Active dunes may be concave downwind (barchan), concave to the windward (parabolic), longitudinal (parallel to the wind), or transerve (at right angle to the wind). Certainly at most, and perhaps at all the active sand dunes, the active sand unconformably overlies and has been derived from older (early Holocene) dunes (Fig. 1.26).

Sand deserts also are formed by sheets of sand without conspicuous dunes, only small mounds at shrubs, or coppice dunes. Excavations at coppice dunes show several stages of dune development marked by changes in form of the plants. Locally on the Colorado Plateau the surfaces of floodplains have become eroded by wind and the sand heaped in mounds, typically with greasewood. Beneath the mounded sand is a pedestal marking the old floodplain surface.

Lake deposits are as characteristic of deserts as they are of glaciated parts of the country. During the Pleistocene there were scores of lakes, especially in the Great Basin. Even Death Valley had a lake 600 feet (183 m) deep. Two unusually large lakes were Lake Bonneville, grandaddy of Great Salt Lake (Stokes 1966) and Lake Lahontan (Fig. 1.27). There is difference of opinion about the meteorological differences between the wet climates of the Pleistocene and the present climate, but the lake deposits in the deserts clearly record that the effective climate was very different. Currently, many of the old, dry lake beds are crusted with salt (Fig. 1.28).

Finally, mention should be made of desert varnish, the widespread stain of iron and manganese oxide. It is forming today at active seeps, but these are very local occurrences where there is water necessary for transporting and depositing the oxides. The extensive coatings of varnish on cliffs (Fig. 1.29) and alluvial fans date from past wet periods, the most recent of which occurred during the middle Holocene. The dating is archeological and a similar record appears in arid land in other parts of the world (Hunt and Mabey 1966). Study of monuments in Egypt indicates practically no deposition of desert varnish during the last 2,000 years but older monuments are stained.

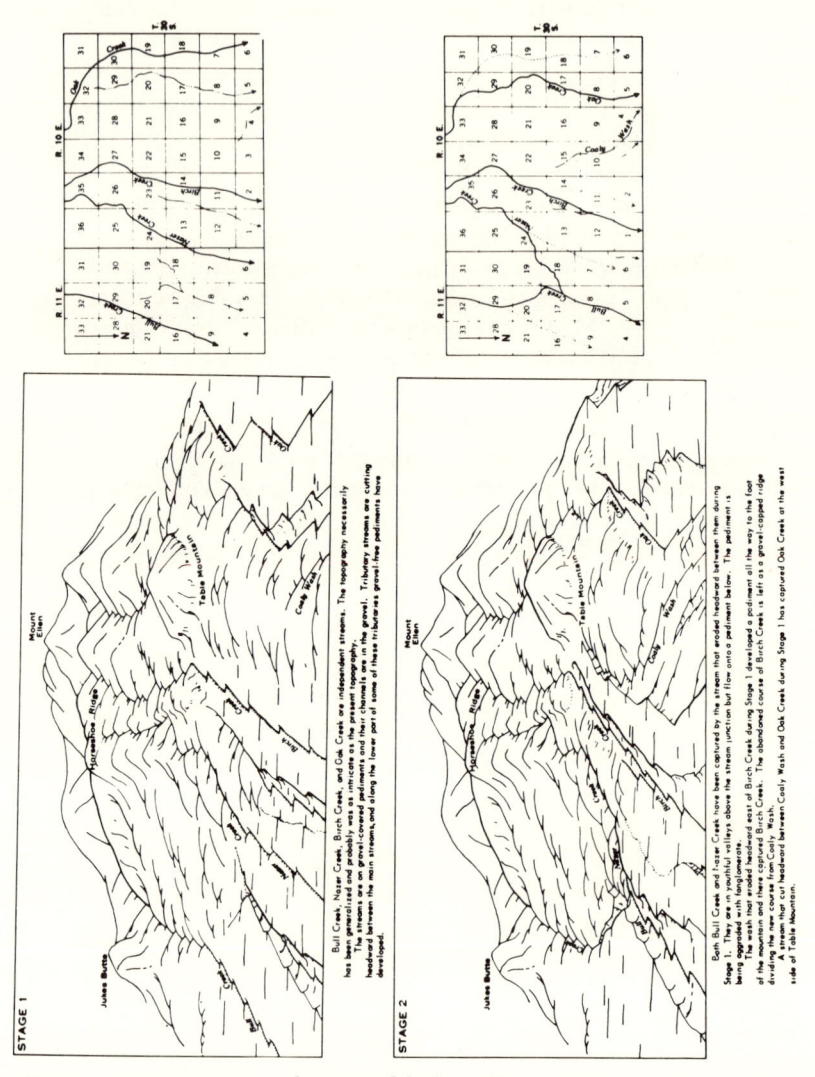

Figure 1.23. Diagrams above and below illustrating four stages in the development of pediments and their gravel cover on the Colorado Plateau.[3]

## STAGE 3

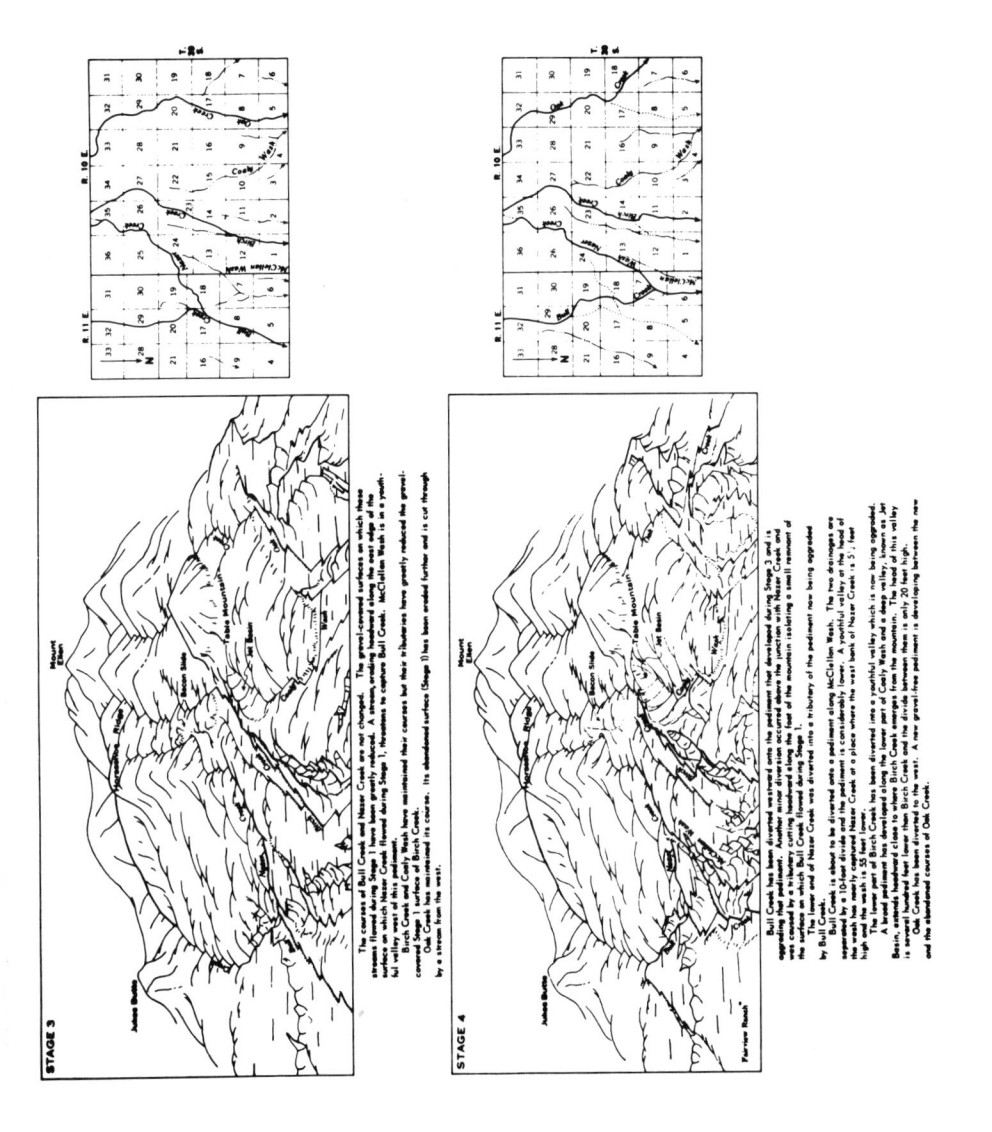

The courses of Bull Creek and Nazer Creek are not changed. The gravel-covered surfaces on which these streams flowed during Stage 1 have been greatly reduced. A stream, eroding headward along the west edge of the surface on which Nazer Creek flowed during Stage 1, threatens to capture Bull Creek. McClellan Wash is in a youthful valley west of this pediment.

Birch Creek and Oak Creek have maintained their courses but their tributaries have greatly reduced the gravel-covered Stage 1 surface of Birch Creek.

Oak Creek has maintained its course. Its abandoned surface (Stage 1) has been eroded further and is cut through by a stream from the west.

## STAGE 4

Bull Creek has been diverted westward onto the pediment that developed during Stage 3 and is aggrading that pediment. Another minor diversion occurred above the junction with Nazer Creek and was caused by a tributary cutting headward along the foot of the mountain isolating a small remnant of the surface on which Bull Creek flowed during Stage 1.

The lower end of Nazer Creek was diverted into a tributary of the pediment now being aggraded by Bull Creek.

Bull Creek is about to be diverted onto a pediment along McClellan Wash. The two drainages are separated by a 10-foot divide and the pediment is considerably lower. A youthful valley at the head of this wash has cut deeply below Nazer Creek at a place where the west bank of Nazer Creek is 55 feet high and the wash is 55 feet lower.

The lower part of Birch Creek has been diverted into a youthful valley which is now being aggraded. A small pediment has developed along the lower part of Cody's Wash and a steep valley, known as Jet Basin, has cut close to the place where Birch Creek emerges from the mountain. The head of this valley is several hundred feet lower than Birch Creek and the divide between them is only 20 feet high.

Oak Creek has been diverted to the west. A new gravel-free pediment is developing between the new and the abandoned courses of Oak Creek.

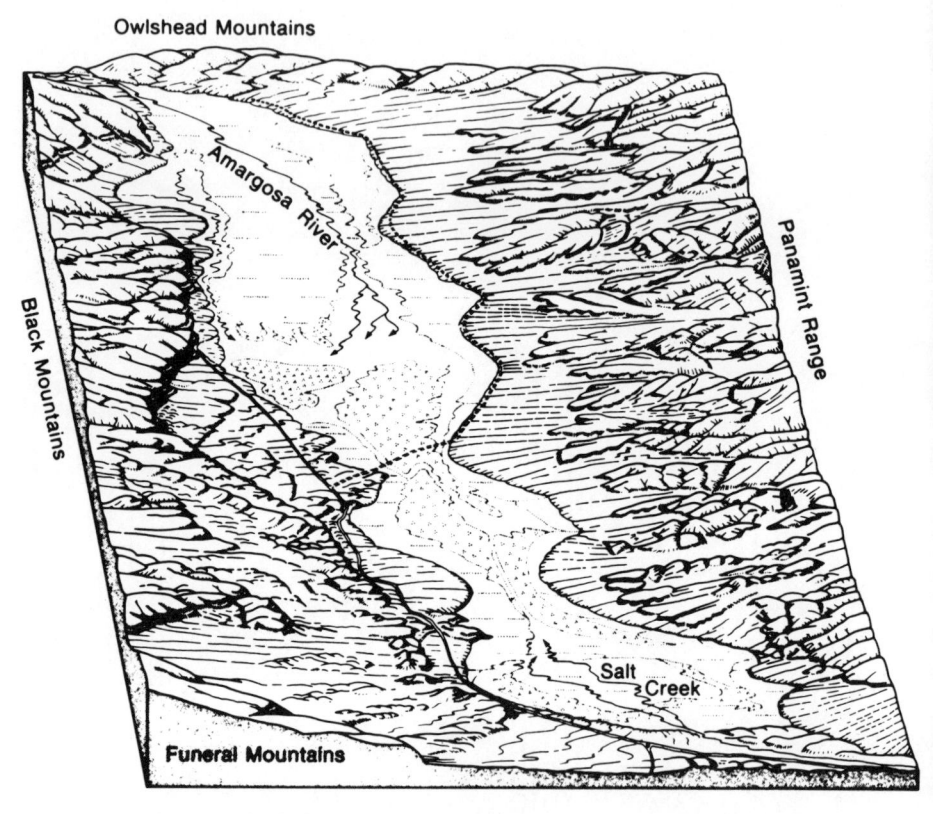

Figure 1.24. Block diagram of a basin in the Basin and Range province. The view is south along Death Valley; from Hunt and Mabey 1956.

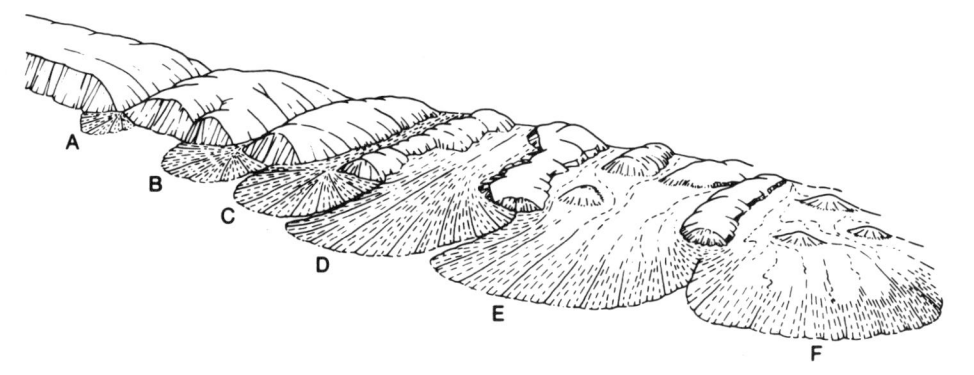

Figure 1.25. Some different forms of gravel fans in the Basin and Range province. Newly formed fault scarps may be without fans or have small ones at the base (A). In the next stage, the mountain front has retreated (B), and the fans may extend up the mountain valley (C). A fault-block mountain being engulfed by its own debris may have a front that no longer is straight because of burial (D), and the fans may even wrap around spurs in the mountains (E). In the final stage (F) the gravel buries all bedrock except isolated hills; from Hunt 1972.[4]

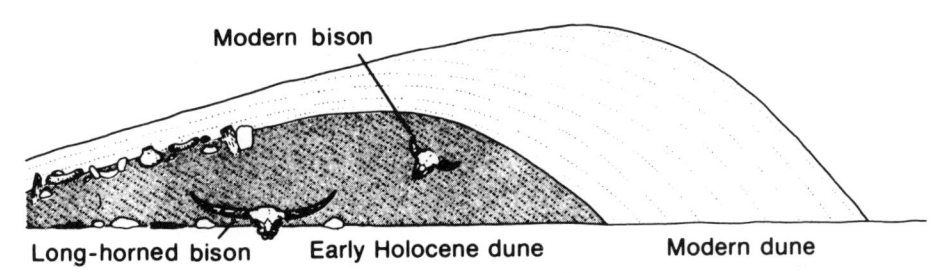

Figure 1.26. Diagrammatic section of sand dunes in the southwestern U.S. deserts illustrating a common stratigraphic sequence of eolian activity. Artifacts and sites of the late-Holocene pottery-making Indians overlie the early Holocene dune but are buried by the loose sand of the presently active dune. The early Holocene sand is weathered and stabilized; in and under it are remains of early Holocene mammals and, rarely, pre-pottery Indians; from Hunt 1972.[4]

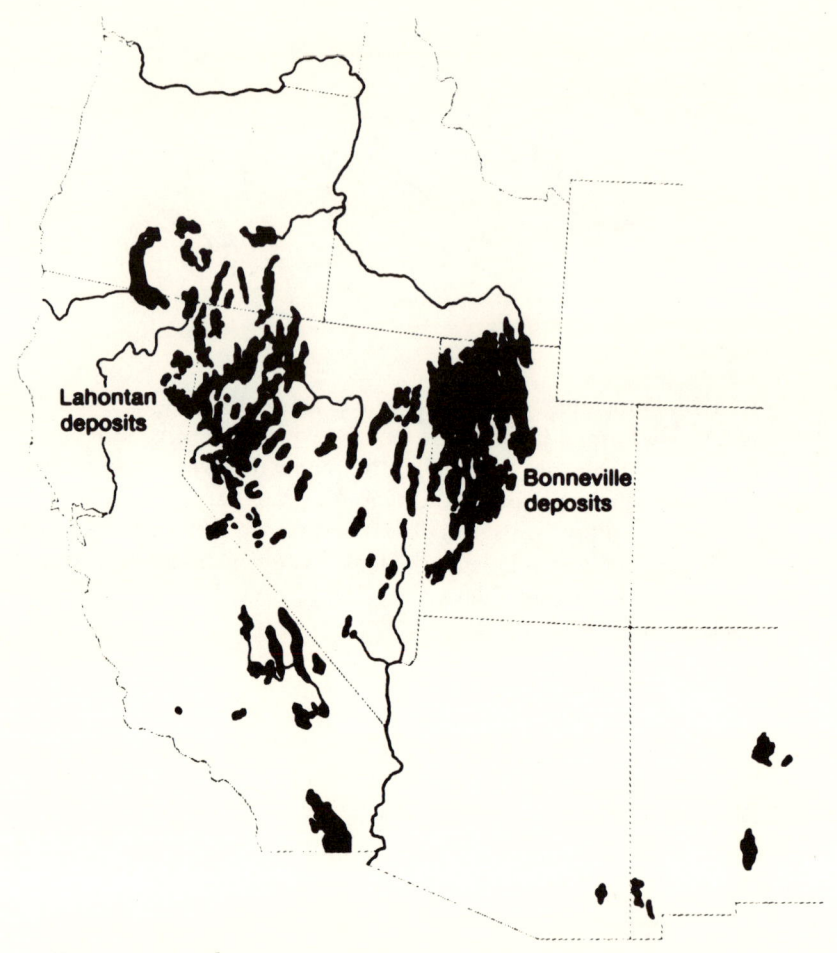

Figure 1.27. Pleistocene lakes in the Great Basin. Only a few of the lakes have survived; most became desiccated during the Holocene and today are ephemeral lakes, that is, playas. During the middle Holocene (ca 3000 B.C. to 1 A.D.) shallow lakes formed at many of the playas; from Meinzer 1923.


Figure 1.28. Diagrams illustrating history of a saltpan in the Basin and Range province. Evaporation of a brine in a dish (A) deposits salts that are zoned in an orderly way with respect to their solubilities, carbonates around the edge (c), an intermediate zone of sulfates (s), and chlorides at the center (h). As the pan becomes tilted by earth movement, the salt rings become crowded towards the low side (B). As floods of fresh water extend into the basin, the salts become restricted in zones where the floods ebb (C); from Hunt and Robinson 1966.

Charles B. Hunt

Figure 1.29. The stain of iron and manganese oxide, known as desert varnish, is being deposited today where seeps discharge onto rock walls. Along canyons the varnish also coats dry rock surfaces, but these are old deposits that are being eroded; blocks fallen from the varnished cliffs leave scars of unvarnished rock. The stain was deposited sometime before A.D. 1. It antedates Anasazi cliff dwellings on the Colorado Plateau, and throughout the arid lands it antedates ceramic sites. Artifacts of the ceramic stage occupations are not stained; whereas, those of old, lithic sites are stained; from Hunt 1972.[4]

## NOTES

1. Figures obtained from *Natural Regions of the United States and Canada*, copyright, W. H. Freeman and Co., reproduced with permission.
2. Figures obtained from U.S. Geological Survey Professional Paper 669.
3. Figures obtained from Geological Survey Professional Paper 228.
4. Figures obtained from *Geology of Soils*, copyright, W. H. Freeman and Co., adapted from Davis 1925, reproduced with permission.
5. Summarized from *Natural Regions of the United States and Canada*, copyright, W. H. Freeman and Co., used with permission.
6. Summarized from Hunt, C. B. 1979. "The Great Basin, an overview and hypothesis of its history," *Rocky Mtn. Assoc. Geol. and Utah Geol. Assoc.*, 1979 Basin and Range Symposium, 1–10.

## REFERENCES

Bancroft, H. H. 1890. *History of Nevada, Colorado, and Wyoming.* San Francisco, The History Company.

Blackwelder, E. 1934. "Origin of the Colorado River," *Geol. Soc. America Bull.*, 45:551–556.

Blair, W. N., and A. K. Armstrong. 1978. "Hualapai Limestone Member of the Muddy Creek Formation: The Youngest Deposit Predating the Grand Canyon, Southeastern Nevada and Northwestern Arizona," *U.S. Geol. Survey Prof. Paper 1111.*

Bradley, W. H. 1936. "Geomorphology of the North Flank of the Uinta Mountains," *U.S. Geol. Survey Prof. Paper 185-L.*

Childs, O. E., and B. W. Beebe (eds). 1963. *Backbone of the Americas.* American Association Petroleum Geologists Memoir 2.

Crittendon, M. D., Jr. 1963. "New Data on the Isostatic Deformation of Lake Bonneville," *U.S. Geol. Survey Prof. Paper 454.*

Darton, N. H. 1925. *A Resume of Arizona Geology.* Arizona Bureau of Mines Bull. 119, 298 p.

Davis, W. M. 1925. "The Basin Range Problem," *National Academy Sci. Proceedings*, 11:387–392.

Fenneman, N. M. 1928. "Physiographic Subdivisions of the United States," *Annals Association American Geographers*, vol. XVIII, 353 p.

Gilbert, G. K. 1876. "The Colorado Plateau Province as a Field for Geological Study," *American Jour. Sci.*, 3rd series, 12:16–24.

Gilbert, G. K. 1890. "Lake Bonneville," *U.S. Geol. Survey Monograph I.*

Gile, L. H., F. F. Peterson, and R. B. Grossman. 1966. "Morphological and Genetic Sequences of Carbonate Accumulation in Desert Soils," *Soil Science* 101:346–360.

Gilluly, J. 1965a. "Tectonic and Igneous Geology of the Northern Shoshone Range, Nevada," *U.S. Geol. Survey Prof. Paper 465.*

Gilluly, J. 1965b. "Volcanism, Tectonism, and Plutonism in Western United States," *Geol. Soc. America Spec. Paper No. 80.*

Hansen, W. R., 1969. *Development of the Green River Drainage System across the Uinta Mountains.* Intermountain Association of Geologists, 16th Annual Field Conference, 93–100.

Hubbs, C. L., and R. R. Miller. 1948. "The Great Basin: Zoological Evidence," *University of Utah Bull.*, 38:18–166.

Hunt, C. B. 1956. "Cenozoic Geology of the Colorado Plateau," *U.S. Geol. Survey Prof. Paper 279*.

Hunt, C. B. 1969a. "John Wesley Powell—His Influence on Geology," *GeoTimes* 14:16–68.

Hunt, C. B. 1969b. "Geologic History of the Colorado River," in *The Colorado River Region and John Wesley Powell, U.S. Geol. Survey Prof. Paper 669*, 59–130.

Hunt, C. B. 1974. *Natural Regions of the United States and Canada*. San Francisco: W. H. Freeman and Co., 725 p.

Hunt, C. B. 1975. *Death Valley: Geology, Ecology, Archeology*. University of California Press, 234 p.

Hunt, C. B. 1979. "The Great Basin, an Overview and Hypotheses of its History," *Rocky Mountain Assoc. Geol. and Utah Geol. Assoc., 1979 Basin and Range Symposium* 1–10.

Hunt, C. B., and D. R. Mabey. 1966. "Stratigraphy and Structure, Death Valley, California," *U.S. Geol. Survey Prof. Paper 494-A*.

Hunt, C. B., and T. W. Robinson. 1966. "Hydrologic Basin, Death Valley, California," *U.S. Geol. Survey Prof. Paper 494-B*.

Ketner, K. B. 1977. "Deposition and Deformation of Lower Paleozoic Western Facies Rocks, Northern Nevada," in *Paleozoic Paleogeography of the Western United States, Pacific Coast Paleogeography Symposium 1, Pacific Section, Soc. Economic Paleontologists and Mineralogists*, Los Angeles, 251–258.

Larson, E. E., M. Ozima, and W. C. Bradley. 1975. "Late Cenozoic Basic Volcanism in Northwestern Colorado and Its Implications Concerning Tectonism and the Origin of the Colorado River System," *Geol. Soc. America Mem.* 144, 155–178.

Longwell, C. R. 1936. "Geology of the Boulder Reservoir Floor, Arizona–Nevada," *Geol. Soc. America Bull.*, 47:1393–1476.

Longwell, C. R. 1946. "How Old is the Colorado River?," *American Jour. Sci.*, 244:817–835.

Luchitta, I. 1972. "Early History of the Colorado River in the Basin and Range Province," *Geol. Soc. America Bull.*, 83:1933–1948.

Lustig, L. K. 1974. "Deserts," in *Encyclopaedia Britannica*, 5:602–615.

Meinzer, O. E. 1922. "Map of the Pleistocene Lakes of the Basin and Range Province and Its Significance," *Geol. Soc. America Bull.*, 33:541–552.

McKee, E. D., and E. H. McKee. 1972. "Pliocene Uplift of the Grand Canyon Region, Time of Drainage Adjustment," *Geol. Soc. America Bull.*, 83:1923–1932.

McKee, E. D., and others. 1967. "Evolution of the Colorado River in Arizona." *Museum Northern Arizona Bull.* 44, 67 p.

Merriam, C. W., and C. A. Anderson. 1942. "Reconnaissance Survey of the Roberts Mountains, Nevada," *Geol. Soc. America Bull.*, 53:1675–1728.

Misch, P. 1960. "Regional Structural Reconnaissance in Central Northeast Nevada and Some Adjacent Areas," in *Guidebook to Geology of East Central Nevada, Intermountain Assoc. Petroleum Geologists, 11th Field Conf.*, 17–42.

Noble, L. 1941. "Structural Features of the Virgin Springs Area, Death Valley, California," *Geol. Soc. America Bull.*, 52:941–1000.

Peirce, H. W. 1976. "Tectonic Significance of Basin and Range Thick Evaporite Deposits," *Arizona Geol. Soc. Digest*, 10:325–339.

Plummer, F. B. 1932. "Evolution of the Physiography of Northwest Texas and Southeastern New Mexico," in *The Geology of Texas, Vol. 1: Stratigraphy, University of Texas Bull.* 3232, 770 p.

Powell, J. W. 1875. *Exploration of the Colorado River of the West, 1869–72*. Washington, D.C.: Government Printing Office, 291 p.

Powell, J. W. 1876. *Report on the Geology of the Eastern Portion of the Uinta Mountains*.

Washington, D.C.: Government Printing Office, 218 p.

Powell, J. W. 1879. *Report on the Lands of the Arid Region of the United States*. U.S. 45th Congress, 2nd sess., House Executive Document 73, 195 p.

Powell, J. W. 1896. *The Physiography of the United States*. American Book Co.

Roberts, R. J. 1965. "Stratigraphy and Structure of the Antler Peak Quadrangle, Humboldt and Lander Peak Quadrangles, Nevada," *U.S. Geol. Survey Prof. Paper 495A*.

Roberts, R. J. 1968. "Tectonic Framework of the Great Basin," in *A Coast to Coast Tectonic Study of the United States, University of Missouri Journal, V. H. McNutt Colloquium*, No. 1, 101–119.

Spieker, E. M. 1946. "Late Mesozoic and Early Cenozoic History of Central Utah," *U.S. Geol. Survey Prof. Paper 205D*.

Stewart, J. H., W. J. Moore, and I. Zietz. 1977. "East-West Patterns of Cenozoic Igneous rocks, Aeromagnetic Anomalies, and Mineral Deposits, Nevada and Utah," *Geol. Soc. America Bull.*, 88:67–77.

Stock, C., and F. D. Bode. 1935. "Occurrence of Lower Oligocene Mammal-Bearing Beds near Death Valley, California," *National Academy Sci. Proceedings*, 21:571–579.

Stokes, W. L. (ed). 1966. "The Great Salt Lake," *Guidebook to the Geology of Utah, Utah Geological Society*, 164 p.

Young, R. A. 1966. *Cenozoic Geology Along the Edge of the Colorado Plateau in Northwestern Arizona*. Ph.D. dissertation, St. Louis: Washington University, 167 p.

Young, R. A., and W. J. Brennan. 1974. "The Peach Springs Tuff: Its Bearing on Structural Evolution of the Colorado Plateau and Development of Cenozoic Drainage in Mohave County, Arizona," *Geol. Soc. America Bull.*, 85:83–90.

# 2

# SOME LAND MANAGEMENT PROBLEMS IN OUR WESTERN U.S. ARID LANDS

Charles B. Hunt

University of Utah
Salt Lake City, Utah

## WATER SUPPLIES AND WASTE DISPOSAL IN THE SOUTHWEST DESERTS

The importance of the Rocky Mountains, other western mountains, and High Plateaus to the water economy of the Southwest deserts can be appreciated by a glance at maps showing the rivers (Fig. 1.2). The Southern Rockies, for example, provide the headwaters for the Colorado, Dolores, San Juan, Rio Grande, and Pecos rivers. This has political implications. New Mexico, for example, is virtually dependent upon Colorado for its surface water, which is a good example of why the Federal government has had to play an increasing role in water management. And even the Colorado River is small compared to rivers in central and eastern United States. It has been said that money is at the root of most evil, but in the Southwest deserts, water is at the root of most evil. Its scarcity is a veritable gold mine for lawyers.

Even with the Rockies and other water sources the runoff from the arid lands averages less than 1 inch (25 mm) per annum. Runoff from the Great Basin is zero. Runoff in the Colorado Plateau and Sonoran and Chihuahuan deserts is barely enough to maintain flow of the rivers that cross those deserts.

Ground-water supplies are obtained from many basins in the Basin and Range province and from certain sandstone units on the Colorado Plateau. At all the urban areas and other areas where ground water is used for irrigation, water levels have seriously declined. Withdrawals exceed the recharge, and unless the States act responsibly in controlling the depletion of the ground-water resource, pressure will build for more Federal intervention.

In addition to water shortage, water quality is a problem, in large part because the high rate of evaporation increases the concentration of salts dissolved in water. By the time the Colorado River reaches Mexico, the water is saline, and the United States has agreed to build a plant for treating the water being delivered to Mexico. Ground-water supplies in the deserts are almost universally hard water and in places sufficiently so to clog pipes with accumulations of calcium carbonate. Man has contributed to water pollution in the deserts. Agriculture contributes fertilizers, herbicides, and pesticides; mines and smelters contribute acid water. The problem is illustrated by graffiti found in towns along the Rio Grande in New Mexico, "Please flush the toilet; the water is needed in Texas."

Flash floods are another hydrologic problem in the deserts. In Arizona the largest flood of record on the Salt River had a peak flow about equal to the largest flood on the Colorado River (Harshberger et al. 1966). Yet, state and municipal governments allow apartments in urban areas to be built in washes subject to flash floods (for example, see Fig. 2.1A and B).

Another kind of problem concerns disposal of radioactive and other toxic wastes. The Water Atlas of the United States indicates that the basins of the Basin and Range province are "well suited" for deep well disposal (Geraghty and Miller 1973). I dissent, having participated in studies that developed evidence for interbasin circulation of ground water in Death Valley (Hunt and Robinson 1966). The evidence casts grave doubts about the safety of the radioactive-waste dump near Beatty, Nevada, located ironically just above Death Valley. Detailed studies of the movement of ground water in that area are underway by the U.S. Geological Survey, but the public is not being informed about progress of the studies. If the public is informed, the chances are that higher priority would be given the studies, because they concern not only that site but principles having a bearing on the movement of ground water in other parts of the Basin and Range province.

## PLANT GEOGRAPHY: FOR HEALTHY GROWTH, PLANTS REQUIRE WATER

Two important studies about plant geography in arid lands were published during the 1890s. One, in Death Valley by F. V. Coville (1893), considered why individual species of plants are restricted to certain habitats and related them to ground conditions. The other study, by C. H. Merriam (1892, 1898), in the Grand Canyon area, equated altitudinal and latitudinal zoning of plants to climatic factors.

Figure 2.1. Inept city and county zoning in the arid regions allows buildings like these apartments (A) to be built in washes subject to flash floods, so Senators and Congressmen obtain funds for the Corps of Engineers to erect dams (B) to protect them. The examples are at Las Cruces, New Mexico, but the problem is commonplace.

The southern parts of the Basin and Range province have the hottest and driest deserts, partly because they are most southerly and partly because they are lowest in altitude. This is Merriam's Lower Sonoran zone and is characterized by creosote bush, many species of cacti and yucca, and various spiney or thorny shrubs and small trees. The western part of the Lower Sonoran zone has its rainfall predominantly during the winter; summers are so hot and dry that J. Ross Browne (1869) reported mules could bray only at midnight. In southern Arizona, precipitation occurs biseasonally, winter and summer. In the Chihuahua Desert of southern New Mexico and west Texas, precipitation is predominantly during the summer growing season.

Plants growing on alluvial fans are xerophytes (Fig. 2.2). Plants on these fans are zoned altitudinally (Fig. 2.3) but the zonation is irregular because differences in ground conditions affect moisture infiltration and retention. Some parts of a fan collect runoff from adjoining areas and receive more than average moisture; other parts have excessive runoff and the ground receives less than the average moisture. The principle is illustrated along most highways where vegetation is comparatively lush along the shoulders because of additional runoff from the pavement.

Other desert plants, phreatophytes, grow where ground water is shallow and within reach of the plant roots. Whereas xerophytes are distributed in orderly patterns according to the quantity of water seeping into particular tracts of ground, phreatophytes are zoned according to the salinity of their supply (Fig. 2.4). Figure 2.5, a transect across the Pecos Valley in New Mexico, illustrates the sensitivity of desert vegetation to differences in conditions.

In the central and northern parts of the Great Basin and on the Colorado Plateau, altitudes average 2,000–3,000 feet (610–914 m) higher than in the southern deserts, and the vegetation is that of Merriam's Upper Sonoran zone. Vegetation there is characterized by sagebrush and its associates. Xerophytic plants there also reflect differences in quantity of water available for plant growth. For example, shale deserts have matsaltbush; whereas, sandy ground has sand sagebrush and curley grass. Figure 2.6 illustrates the plant geography that is typical of gravel-covered pediments on the Colorado Plateau where the altitudinal zoning is modified by availability of perched water along buried channels under the gravel cap.

Another principle of plant geography, the effect of microclimate, is illustrated by the way species adapt to conditions near the limit of their range. At their northern limit, southern species seed south-facing slopes; at the southern limit, northern species seed north-facing slopes. Some of the changes in plant geography that reflect the Pleistocene and Holocene climatic changes are described in the papers by Van Devender and Spaulding and Axelrod in this symposium volume.

## LAND MANAGEMENT IN DESERTS

Powell's (1879) report on the arid regions was the first attempt to educate Americans that the arid lands had to be developed and managed differently from the humid, eastern parts of the country. Today, because of a population explosion, particularly in the western U.S., pressures on the arid lands are increasing exponentially. Doubling the population more than doubles the problems. In Powell's day practically all the arid region was wilderness. Human population of the arid-land states was only 1.75 million. Today, those states approach fifty million, a twenty-five-fold increase that is five times the national average, and there is controversy about how the arid land should be managed. One issue, for example, is the degree to which remnants of Powell's wilderness should be preserved.

Population pressure on land of all kinds is a global problem and much worse in many parts of the world than in the U.S. Foolishly though, we are not learning either from our own experience or the experience of others. Our deserts can withstand drought, but how many offroad vehicles (Fig. 2.7)? And how many livestock? And should there be any restrictions on mining and other developments? And who should decide such questions? Obviously, the interests of those using the lands should be considered, but leaving the decisions to such special interest groups would be, as James Thurber expressed it, "Government of the orioles, by the orioles, and for the foxes."

Many parts of Powell's wilderness had been farmed by irrigation by Indians a thousand years earlier. At many or most of those places the land use, perhaps coupled with drought, led to erosion (Fig. 2.8). This pattern of land use followed by erosion was repeated during the 1880s and 1890s when the new generation of westerners began crowding onto the land.

The two land-use histories a thousand years apart suggest that the use was the cause of the erosion, but geology records similar episodes of erosion long before people were using the lands. There still is difference of opinion whether land use caused the erosion or simply triggered an event that was inevitable because of climatic conditions. We can only conclude that arid lands erode easily and need to be managed with care, yet we do not know just what is meant by 'being careful.' But certainly the solution is not to abandon controls as proposed by the "sagebrush rebellion."

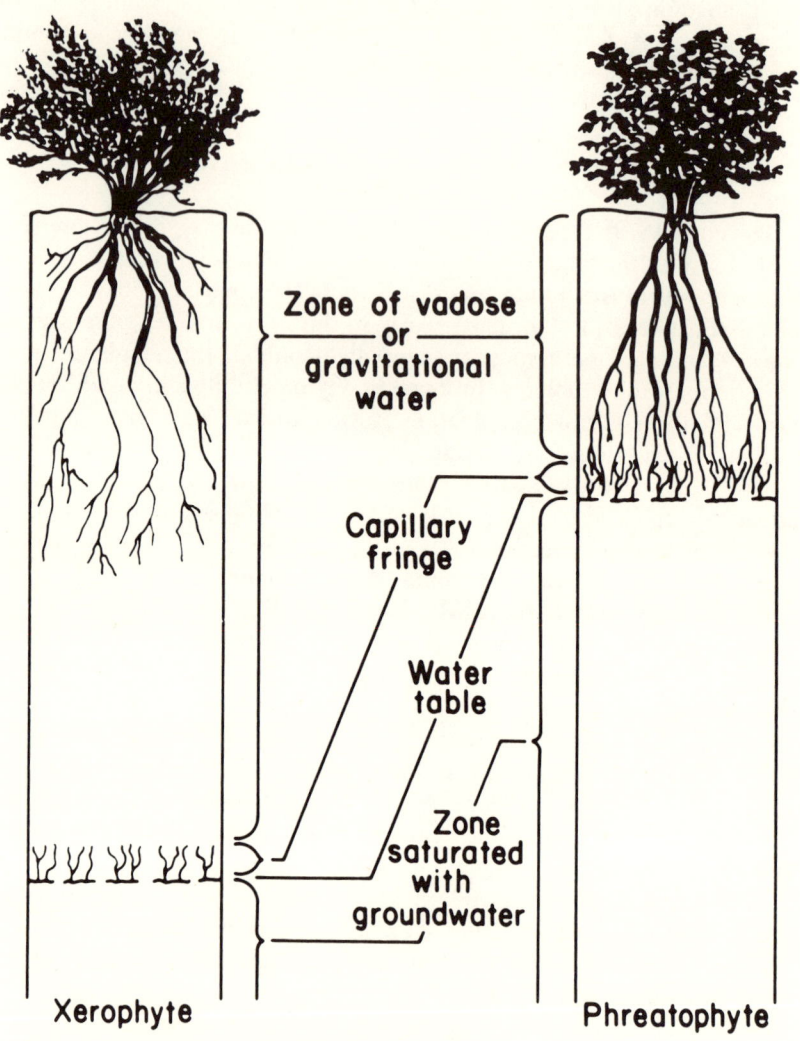

Figure 2.2. Water in the ground is available to plant roots in at least two basic ways. The top of the zone saturated with groundwater is referred to as the water table. A capillary fringe rises upward from it. Plants that send their roots down to this zone have a perennial water supply and are known as phreatophytes. The zone above the capillary fringe is wet only when water seeps downward through it, after rains or floods. Plants that root in this zone must be capable of surviving droughts and are known as xerophytes; from Hunt 1974.[1]

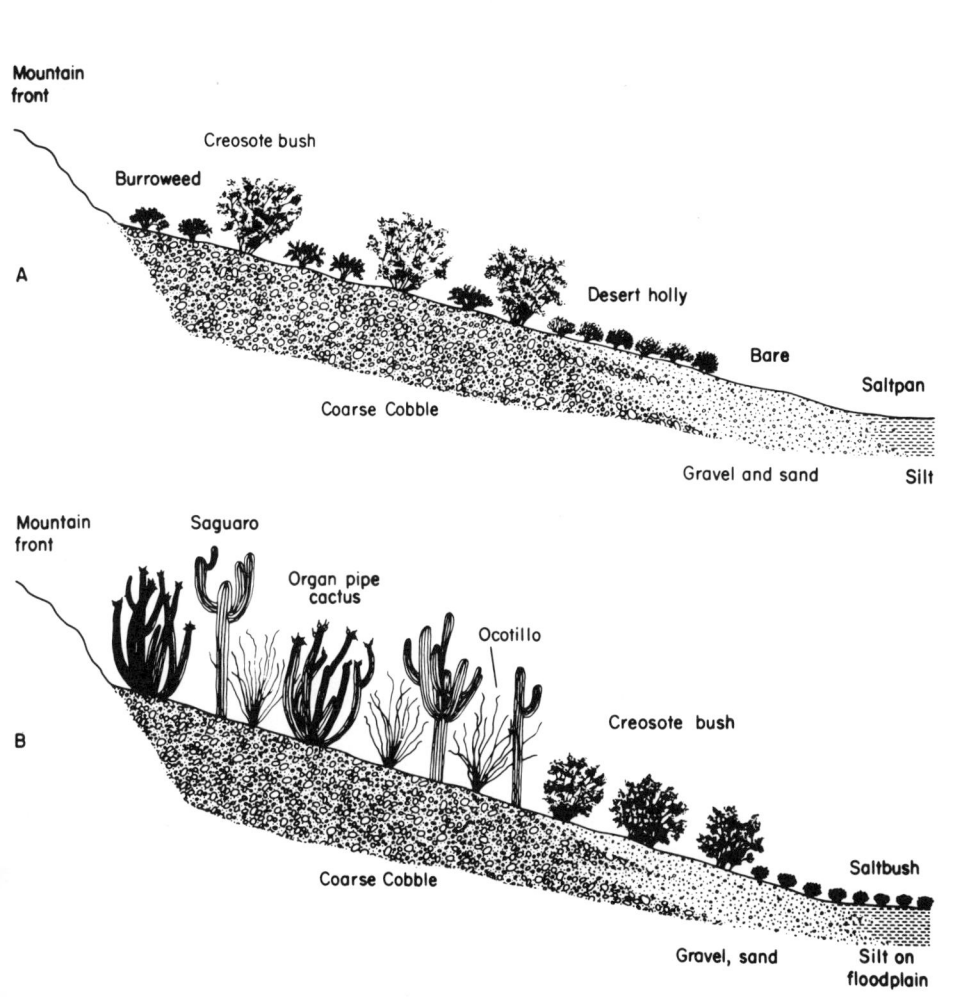

Figure 2.3. Vegetation on the alluvial fans in the Basin and Range province is zoned altitudinally, in part, because of temperature differences on the fans and, in part, because of differences in the kind of ground affect moisture infiltration and retention. Species characteristic of the low parts of the fans may range to the higher parts and consequently the number of species increases upward. (A) is transect typical of Death Valley and the Mojave Desert; (B) is in the Organpipe Cactus National Monument and is typical of the Sonoran Desert. Both transects are 5 to 10 mi (8–16 km) long; from Hunt 1974.[1]

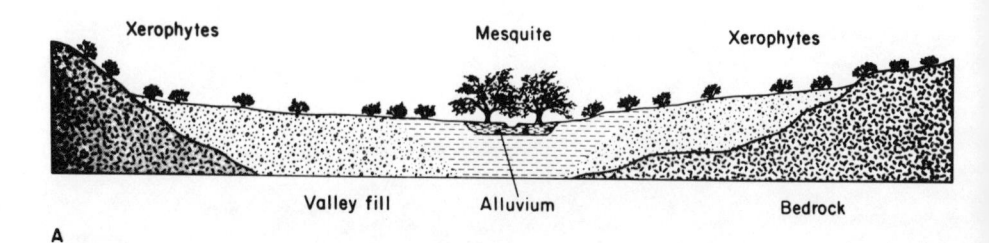

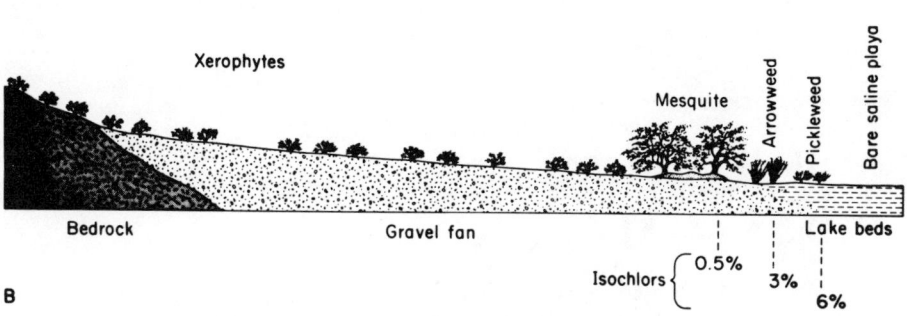

Figure 2.4. Diagrams illustrating how ground-water conditions are indicated by stands of phreatophytes in the southern deserts. (A) Mesquite grows where there is ground water or frequent recharge of the vadose zone in alluvium along a stream. The bordering fans are wet only infrequently and have stands of xerophytes. (B) Saline playas have bordering springs with phreatophytes that are zoned with respect to their salinity tolerances. The bordering fans and mountainsides have xerophytes; from Hunt 1974.[1]

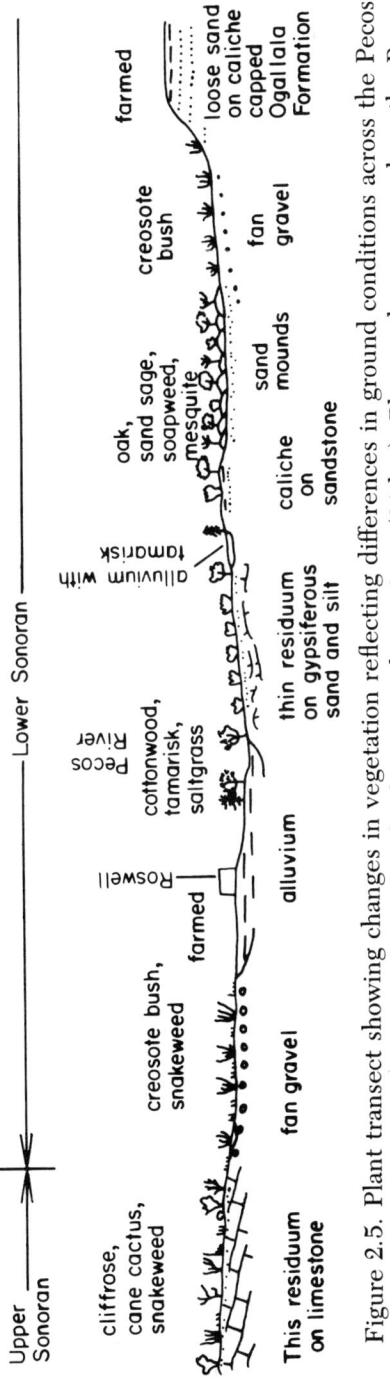

Figure 2.5. Plant transect showing changes in vegetation reflecting differences in ground conditions across the Pecos River valley, near Roswell, New Mexico; length of transect about 40 mi (64 km). Phreatophytes grow along the Pecos River and other alluvial valleys. Each of the six different kinds of xeric ground has a distinctive stand of xerophytes, which reflect differences in infiltration and retention of moisture.

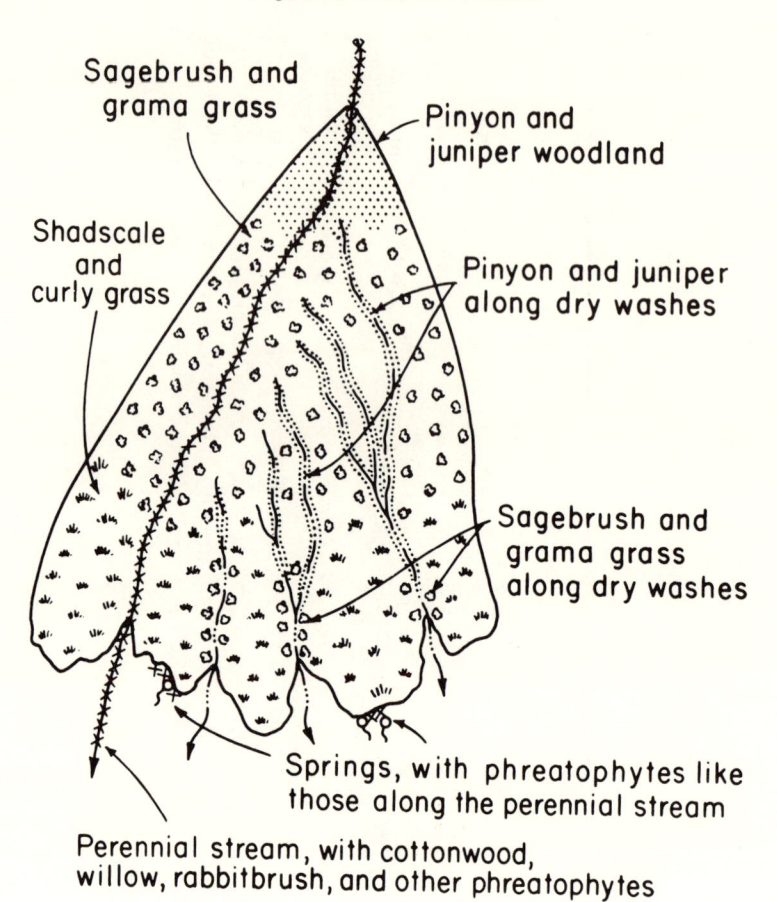

Figure 2.6. Vegetation map typical of gravel-covered pediments near the foot of mountains and high plateaus on the Colorado Plateau. Altitudinal zoning is marked by pinyon-juniper woodland on the high parts, sagebrush and grama grass below the woodland, and shadscale and curley grass below the sage. Each of the upper zones extends downslope along washes that collect runoff from neighboring areas. Perennial streams and springs are marked by phreatophytes; from Hunt 1974.[1]

Figure 2.7. Arid lands can withstand drought, but how many offroad vehicles (ORVs)? And how many livestock? And how much mining or other land use?

The arid lands today also are confronted with problems of urban sprawl. Populations in the Tucson–Phoenix areas of southern Arizona have increased 100-fold. The El Paso, Texas and Albuquerque, New Mexico areas have increased 50-fold. The Denver, Colorado and Salt Lake City, Utah corridors have increased 15-fold. The fact is the West now is dude Marlboro country and no longer qualifies as Bull Durham country. The noisy participants in the 'sagebrush rebellion' prefer to damn the Feds rather than think out their problem. Their extravagant protests may satisfy emotions but will not stand elementary analysis. Five case histories of restrictive legislative actions, or proposed action, illustrate this.

*First:* Who opposed Powell's recommendations for managing the arid lands? Wallace Stegner (1954), who analyzed the political battles that swirled around Powell, wrote: ". . . western Senators and Congressmen . . . stomped his arid regions proposal to death in 1879." There simply were too many like Gilpin of Colorado wanting to exploit the West's potentialities, a viewpoint still reflected by those "sagebrush rebels" who

Figure 2.8. At places on the Colorado Plateau, prehistoric land use by Indians was followed by erosion. At this place (floodplain of Bull Creek north of the Henry Mountains, Utah) the occupation layer (ca. 900 A.D., marked by stones) is 6 to 12 in (152 to 305 mm) higher than the rest of the floodplain, the surface of which has been eroded by wind, and the silt has been blown from the surface and heaped in mounds held by greasewood. Each mound of eolian material is on a pedestal of the old alluvium.

do not recognize the facts of population pressure and still yearn for the halcyon days of Wyatt Earp, Billy the Kid, and Butch Cassidy.

*Second:* Forested lands became protected as forest reserves in 1891. Western Congressmen, then as now, opposed to Federal land management, attached a rider to the Agricultural Appropriation Bill in 1907 prohibiting further additions to the Forest Reserves (now National Forests) by presidential proclamation. Theodore Roosevelt was president, and he signed the bill. But before signing he added, by proclamation, another 15.5 million acres (approximately 6.3 hectares) to the established forests. So, in this matter he could say with a smile, as he did about the Panama Canal, "I just took it."

According to Dean Box at Utah State University (1978, p. 16) "With the establishment of grazing regulations in 1905, the condition of the National Forest rangelands improved and has continued to the present time. . . . Today they are in the best condition since the turn of the century."

*Third:* While forested lands improved, nonforested lands barely survived the abuses of nonmanagement. There were no controls on grazing or other use and the over-used lands became devastated when drought struck during the 1920s and 1930s (Fig. 2.9). These conditions led to the Taylor Grazing Act of 1934. Both the legislation and its enforcement were by westerners and not those uninformed easterners so castigated by the western press. Congressman Taylor was from Colorado. The first director and first assistant director were westerners. And administration was by grazing districts that utilized advisory committees of local ranchers acquainted with the district.

*Fourth:* The report of the Public Land Law Review Commission (1970) has been the basis for most arid-lands legislation during the last decade. The Commission had to reconcile such diverse interests as the national public, the regional public having ready access to the public lands (mostly the arid lands), and their resources include such diverse activities as:
- mining
- petroleum exploration and development
- pipelines and highways
- lumbering
- cattle grazing
- sheep grazing
- agriculture
- water supply and watershed protection

Figure 2.9. Shale deserts and alluvial floodplains are especially susceptible to arroyo cutting. Moreover, floodplains were generally the places favored for early settlements because the rich land was flat and easily tilled, and most streams had sufficient water for irrigation. In nearly every valley, however, agriculture was followed by floods and the start of arroyo cutting.

- fish and wildlife needs
- recreation.

These are not cozy bedfellows. There has been infighting within these activities, as between cattle and sheep interests and between motorcycle or other ORV (off-road vehicle) and hiking clubs.

The Commission's study utilized panels of experts in each field by including representatives of the numerous interested organizations. Moreover, thirteen of the nineteen members of the Commission, including both the chairman and vice-chairman, were from the arid-land states. Yet, westerners complain that Washington is unfair to their states. Headlines in the Salt Lake Tribune complain:

"U.S. agencies determine Utah Land Policy," and

"Game's fixed in Washington. Utah plays against stacked deck in land policy."

The Commission's report is comprehensive and, by taking a national rather than provincial stance, the report is so reasonable no particular interest is given unfair advantage over another. Critics, like those agitating for the "sagebrush rebellion" obviously represent special interests. They seek to be the foxes to which James Thurber alluded.

*Fifth:* When Congress began enacting the Commission's recommendations, maximum consideration was given to the regional public having ready access to the public lands. The Federal Land Policy and Management Act of 1976 specifically provides that federal land-management agencies coordinate their plans with state enacted plans. But no intermountain state has a land-development plan. My adopted state, Utah, has twice rejected such state planning. In the mid-forties the legislature killed a proposal that had been submitted by the Utah Academy of Sciences (Cottam 1945). And about seven years ago Utahans voted down a proposition for state planning that had been entered on the ballot. Westerners have not been able to agree on planning for themselves and by default have left all initiative and action to Washington.

And who, except the federal government, is trying to correct the rampant air pollution in the West? It seems elementary that air so dirty that it blocks out a mountain is hazardous to your health. Yet, industry has a standard reply to every proposal to curb emissions, "Rules too stifling; we'll move." Each state has been proved helpless in the face of loss of economic base and loss of jobs. So again we turn to the federal government to obtain uniform rules.

Water problems in the arid lands are not merely those of scarcity; floods are a problem too, as witness the Big Thompson flood in Colorado in 1976 and the Teton Dam failure in 1977. Yet, the states persist in neglecting their responsibilities and permit apartments to be built in washes subject to flash floods (Fig. 2.1A). And then their congressmen obtain funds for the Corps of Engineers to erect dams to protect such buildings (Fig. 2.1B). Western congressmen object to their state's paying 10 percent of the cost of reclamation projects like the Central Utah and Central Arizona projects. They practically admit the projects are uneconomic, pork-barrel projects by asserting "that 10 percent would break us." We can be certain, though, that projects by the Bureau of Reclamation and Corps of Engineers would be scrutinized more closely if the states did pay a substantial percentage of the cost.

It would seem elementary that in a region where water is scarce every effort would be made to conserve the water supplies, both surface and ground water. But because of subsidy by the Bureau of Reclamation and Corps of Engineers, water still is cheap and there has been little incentive to encourage conservation. Yet, urban areas that have become sprawling metropolises, like the urban corridor at Denver, Colorado, and the similar one in the Salt Lake City, Utah area, probably could meet 10 to 20 percent of their water needs by having parts of yards and parking strips landscaped in harmony with the desert environment instead of trying to make them look like a Washington, D.C. suburb.

Would overall public land management be improved if the federal land management agencies were together in one department? The Public Land Law Review Commission recommended that, but bureaucratic interests, which are as suspect as those of the "sagebrush rebellion," brought pressure on the 96th Congress to say 'No.'

I share the common criticism about the growing federal bureaucracy, but I am sure there is nothing wrong with it that a 10 percent cut in appropriations won't cure. I don't know the solution to land management problems in the arid lands. I do know that damning the Feds and "uninformed easterners" will not solve those problems. The solutions adopted will have to consider the facts of the region's physiography and the facts of population pressure in this last quarter of the twentieth century.

## NOTE

1. Figures obtained from *Natural Regions of the United States and Canada*, copyright W. H. Freeman and Co., reproduced with permission.

## REFERENCES

Browne, J. 1869. *Adventures in the Apache country*. London, 292 p.
Cottam, W. P. 1945. *Resource problems of Utah*. Proc. Utah Acad. Science, Arts and Letters, 13 p.
Coville, F. V. 1893. *Botany of the Death Valley Expedition*. U.S. National Herbarium Contribution, vol. 4, 363 p.
Geraghty, J. J., and D. W. Miller. 1973. *Water Atlas of the United States*. Water Information Center Publication, 119 plates.
Harshbarger, J. W., D. D. Lewis, H. E. Skibitzke, and W. L. Heckler, and L. R. Kister. 1966. "Arizona Water," *U.S. Geol. Survey Water-Supply Paper 1648*.
Hunt, C. B., and T. W. Robinson. 1966. "Hydrologic Basin, Death Valley, California," *U.S. Geol. Survey Prof. Paper 494-B*.
Merriam, C. H. 1892. "The Geographic Distribution of Life in North America," *Washington Bio. Soc. Proceedings*, 7:1–64.
Merriam, C. H. 1898. "Life Zones and Crop Zones of the United States," *U.S. Division Biological Survey Bull*. vol. 10, 79 p.
Powell, J. W. 1879. *Report on the Lands of the Arid Region of the United States*. U.S. 45th Congress, 2nd sess., House Executive Document 73, 195 p.
Public Land Law Review Commission. 1970. *One Third of the Nation's Land, a Report to the President and to the Congress*. Washington, D.C.: Government Printing Office, 342 p.
Stegner, W. 1954. *Beyond the Hundredth Meridian*. Boston: Houghton Mifflin, 438 p.

# 3

# THE PLATE TECTONIC SETTING OF CORDILLERAN DESERTS

Peter J. Coney

University of Arizona
Tucson, Arizona

## INTRODUCTION

The great deserts of the American Southwest are for the most part coincident with the Basin and Range province (Stewart 1978) of the southwestern part of the North American Cordillera (Fig. 3.1). This region includes the northern Basin and Range of Nevada and western Utah, the Arizona–Sonora Basin and Range of southwestern United States and northwestern Mexico, and the smaller Mohave desert of southern California. The northern Basin and Range is bounded on the west by the Sierra Nevada Mountains and on the east by the Colorado Plateau. The northern boundary, which is quite transitional, is the Columbia Plateau and the mountains north of the Snake River plain. The Arizona–Sonora Basin and Range lies east of the Peninsular Ranges of southern California and the Gulf of California and south of the Colorado Plateau. Its eastern boundary is clearly defined only in Sonora, where it is the Sierra Madre Occidental. Northward the province extends eastward into southern New Mexico and Chihuahua and then extends northward as far as Colorado as the narrow Rio Grande rift. The Mojave desert is largely that region east of the San Andreas fault, south of the Garlock fault, and west of the Colorado River.

The distinctive desert landscapes are most characterized by a basin and range topography and a general elevation less than surrounding provinces. This lower general elevation, particularly in the broad basins, and the surrounding highlands, particularly on the west, have induced the recent climatic severity. Both the distinctive topography of basin and range and the lower relative elevation are exceedingly young, certainly no older

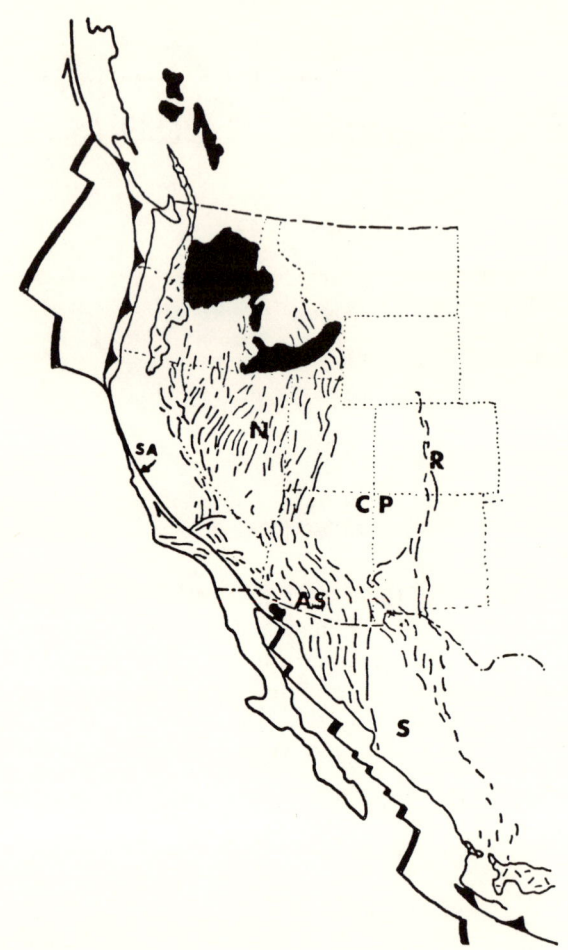

Figure 3.1. The Late Cenozoic Basin and Range province. The short wavy dashed lines are the generalized distribution of Basin and Range block faults. N = Northern Basin and Range, AS = Arizona–Sonora Basin and Range, R = Rio Grande rift, CP = Colorado Plateau, S = Sierra Madre Occidental, SA = San Andres fault. Heavy barbed lines are active trenches, connected heavy black lines are the spreading centers, black areas are Late Cenozoic basalt fields. Short dash pattern are active magmatic arcs.

than the past 17–20 m.y. (million years), and represent less than 1 percent of the recorded geologic history of the region. Both are also clearly the result of widespread regional uplift and extensional block-faulting, and associated strike-slip faulting, which collapsed and fragmented large segments of a rising southwestern Cordillera in Late Tertiary time. These Late Tertiary events are the result of an accident of plate tectonic geometry—namely, progressive collision of the Cordilleran margin with the East Pacific Rise. This accident produced a unique tectonic-physiographic province. Indeed, there is nothing quite like the Basin and Range province anywhere else on our planet, and the uniqueness is commensurate with the accident which produced it. The province has been much debated since the early explorations, and to this day its uniqueness is still much discussed.

## PRE-LATE TERTIARY TECTONIC EVOLUTION

The pre-Late Tertiary tectonic evolution of southwestern North America has been dominated by a succession of variable plate tectonic settings since Late Precambrian time (Dickinson 1977; Coney 1978a, 1978b). The purpose in reviewing briefly this prolonged prelude to Late Tertiary events is to provide the reader with a perspective background on what later transpired and to examine what elements, if any, produced by the early history may have influenced development of the Basin and Range province in Late Tertiary time.

From Late Precambrian through Middle Paleozoic, the western edge of North America was a passive intra-plate continental margin much like our present Atlantic coastal plain and continental shelf (Fig. 3.2). Across this margin, at least from southern California northward, a westward thickening marine miogeoclinal sedimentary terrace formed which faced a paleo-Pacific Ocean. A similar margin was evolving in the region of the present Gulf of Mexico. Inboard of the two continental shelves and extending across Arizona–New Mexico and for some unknown distance into Mexico was a stable cratonic interior platform. Continental freeboard was very low and during much of the time this part of North America was awash with shallow shifting seas (Peirce 1976).

The paleo-Pacific margin shelf-slope break, or seaward edge of the continental shelf, extended along a line roughly from the Idaho–Oregon border southwestward toward the present central Sierra Nevada Mountains. The importance of this is that most of the western half of the northern Basin and Range in Nevada does not lie on ancient North American continental basement like the eastern half in eastern Nevada and Utah, and the entire southern Basin and Range do. In contrast, the eastern hinge

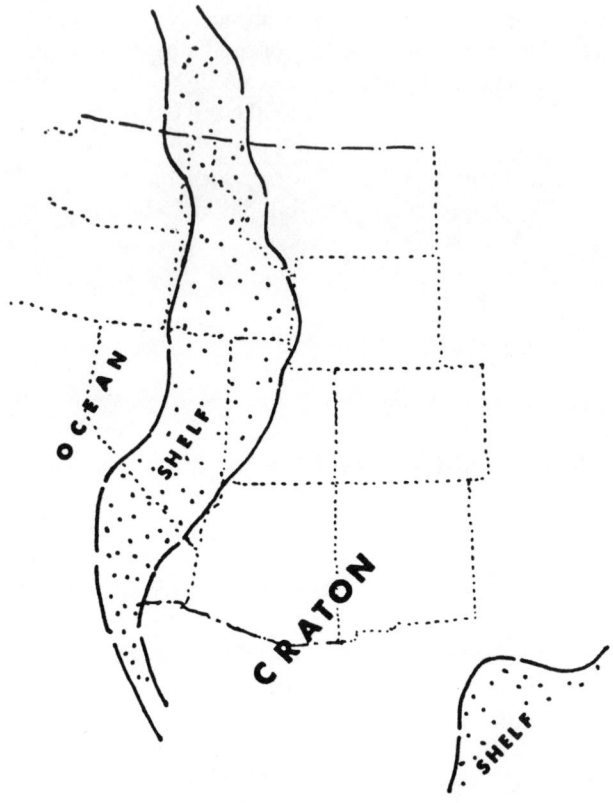

Figure 3.2. Major features of Paleozoic time. The dotted areas are the major continental terrace accumulations that formed on the margins of North America's cratonic interior platform.

line of the early Paleozoic westward thickening miogeocline roughly follows the present eastern edge of the Basin and Range province from the Snake River plain southwestward to southern Nevada along what is known as the Wasatch line. This boundary is also, of course, the western edge of the Colorado Plateau. In contrast, the northern edge of the Arizona–Sonoran Basin and Range is not a noticeable discontinuity in Paleozoic stratigraphy. The Paleozoic formations of the Grand Canyon on the Colorado Plateau are essentially identical to those in the Basin and Range to the south, and in both places they are part of the thin interior cratonic sequence of southwestern North America (Peirce 1976).

In Late Paleozoic to earliest Mesozoic time, the Pacific margin was disturbed twice by Late Devonian–Mississippian Antler deformation and Triassic Sonoma deformation. Oceanic materials were accreted to the Pacific margin in both events, but the effects were felt only in Nevada. In contrast, collisional events along the eastern and southern margin of North America, presumably related to suturing of Africa–South America against that margin, produced widespread intraplate faulting and formation of deep intracratonic basins and adjacent uplifts over much of southwestern North America in mostly Pennsylvanian to early Permian time. This event is known as the Ancestral Rockies in the eastern Cordillera. Except in New Mexico and adjacent Mexico and in western Utah, none of this affected what today is the Basin and Range province.

During Jurassic time the Pacific margin of North America became convergent and a magmatic arc stretched through Mexico, across southern Arizona and northward into eastern California (Fig. 3.3). A trench is inferred to have lain southwest of the arc. By Middle to Late Jurassic time Africa–South America was separating from North America and the Atlantic Ocean and Gulf of Mexico opened. South America, however, remained attached to North America through Mexico, and the separation transformed a large segment of the southern Cordillera southeastward along the Mojave-Sonora "megashear" or transform fault (Silver and Anderson 1974). Eventually, in latest Jurassic or earliest Cretaceous time, South America finally broke free from North America to open a proto-Caribbean Sea. As a result of the final separation, motion on the Mojave-Sonora megashear ceased.

In Late Jurassic time magmatic activity waned then flared up again far in the southwesern U.S. in Early Cretaceous time (Fig. 3.4). This new magmatic activity produced an enormous volcano-plutonic complex along what is now the Peninsular batholith of Baja California and southern California and the Sierra Nevada batholith in central California. A trench lay to the southwest of the magmatic arc and the Franciscan assemblage was accreted to North America's Pacific margin. The massive plutonic addition to the crust formed the foundation of the magmatic arc and to

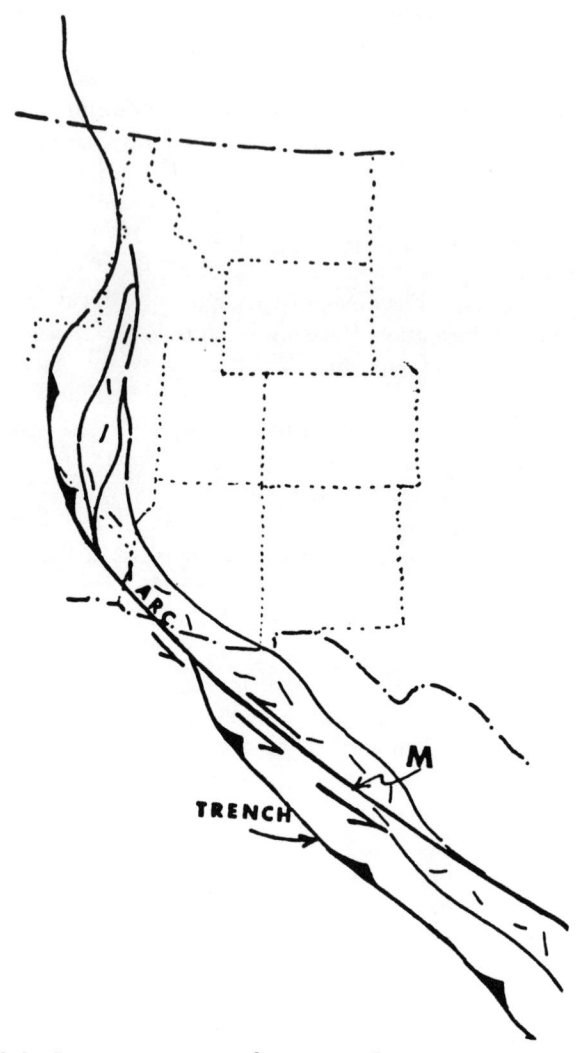

Figure 3.3. Jurassic tectonic features. The Jurassic magmatic arc is shown by dashed pattern. M = the Sonora–Mojave megashear or transform fault.

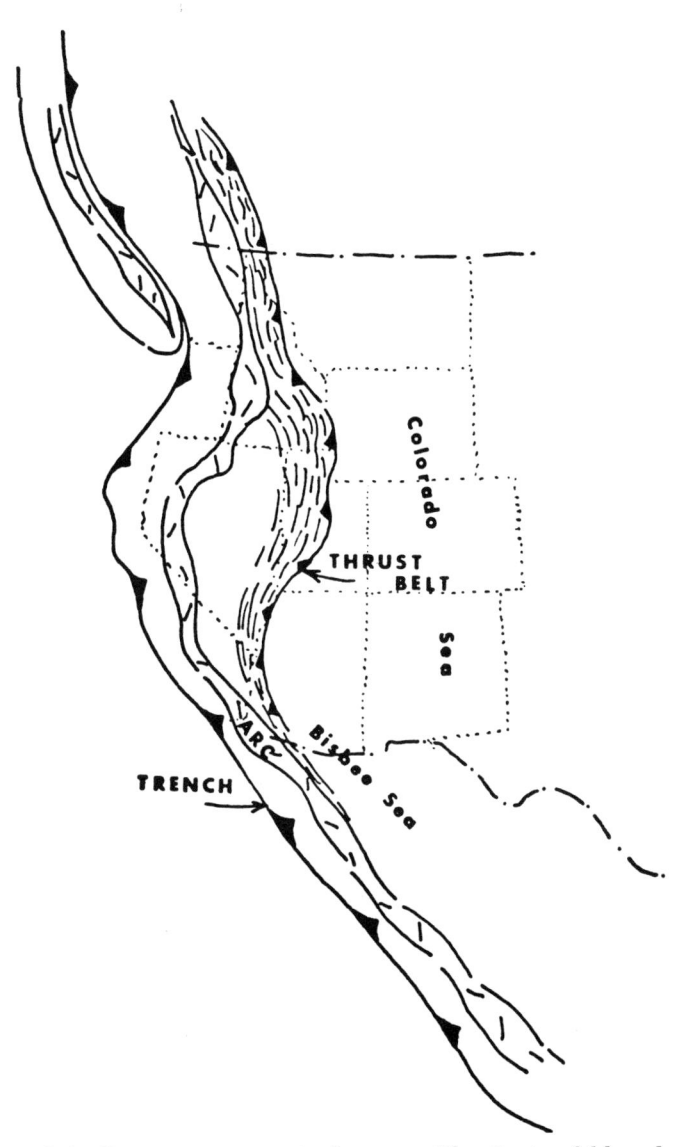

Figure 3.4. Cretaceous tectonic features. The Sevier fold and thrust belt is shown by small barbed line and irregular wavy line patterns. The Cretaceous magmatic arc trend is shown in dashed pattern.

this day is the western margin of the Basin and Range province from northwestern Mexico to Nevada.

East of the magmatic arc paleogeography was complex. From at least southern Nevada northward, arc-rear thrusting took place and produced the east-vergent folds and low-angle thrust faults of the Sevier orogenic belt (Armstrong 1968). Thrusting extended to the eastern edge of the Paleozoic miogeocline along the Wasatch line and debris from the deformation spread eastward across what is today the Colorado Plateau and Rocky Mountains into a vast interior foreland sea. This sea lapped southward onto an ancestral Mogollon highland in central Arizona. Southward, extending from the southeast out of the now completely opened Gulf of Mexico, was the Bisbee sea (Hayes 1970). At its maximum extent it covered most of south-central and southeastern Arizona and much of northeastern Mexico as far west as Sonora. The embayment must have merged with the Rocky Mountain sea somewhere to the east, but the peninsulalike Mogollon highland seems to have separated the two in central Arizona and New Mexico. The Bisbee sea lapped across an already deformed Jurassic arc terrane in Sonora and southern Arizona and across a varied Precambrian–Paleozoic terrane northward.

During Late Cretaceous time (Fig. 3.5) the magmatic arc along the Pacific margin began an eastward sweep (Coney and Reynolds 1977). In the north it swept to near extinction, but scattered igneous activity reached central Colorado. In the south the sweep stayed alive and reached central New Mexico, west Texas, and eastern Mexico. This eastward sweep was accompanied by, or shortly followed, intense Laramide compressive deformation (Coney 1976). In the north, enormous crustal folds and faults affected the entire Colorado Plateau and Rocky Mountains east of the Sevier orogenic belt. In the south, it severely deformed southern Arizona (Davis 1979), Sonora, and southeastern New Mexico, and produced the Sierra Madre Oriental of eastern Mexico. Once again the two major parts of the Basin and Range province were affected differently. The northern Basin and Range lay largely west of the Laramide destruction, but the Arizona–Sonora region was in the midst of it. Most of the great southwestern copper deposits, which are associated with Laramide plutons, formed at this time. The eastward sweep of magmatic arc activity is believed to be the result of a progressive flattening in dip of the Late Cretaceous to Early Tertiary subducting slab of Farallon plate beneath southwestern North America.

In Eocene time Laramide deformation ceased and was followed by widespread erosion (Epis and Chapin 1975) and an abrupt return sweep of the magmatic arc toward the Pacific margin during Middle Tertiary time (Coney and Reynolds 1977) (Fig. 3.6). Vast outbursts of ignimbrites from fissures and calderas occurred on a scale rarely seen anywhere on

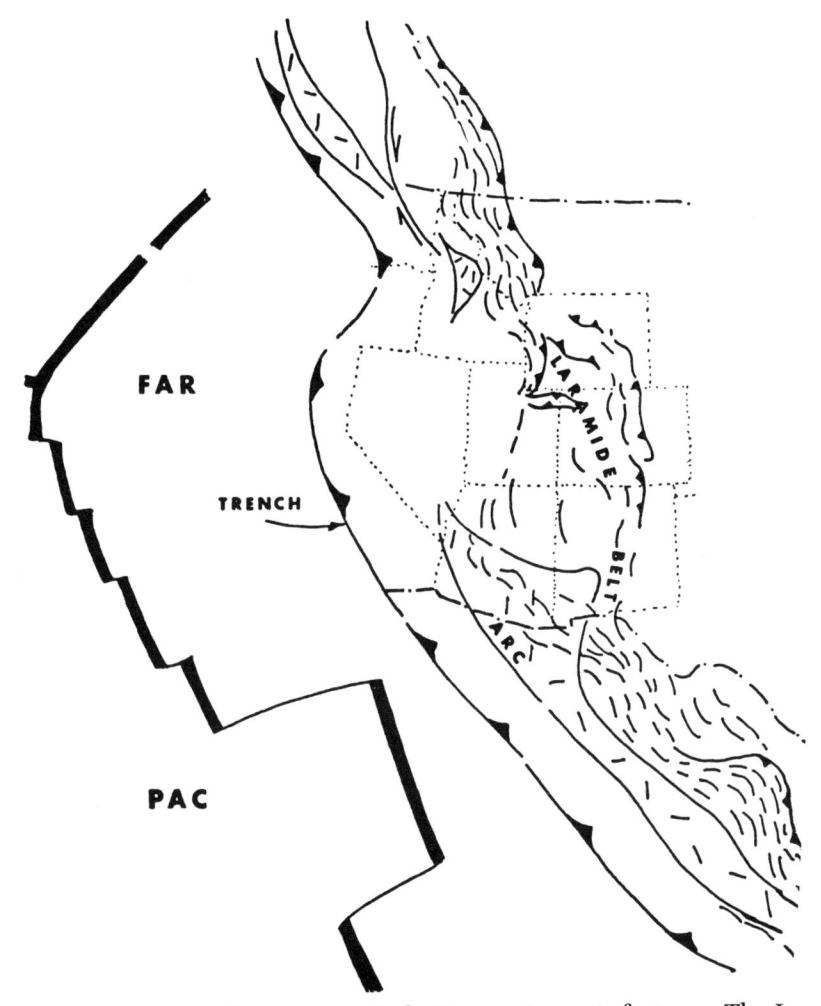

Figure 3.5. Late Cretaceous–Early Tertiary tectonic features. The Laramide fold and thrust belt is shown by small barbed lines and wavy lines. Laramide magmatic arcs shown by dashed pattern. The heavy black line offshore is the East Pacific Rise. FAR = Farallon plate, PAC = Pacific plate. The position of the East Pacific Rise is that of about 40 million years ago at the end of Laramide time.

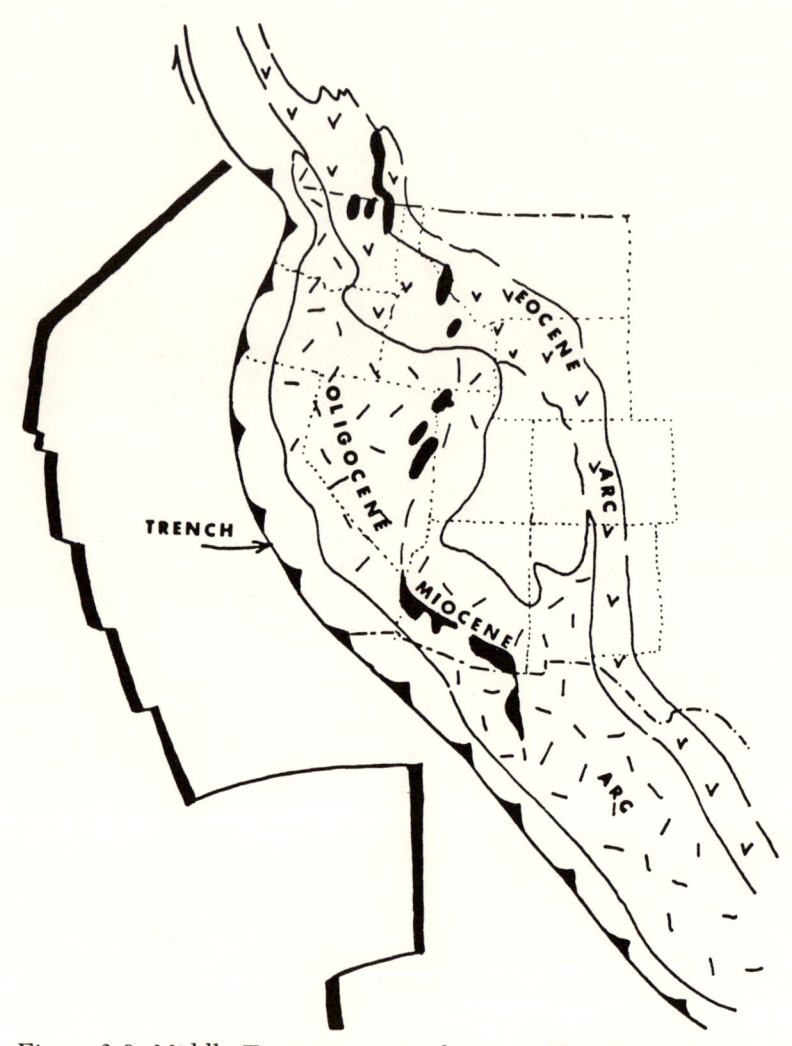

Figure 3.6. Middle Tertiary tectonic features. The Eocene magmatic arc trend is shown in V pattern. The Oligocene-Miocene magmatic arc trend is shown in dashed pattern. Black areas are metamorphic core complexes. Heavy black line is the East Pacific Rise at the beginning of a period about 40 million years ago.

the planet (Elston 1976). This event was a massive thermal disturbance which seems to have melted large segments of the crust and was accompanied by widespread shallow metamorphism. There was also a large amount of low-angle listric normal faulting (Anderson 1971). This activity is particularly restricted to the region that in later Tertiary time was to become the Basin and Range province. For example, the Colorado Plateau escaped it. Very large extensional terranes formed (Davis and Coney 1979). These terranes were floored by cataclastically deforming basement gneiss, early to Middle Tertiary plutons, and attenuating Phanerazoic rocks. Progressively, there was also widespread deposition of continental red-beds, particularly in Arizona and Sonora, which interfingered with distal volcanic outfalls. Some of these metamorphic terranes eventually domed and arched, causing late denudational sliding of the extended cover rocks to produce a belt of so-called metamorphic core complexes strung like beads through the Basin and Range province. It is important to realize that although the later Basin and Range block faulting is clearly younger than the events described above, the Basin and Range province essentially developed in the same region that suffered the Middle Tertiary thermal disturbance. At least in Arizona, the evidence seems clear that the first differentiation of the Colorado Plateau from what was to become the Basin and Range province in later Tertiary time occurred at the initiation of the Middle Tertiary thermal disturbance. It is at this time that we see the first reversal of drainage causing streams to flow off the Plateau rather than onto it as had been the case in Laramide time (Peirce et al. 1979).

## LATE TERTIARY TECTONIC EVOLUTION

Late Tertiary plate tectonics of southwestern North America evolved from Late Mesozoic to Early Tertiary plate configurations (Atwater 1970). By Late Cretaceous time we know at least three major plates paved the Pacific Ocean. They were the Pacific, Farallon, and Kula plates. Spreading centers lay between them and a trench was along the Pacific margin of North America. The trench was subducting mostly Farallon plate as that plate spread northeastward from the East Pacific Rise. During Late Cretaceous through Middle Tertiary time, the rise slowly approached the Pacific margin trench of North America and progressively younger and hotter oceanic crust entered the subduction zone and descended beneath North America's margin. Sometime after 30 m.y. ago, but before 20 m.y. ago, the East Pacific Rise made initial contact with the North American trench, probably in the vicinity of southern California–northern Baja California. This placed a northwestward-moving Pacific plate directly in contact with North America's westward-moving margin, and the vector subtraction of these two motions produced right strike-slip transform faults between the two plates trending north-northwesterly parallel to the Pacific margin. As more and more of the rise crest was annihilated, the transform boundary grew both north and south, and subduction and arc activity ceased between the two separating triple junctions. This must have produced a growing subducted slab "window" beneath the region northeast of the growing transform boundary (Dickinson and Snyder 1979).

The transform fault boundary, which probably initially lay offshore, was nearly 1,000 km long before Basin and Range rifting began near 17 m.y. ago in Miocene time. In any event, this accident of plate geometry, namely collision of North America with the East Pacific Rise, has continued to the present and all of Basin and Range rifting has evolved since that collision. The only apparent major interruption in this progressive evolution was when the transform margin jumped inboard to open up the Gulf of California and initiate the San Andreas transform system near 6 m.y. ago. This transferred Baja California and much of western California south of Cape Mendocino to the Pacific plate.

## DISCUSSION

The basic dilemma of the Basin and Range province is why such widespread rifting and collapse should have taken place when and where it did, particularly so far inboard of the Pacific margin transform faults. Since 1970 (Atwater 1970) there has been little doubt that the phenomenon is somehow related to the plate interactions described above between the North America, Farallon, and Pacific plates. The problem is exactly how it is related to those interactions, and why the tectonic response has been so puzzlingly distinctive. Related to this is a broader tectonic problem. That is how the Basin and Range relates to Late Tertiary tectonics of the entire central and southern Cordillera, particularly the Colorado Plateau and the southern Rocky Mountains.

The Basin and Range suffered extensional block faulting over a wide area (Stewart 1978) accompanied by scattered bimodal basalt-rhyolite volcanism (Christiansen and Lipman 1972). There was also some strike-slip faulting, particularly in the western part of the province, associated with growing transform faults along the Pacific margin. All this activity began, in some sectors at least, by 17 m.y. ago (Eberly and Stanley 1978) and continued, in some sectors at least, to the present time (Stewart 1978). This activity clearly postdates Early to Middle Tertiary explosive arc magmatism and shallow metamorphism. It also clearly postdates Early to Middle Tertiary listric normal faulting, and it is important that directions of faulting in the two periods are usually distinctly different. It is obvious, however, that the general coincidence of the Basin and Range province with the area affected by the Early to Middle Tertiary thermal disturbance is very conspicuous. For example, the Colorado Plateau for the most part escaped both.

The Basin and Range province is underlain by relatively thin (25 km thick) crust and seems to experience higher heat flow than adjacent regions (Thompson and Burke 1974). The differentiation between the Basin and Range and adjacent provinces is particularly well known with regards to the Colorado Plateau, which has a crust nearly 40 km thick, and the Sierra Nevada Mountains, which have a crust nearly 50 km thick. Both provinces have lower heat flow values. A related geophysical fact is that the Bouguer gravity is slightly to considerably higher and the general elevation slightly to considerably lower in the Basin and Range as compared to the adjoining Colorado Plateau (Eaton et al. 1978). The distinction is most clear between the Arizona–Sonora sector and the Plateau, but less obvious in the Nevada–Utah sector. What is more important, however, is that general elevation is significantly higher and the Bouguer gravity is significantly lower than might be expected over the entire region of the Basin and Range, Colorado Plateau, and Rocky Mountains. This suggests the Basin and Range province is simply a slightly collapsed part of a massive regional uplift which affects the entire Cordillera and even the Great Plains, as inspection of a continental relief map reveals.

The evidence is incomplete and usually controversial, but it would appear the massive uplift of the Cordillera grew exponentially since Early Tertiary time. For example, certain floral evidence (Axelrod 1966, Axelrod and Bailey 1976, see Axelrod this volume), suggests the region was quite low in Eocene time, but it is certainly anomalously high today. It would appear that as the entire southern Cordillera rose, the fragmentation and partial collapse of the Basin and Range was simply superimposed on the general uplift. The Basin and Range was partially left behind, so to speak, as the Cordillera was uplifted.

There has been some discussion as to whether the Basin and Range province is time transgressive and has grown northward following growth of the San Andreas transform as the Mendocino triple junction migrates northward with the Pacific plate (Dickinson and Snyder 1979). The issue is critical, since if the rifting is directly linked to the transform margin it should migrate with it. Unfortunately, although the meager data faintly supports such a migration it is not entirely conclusive. It is obvious that large parts of the Arizona–Sonora desert region are not as recently active today as, say, the Great Basin of Nevada and Utah. This is manifested by much wider pedimentation in the Arizona–Sonora desert and a lack of evidence for recent faulting except on the eastern and northeastern margins. Also, the general elevation there is significantly lower and the gravity significantly higher than in the northern Basin and Range. This can suggest the Arizona–Sonora sector is now quiescent and perhaps cooling, but it does not necessarily prove it started earlier. The quiescence may coincide with the opening of the Gulf of California. This may have concentrated strain in the Gulf of California spreading centers; whereas before, it was spread over the entire region, as it still is to the north in Nevada–Utah. In any event, the Basin and Range province extends far to the north of the eastward projection of the Mendocino fracture zone. This marks the northern edge of the slab-free region and the most northerly point of the present San Andreas fault.

Another important fact, often ignored in regional interpretations of the Basin and Range province, is that the Rio Grande rift is part of the system. In spite of the fact that it is far to the east of the Basin and Range of Nevada–Utah, it is linked to the greater province through southern New Mexico and southeastern Arizona. Most important, it has the same basic structural geometry and the same timing (Kelley 1979). The timing is particularly significant in that geologic evidence where best known suggests the major block faulting is certainly post-20 m.y. in age, just as it is everywhere else in the Basin and Range province. It would seem that whatever model of genesis is proposed for the "classic" Basin and Range province must also explain the Rio Grande rift.

## CONCLUSIONS

It is very clear that the Basin and Range province and all its relatives, such as the Rio Grande rift, are due to Late Tertiary regional extension (Smith 1978). The extension explains the thin crust and lithosphere and the higher heat flow, and is compatible with the normal faulting, present seismicity and relative general elevation. The amount of extension is much debated. Estimates have ranged from about 10 percent to over 100 percent, but it is probably in the range of 15 percent to no more than 30 percent (Stewart 1978). If the extension were much more than 30 percent, some will argue, the region would be below sea level, although the higher lithospheric temperatures due to lithosphere thinning and accompanying igneous activity no doubt counteract the effect. The extension and collapse of the Basin and Range province was superimposed on a massive uplift of the Cordillera which has accelerated in Late Tertiary time. The uplift is probably largely of thermal origin.

The timing of extensional block faulting correlates only imperfectly with plate geometry evolution along the Pacific margin, but seems to be inescapably related to it. The tectonic response was affected by inherited crustal history, particularly thermal, and inherited physical properties.

For example, the faulting avoids large batholith complexes such as the Sierra Nevada–Peninsular batholiths and the Sierra Madre Occidental, no doubt underlain by a batholith. On the other hand, the province mimicked the large region of Middle Tertiary thermal disturbance. For some still obscure reason, both avoided the Colorado Plateau.

There have been many explanations proposed for the Basin and Range province. For example, see Stewart (1978) for a review. There are four critical concepts, however, that have been suggested which when summed probably explain much of the problem. The first is Atwater's (1970) concept of a broad transform-rift boundary evolving out of the collision of North America and the Pacific plate as the East Pacific Rise was extinguished and the San Andreas transform grew. The gross timing and distribution of the province is broadly consistent with this model. The second concept is collapse of a low-dipping subducted slab of Farallon plate (Coney and Reynolds 1977) after Eocene time, which seems to explain the Early to Middle Tertiary retrograde sweep of the magmatic arc and resulting thermal disturbance upon which the Basin and Range was later superimposed. The third concept is that of a slab-window (Dickinson and Snyder 1979) beneath the southwestern Cordillera geometrically required by growth of the San Andreas transform as subduction ceased along its trend. This would allow hot asthenosphere to well up into the window and contribute to the uplift observed. Finally, there is the concept of North America progressively overriding younger and hotter Farallon plate (Damon 1979). This offers an explanation for the massive uplift of the Cordillera and the western Great Plains upon which the Basin and Range was eventually superimposed. An integrated rigorous quantification of all these concepts is difficult, but nonetheless qualitatively appealing.

It should be quite obvious from this review that a contrast exists between the two major subdivisions of the Basin and Range province. Although both share the distinctive characteristics of tilted blocks and basins and a grossly similar physiography, it has long been recognized that the Arizona–Sonora desert has wider pedimentation, a lower elevation, and a much "older" appearance than its northern partner in Nevada–Utah. The contrast is much deeper, however, than present physiography and geophysics, and includes tectonic history extending back into Precambrian time. It is the tectonic history that deserves emphasis here.

Recall that almost one-third of the Nevada–Utah sector does not lie on North American Precambrian basement; whereas, almost all of the Arizona–Sonora sector seems to do so. Similarly, the northern sector was a thick Paleozoic miogeocline, whereas the southern sector was a thin Paleozoic platform. Lower Mesozoic history was very different in the two subdivisions, and in Cretaceous time almost all of the Nevada–Utah sector was within the Sevier orogenic belt while the Arizona–Sonora region was largely a shallow marine embayment. In Late Cretaceous–Early Tertiary time the Nevada–Utah Basin and Range was totally west of Laramide plutonism and deformation, while the Arizona–Sonora region was in the midst of it. It is not until Early to Middle Tertiary time that the two subdivisions begin to share tectonic history. They both suffered the rapidly shifting, intense volcanism and shallow metamorphism so characteristic of this puzzling time.

If the Basin and Range province has been produced by extension, it must have extended at some rate. This means that large segments of the North American Cordillera have moved westward and northwestward at a velocity slightly but significantly greater than, and in part independently of, the rest of the North American plate. This somewhat trivial observation is nonetheless very important, because it leaves us with the ultimate dilemma. This is whether these independent motions are fundamentally active or passive in origin (Christiansen and McKee 1978). In other words, are the cumulative tectonics of the southern Cordillera the result of kinematic and thermal response to passive plate geometric accidents; or, are they due to some deep-seated active convective process below? The question is similar, and obviously related to, the problem of plate dynamics on a global scale, and it cannot be answered here. Nevertheless, either separately or taken together, the four concepts of Basin and Range province evolution discussed earlier are basically passive in character and when combined with the elements of tectonic inheritance discussed above and the natural complexity of intraplate continental tectonic response seem propitious at this time.

## REFERENCES

Anderson, R. E. 1971. "Thin Skin Distension in Tertiary Rocks of Southeastern Nevada." *Geol. Soc. America Bull.*, 82:43–58.

Armstrong, R. L. 1968. "Sevier Orogenic Belt in Nevada and Utah." *Geol. Soc. America Bull.*, 79:429–458.

Atwater, T. 1970. "Implications of Plate Tectonics for the Cenozoic Tectonic Evolution of Western North America." *Geol. Soc. America Bull.*, 81:3513–3536.

Axelrod, D. I. 1966. "The Eocene Copper Basin Flora of Northwestern Nevada." *California Univ. Pubs. Geol. Sci.*, Vol. 59, 125 p.

Axelrod, D. I., and H. P. Bailey. 1976. "Tertiary Vegetation, Climate, and Altitude of the Rio Grande Depression, New Mexico–Colorado." *Paleogeology*, 2:235–254.

Christiansen, R. L., and P. W. Lipman. 1972. "Cenozoic Volcanism and Plate Tectonic Evolution of Western United States: II. Late Cenozoic." *Trans. Roy. Soc. London*, 271:249–284.

Christiansen, R. L., and E. H. McKee. 1978. "Late Cenozoic Volcanic and Tectonic Evolution of the Great Basin and Columbia Intermontene Region," in R. B. Smith and G. P. Eaton (eds). *Cenozoic Tectonics and Regional Geophysics of the Western Cordillera*, Geol. Soc. America Mem. 152, 283–312.

Coney, P. J. 1976. "Plate Tectonics and the Laramide Orogeny." *New Mexico Geol. Soc. Spec. Pub. No. 6*, 5–10.

Coney, P. J. 1978a. "Mesozoic–Cenozoic Cordillera Plate Tectonics," *Geol. Soc. America Mem. 152*, 33–50.

Coney, P. J. 1978b. "The Plate Tectonic Setting of Southeastern Arizona." *New Mexico Geol. Soc. Guidebook: 29th Field Conf.*, 285–290.

Coney, P. J., and S. J. Reynolds. 1977. "Cordillera Benioff Tours." *Nature*, 270:403–406.

Damon, P. E. 1979. "Continental Uplift at Convergent Boundaries." *Tectonophysics*, 61:307–319.

Davis, G. H. 1979. "Laramide Folding and Faulting in Southeastern Arizona." *American Jour. Sci.*, in press.

Davis, G. H., and P. J. Coney. 1979. "Geological Development of Cordilleran Metamorphic Core Complexes." *Geology*, 7:120–124.

Dickinson, W. R. 1977. "Paleozoic Plate Tectonics and the Evolution of the Cordilleran Continental Margin," in J. N. Stewart, C. H. Stevens, and A. E. Fritsche (eds.), *Paleozoic Paleogeography of the Western United States: Soc. Econ. Paleontol. Mineral., Pacific Soc. Pacific Coast Paleogeography Symp. 1*, 137–155.

Dickinson, W. R. and W. S. Snyder. 1979. "Geometry of Subducted Slabs Related to San Andreas Transform." *Jour. of Geology*, 87:609:627.

Eberly, L. D., and T. B. Stanley, Jr. 1978. "Cenozoic Stratigraphy and Geologic History of Southwestern Arizona." *Geol. Soc. America Bull.*, 89:921–940.

Elston, W. E. 1976. "Tectonic Significance of Mid-Tertiary Volcanism in the Basin and Range Province," in W. E. Elston and S. A. Northrop (eds). *Cenozoic Volcanism in Southwestern New Mexico, New Mexico Geol. Soc. Spec. Pub. 5*, 93–151.

Epis, R. C., and C. E. Chapin. 1975. "Geomorphic and Tectonic Implications of the Post-Laramide, Late Eocene Erosion Surfaces in the Southern Rocky Mountains." *Geol. Soc. America Mem. 144*, 1–40.

Hayes, P. T. 1970. "Cretaceous Paleogeography of Southeastern Arizona and Adjacent Areas." *U.S. Geol. Survey Prof. Paper 658B*, 42 p.

Kelley, V. C. 1979. "Tectonics, Middle Rio Grande Rift, New Mexico," in R. E. Reicker (ed). *Rio Grande Rift: Tectonics and Magmatism, Amer. Geophys. Union*, Washington, D.C., 57–40.

Peirce, H. W. 1976. "Elements of Paleozoic Tectonics in Arizona." *Arizona Geol. Soc. Digest*, 10:37–58.

Peirce, H. W., P. E. Damon, and M. Shedigulich. 1979. "An Oligocene (?) Colorado Plateau Ridge in Arizona." *Tectonophysics*, 61:1–24.

Smith, R. B. 1978. "Seismicity, Crustal Structure, and Intraplate Tectonics of the Interior of the Western Cordillera," in R. B. Smith and G. E. Eaton (eds). *Cenozoic Tectonics and Regional Geophysics of the Western Cordillera, Geol. Soc. America Mem. 152*, 111–144.

Stewart, J. H. 1978. "Basin-Range Structure in Western North America A Review," in R. B. Smith and E. E. Eaton (eds). *Cenozoic Tectonics and Regional Geophysics of the Western Cordillera, Geol. Soc. America Mem. 152*, 1–31.

Silver, L. T., and T. N. Anderson. 1974. "Possible Left-lateral Early to Middle Mesozoic Disruption of the Southwestern North American Craton Margin." *Geol. Soc. America, Abstracts with Programs*, 6:955–956.

Thompson, G. A., and D. B. Burke. 1974. "Regional Geophysics of the Basin and Range Province." *Earth and Planetary Sci., Ann. Rev.*, 2:213–238.

# Landscape Evolution

# 4

# EFFECT OF CALICHE ON DESERT PROCESSES

Laurence H. Lattman

University of Utah
Salt Lake City, Utah

## INTRODUCTION

Caliche is one of several types of cement deposited in and on unconsolidated deposits in arid and semiarid areas. Caliche is dominantly (commonly over 80 percent) calcium carbonate and contains varying amounts of silica, ferruginous material, and clay.

Caliche of interest in this paper forms by pedogenic processes (Gile et al. 1966) or on subaerial surfaces (Lattman 1973). In the southwestern United States caliche is forming today in areas having between about 4 to 18 inches (10 to 46 cm) of rainfall but it can form elsewhere in areas of higher rainfall (Reeves 1976).

Lattman (1973) believed that parent material is an important factor in formation of caliche and, in the Las Vegas, Nevada area, demonstrated that alluvial fans in the same drainage basin show markedly different degrees of calichification depending on mineralogy of the detrital material. Decreasing calichification occurred on fans derived from limestone and dolomite, basic igneous rocks (Fig. 4.1), interbedded clastic sediments, and acid igneous rocks. Calcareous eolian dust and other atmospheric sources also result in caliche deposition (Gardner 1972).

Caliche can form rapidly, and on carbonate material in the Spring Mountains of southern Nevada cementation in six months progresses to the point where a hammer is needed to separate the limestone clasts. The general rate of caliche formation is too variable to assign numerical values. The rate depends on climate, parent material, supply of calcium carbonate, and topography.

Figure 4.1. Massive caliche horizons developed on basaltic and andesitic fan detritus, McCollough Mountains, Clark County, Nevada. Note dark basaltic boulders on surface and vertical, free face maintained by case-hardened caliche.

## TYPES OF CALICHE

Pedogenic caliche goes through a sequential development (Gile et al. 1966) from thin stringers and pebble coatings to horizons in which the cement forms a continuum filling most of the pore spaces. The cement varies from soft and "punky" to massive, well-indurated petrocalcic horizons that are true limestones. In addition, the caliche may occur as, or contain, nodules, pisolites, plates, and hard laminar layers. The laminar layers, which are extremely well indurated may form within the soil (Gile et al. 1966) or at the surface (Fig. 4.2) in shallow, ephemeral lakes (Lattman 1973).

Caliche is of very variable thickness and may consist of several superposed horizons. It may be a few inches thick to several tens of feet thick (Bretz and Horberg 1949) and be quite variable in induration throughout its vertical extent. A single caliche horizon traced laterally may how extreme differences in thickness and degree of induration, horizontally and vertically (Yaalon and Singer 1974). Locally, extremely thick and well-

Figure 4.2. Well-indurated, laminar caliche forming in shallow depression on fan surface. This discontinuous layer contains algal remains and is impervious and very resistant.

indurated caliches may be derived from gypsiferrous deposits (Lattman and Lauffenberger 1974).

A special property of caliche is its ability to locally harden where exposed at the surface, on slopes ranging from horizontal to vertical (Fig. 4.3), in regions of greater than about 4 inches (10 cm) rainfall. The caliche is apparently dissolved and reprecipitated causing hard surface induration. With time this induration extends inward and a tough, hard caliche may be formed from a soft one. The rate of case hardening appears to be controlled by many of the same factors that control caliche formation.

## WEATHERING OF CALICHE

In arid and semiarid regions, caliche weathers primarily by mechanical processes. In the higher mountain country (for example, in southern Nevada) freeze-thaw action breaks indurated caliche horizons into angular fragments up to 2 inches (5 cm) long. These fragments may be recemented to form a new caliche layer (Fig. 4.4). On vertical or very steep slopes,

Figure 4.3. Vertical, case-hardened caliche forming a free face, Kyle Canyon, Clark County, Nevada. A white caliche layer is visible at the very top of the vertical face and serves as a caprock. Case hardening below the caprock maintains the free face; compare with Figure 4.1

case hardened caliche breaks off in blocks from the well-indurated layers undermined along intervening less indurated layers (Lattman and Simonberg 1971).

On nearly horizontal or low relief surfaces the caliche is extremely resistant to weathering and in fact may undergo induration rather than breakup upon exposure to subaerial processes. There is some mechanical breaking but this is commonly less rapid than the formation and induration.

Solution weathering of caliche, unless there is major, long-term climatic change to moister conditions, is rarely significant. Small, local solution pitting or lapis development does occur but again, case hardening may exceed solution in importance and preserve the caliche.

Caliche horizons, especially the well-indurated ones, are subject to jointing even though underlying, uncemented material may show no joints. On steep to vertical exposures these joint blocks may be detached and

Figure 4.4. Fragments of mechanically distinegrated caliche recemented into a new caliche layer on an almost horizontal surface.

fall. Case-hardened, vertical exposures may "spall off" in large slabs if undercut by running water.

Finally, of course, long term major climatic change to moister conditions would destroy an exposed or near-surface caliche.

## ROLE OF CALICHE IN DESERT LANDFORMS

Caliche affects desert landform processes in several ways which are classed into several groups for clarity of explanation. These effects are divided into caprock action, slope stabilization, and infiltration effects.

### Caprock Action

Caliche, once formed, acts as a very resistant caprock under arid and semiarid conditions. This caprock forms a free face and results therefore in parallel retreat of slopes. This in turn forms buttes, mesas, and preserves broad calichified surfaces for long periods of time. The preservation

Figure 4.5. A white caliche caprock developed on weak playa beds holds up the surface of Mormon Mesa, Nevada.

of Mormon Mesa, Nevada by a dense caliche caprock (Fig. 4.5) has been described by Gardner (1972). Lattman (1973) studied incised alluvial fans of the Las Vegas region which drain to a common base level. The well calichified fans showed several surfaces separated vertically and converging downfan. Each surface was calichified. Fans which had little or no caliche development exhibited a single, rolling surface with no free faces exposed. As the number of surfaces preserved on a fan appeared to be a function mostly of rapidity and degree of caliche formation, it appeared that correlation of surfaces from fan to fan was dubious at best.

Buried caliches exposed by incision produce breaks-in-slope. These free faces, resulting in step-like slopes, may be quite numerous and obviously affect slope evolution (Fig. 4.6).

The caprock action of a caliche depends on thickness, hardness (and induration), and relative weakness of underlying rock. The most effective caprocks are petrocalcic horizons, siliceous caliches, and caliche cementing resistant gravel. It is probable that caliche, as well as gravel, sod cover, and other crusts of non-calcareous origins are responsible for free face development in many arid and semiarid regions and cause parallel retreat of slopes to be a major landform process under these climates.

Figure 4.6. A break-in-slope formed by exposure of a buried caliche. The break-in-slope is visible about one half way down the case-hardened gully wall.

## Slope Stabilization

Calcium carbonate cement forms on all slope angles up to vertical. In areas of calcareous detritus this cementation forms within a matter of months and is very effective in stabilizing slopes that would otherwise fail or continuously shower loose clasts to the foot of the slope. Highway engineers are aware of this and consider it in highway design and location. It is one of the characteristics of a caliche covered or case-hardened steep slope that it holds small fragments well but fails locally by large calichified blocks or slabs falling. No studies have been made, to the author's knowledge, of rate of slope retreat as a function of caliche development.

## Infiltration Effects

The formation of caliche inhibits infiltration into a topographic surface. The degree of this inhibition is a function of density and induration of the caliche. Petrocalcic horizons, laminar layers, and case-hardened layers cause the greatest inhibition. Gullies and washes in caliche areas commonly show well-indurated cementation of their beds, as well as their banks. Thus, calichification tends to seal the surface.

In the Las Vegas, Nevada region, downfan flooding of calichified fans is much greater in magnitude and frequency than flooding on non-calichified fans. Additionally, the calichified fans show the effects of sheetflow much better developed relative to incision, than do the uncalichified fans. These effects are shown on the inferfluve areas by preferred orientation of elongate pebbles, crag and tail development around boulders, etc. Cooley et al. (1973), studied the effect of caliche on infiltration into fans of the Las Vegas area and concluded that a major factor in flooding characteristics was the depth of burial of the caliche horizon; they found that laminar layers and surface case hardened layers were the most significant in reducing infiltration.

## SUMMARY

Caliche, where formed or forming, clearly has a very significant effect on desert processes and landforms. Its presence causes stronger local relief and steep slopes in an area that might develop a gentler, more rolling topography in the absence of caliche. Caliche favors the development of butte and mesa topography (at all scales) and parallel retreat of slopes. Flooding and sheetflow are increased by the development of caliche.

## REFERENCES

Bretz, J. H., and L. Horberg. 1949. "Caliche in Southeastern New Mexico." *Jour. Geology*, 57:491–511.

Cooley, R. L., G. W. Fiero, L. H. Lattman, and A. L. Mindling. 1973. *Influence of Surface and Near-surface Caliche Distribution on Infiltration Characteristics and Flooding, Las Vegas Area, Nevada.* Desert Research Institute, University of Nevada System, Project Report No. 21, 41 p.

Gardner, L. R. 1972. "Origin of the Mormon Mesa Caliche, Clark Country, Nevada." *Bull. Geol. Soc. Amer.*, 83:143–156.

Gile, L. H., F. F. Peterson, and R. B. Grossman. 1966. "Morphological and Genetic Sequences of Carbonate Accumulation in Desert Soils." *Soil Science*, 191:347–360.

Lattman, L. H. 1973. "Calcium Carbonate Cementation of Alluvial Fans in Southern Nevada." *Bull. Geol. Soc. Amer.*, 24:3013–3028.

Lattman, L. H., and S. K. Lauffenberger. 1974. "Proposed Role of Gypsum in the Formation of Caliche. *Zeit. Geomorph.*, 30:140–149.

Lattman, L. H., and E. M. Simonberg. 1971. "Case-hardening of Carbonate Alluvium and Colluvium, Spring Mountains, Nevada." *Jour. Sed. Petrology*, 41:274–281.

Reeves, C. C. Jr. 1976. *Caliche*. Lubbock, Texas: Estacado Books, 233 p.

Yaalon, D. H., and S. Singer. 1974. "Vertical Variation in Strength and Porosity of Calcrete (Nari) on Chalk, Shefela, Israel and Interpretation of Its Origin." *Jour. Sed. Petrology*, 44:1016–1023.

# Development of Vegetation and Climatic History

# 5

# PALEOBOTANICAL HISTORY OF THE WESTERN DESERTS[1]

Daniel I. Axelrod

University of California
Davis, California

## INTRODUCTION

The flora and vegetation of the three western deserts of North America (the Great Basin, Mohave, and Sonoran) were described by Shreve (1942). As he notes, the Great Basin is dominated by low, semiwoody, half-shrubs that form a rather monotonous cover of *Artemisia, Chrysopsis, Ephedra, Ericameria, Eurotia, Grayia, Hazardia, Lycium, Tetradymia*, and others. Mohave Desert vegetation is a mixture of woody and semiwoody taxa with mixed stands of *Atriplex, Cassia, Encelia, Dalea, Franseria, Haplopappus, Larrea, Lycium, Tetradymia*, and *Yucca*. The Sonoran is an arboreal desert, typified by small trees and associated woody shrubs, distributed in *Acalypha, Acacia, Agave, Bursera, Calliandra, Cercidium, Fouquieria, Lycium, Olynea, Prosopis, Washingtonia*, and many others.

The relatively sharp boundaries between the present deserts reflect major topographic-climatic differences. Elevation decreases southward, from the higher Great Basin, to the intermediate Mohave, to the lower Sonoran Desert. This is accompanied by a gradual decrease in precipitation and a rise in temperature (Fig. 5.1). Precipitation is distributed as winter rain and snow in the Great Basin, but snow is not as frequent or widespread in the Mohave region. Winters are considerably milder in the Sonoran province, with frost rare along its northern border and absent farther south. Summer rains increase in frequence south of the Mohave, and are especially characteristic of the Sonoran Desert south of the border and in Arizona.

The historical development of the three provinces can be deciphered

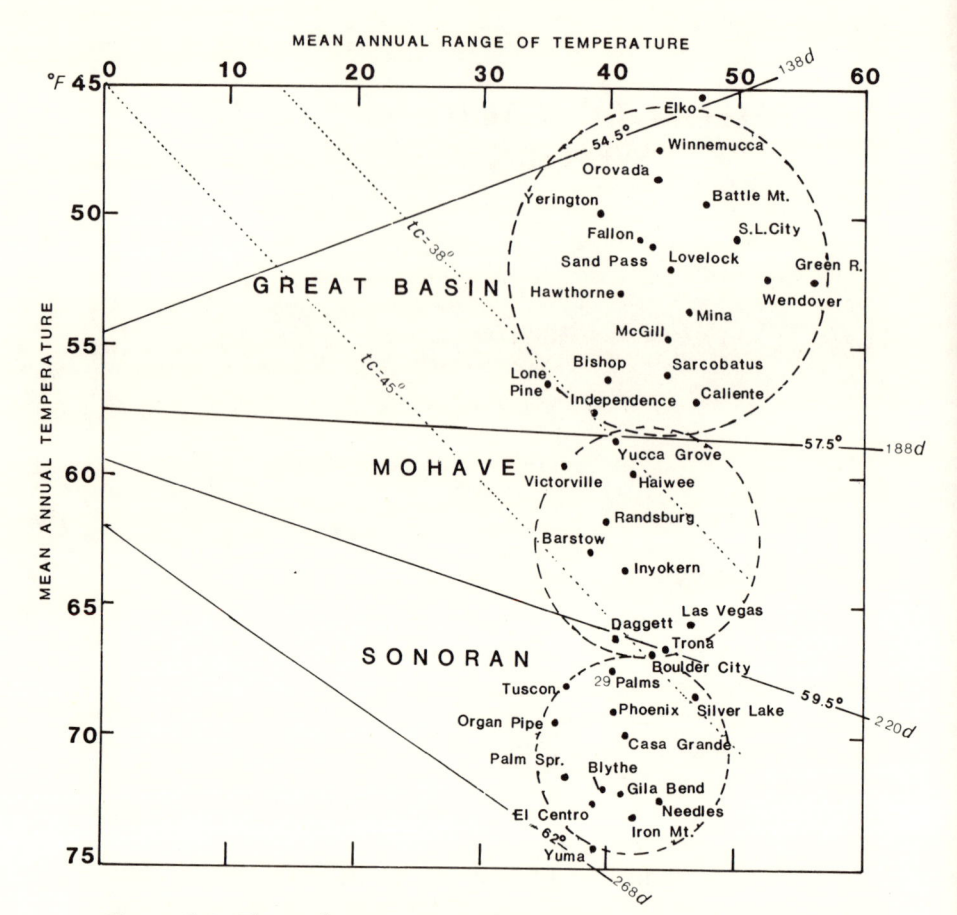

Figure 5.1. Thermal parameters of the western deserts. They are separated by the mean temperature of the coldest month *(tc)*. A change in "warmth" of climate *(W)* also characterizes the shift from one desert to another. W 57.5°F (188 days *(d)* warmer than 57.5°) separates the Great Basin and Mohave; whereas, W 59.5°F (220 days *(d)* warmer than 59.5°) largely distinguishes the Mohave from the Sonoran Desert. Warmth at the southern margin of the Sonoran Desert in the United States at low elevations (e.g., Yuma—200 ft (61 m)) is approximately W 62°F (268 days *(d)* warmer than 62°F).

from Miocene and younger floras scattered over the region. Each flora represents an accumulation of fossil plants preserved chiefly in tuffaceous sedimentary rocks as impressions of leaves, winged seeds, leafy branchlets, and cones. The sediments and their included fossils accumulated near the shores of lakes that earlier occupied the region. Although the rocks were buried deeply, they have been exposed by later uplift and erosion. The fossil plants of Miocene and younger age are very similar to living taxa whose environmental requirements are known. Hence, they provide a reliable basis for interpreting the changes in vegetation and, by inference, in climate over the region during the past 18–20 m.y. The progressive changes that they reveal provide the basis for interpreting the age and origin of desert vegetation.

The following summary of earlier work makes reference to only a sufficient number of fossil floras in each province so that the sequence of change over the present desert region can be outlined. Complete references to earlier literature are in the papers listed in the abbreviated bibliography.

## THE TREND TO DRIER CLIMATE DURING TERTIARY TIME

The guiding principle for interpreting the evolution of desert taxa and desert vegetation is that there was a general trend to increased aridity during Tertiary time. The shift to drier, and also colder, climate is shown by sequences of fossil floras preserved in rocks in central California, southern California, eastern Oregon, western Nevada, the High Plains, and other regions as well. The trend was the result of several factors acting in concert which are briefly recalled below.

First, plate movements were responsible for the gradual closing of the Arctic basin, for movement of Antarctica into a polar position by the Tertiary and for its uplift to produce an ice sheet 14–10 m.y. ago. As a result, polar regions were becoming progressively colder. Seaways which had covered much of North America into the close of the Late Cretaceous were retreating throughout the Tertiary. As more land area was exposed, ranges and extremes of temperature increased, and the amount of moisture available from warm shelf seas was lowered. Major mountain building commenced during the later Tertiary. The uplift of the Cascade–Sierran axis and the Transverse and Peninsular ranges imposed a major rainshadow over the region to the east, reducing precipitation and increasing ranges of temperature there. In addition, uplift of the Rocky Mountains and the Sierra Madre of Mexico created a rainshadow for storms moving northwestward from the Gulf of Mexico. Thus, the present western deserts lie in a double rainshadow that came into existence in the late Tertiary and early Quaternary, and which has effectively blocked summer rain from more southerly, warmer regions. At the same time, the progressive chilling of the oceans had a two-fold effect. As chilling progressed along the Pacific coast and the California Current gained strength, tropical storms moving up the west coast of Mexico would dissipate as they encountered the colder water which was spreading progressively farther south. As a result, moist warm-air masses moving north were now confined to successively lower latitudes. In addition, normal convectional showers from the warm ocean decreased in frequency as the ocean chilled. Furthermore, since saturated air masses (fog) moving onshore in summer were crossing progressively colder water, they were stable because they were moving onto warmer lands. As a result, precipitation was gradually decreasing during the warm season, thus adding to the lengthening period of drought.

As total precipitation decreased over the interior, forests and woodlands retreated. Decreased summer rain was a critical factor eliminating mesic forest trees (that now survive in the eastern United States and eastern Asia), and dry tropic taxa (that now survive in Mexico). The latter were also affected by the colder climate, one inimical to frost-sensitive, subtropical alliances. Thus, by the close of the Tertiary modern-type forests and woodlands had largely been eliminated from the lowlands of the developing desert region, retreating into bordering mountains where moisture was adequate, or becoming extinct in the region as their tolerances for cold or summer moisture (or both) were exceeded.

## SEQUENCES OF FOSSIL FLORAS

### Great Basin

Fossil floras from the northern part of the Great Basin reveal a forested region during the Miocene. This is shown by the 49-Camp flora from the northwest corner of Nevada and by similar floras near Paradise Valley and Pyramid Lake, all about 15–14 m.y. old. They are dominated by deciduous hardwoods, including species of *Acer* (cf. *grandidentatum, macrophyllum, negundo, rubrum*), *Ailanthus, Betula, Carya, Cedrela, Diospyros, Fagus, Nyssa, Persea, Platanus, Sassafras, Tilia, Ulmus,* and *Zelkova*. In addition, a few conifers are present, indicating an ecotone with respect to cooler climate at slightly higher levels where species of *Abies (concolor), Pinus (ponderosa), Chamaecyparis,* and *Ginkgo* contributed to a mixed conifer-hardwood forest.

In west-central Nevada near Middlegate, three large Miocene floras reveal a mixed conifer hardwood forest in this area which had a somewhat higher elevation. *Sequoiadendron* is associated with species of *Abies, Larix, Picea, Pinus, Pseudotsuga, Tsuga,* and *Chamaecyparis*. Their associates incuded species of *Acer, Alnus, Betula, Castanopsis, Crataegus, Hydrangea, Mahonia, Platanus, Populus, Prunus, Robinia, Rhus,* and *Sorbus*. Exotic deciduous hardwoods are not as abundant in this area as to the west and north. Only rare specimens of *Acer, Betula, Cedrela, Diospyros, Hydrangea,* and *Platanus* have been encountered in the large samples. Their rarity may reflect their more interior location as well as a position in the lee of a low range where a rainshadow could reduce summer precipitation over the basin. Sclerophyllous taxa are notably more frequent in the floras near Middlegate, including *Arbutus, Cercocarpus, Ceanothus, Lyonothamnus, Mahonia, Photinia,* and *Quercus*. This is consistent with their more interior position under a climate with warmer summers and less summer precipitation. Similar vegetation extended into southwestern Nevada, as shown by the lower Fingerrock flora from the Cedar Mountain area west of Mina. Conifers include species of *Abies, Chamaecyparis, Glyptostrobus, Larix, Picea, Pinus,* and *Tsuga,* together with species of *Acer, Amelanchier, Betula, Carya, Mahonia, Platanus, Prunus, Quercus* (black oak, maul oak), *Ulmus,* and *Zelkova*. Sclerophylls are well represented, notably *Cercocarpus, Garrya, Lyonothamnus, Mahonia, Photinia,* and also several woody legumes.

It is evident that in proceeding southward through the province in the time from 18 to 14 m.y. ago precipitation gradually decreased from near 40–45 inches (1,016–1,143 mm) in the north to 30–35 inches (762–889 mm) in the south-central part. Ths was accompanied by greater drought stress and warmth southward, as judged from the increasing numbers of sclerophyllous taxa (both trees and shrubs). The central Great Basin forests lived at a moderately higher elevation and exotic deciduous hardwoods decrease in diversity and abundance as the amount of summer rain decreased southward. This may reflect the presence of a low Sierran rise to the west, creating a moderate rainshadow over the central part of the province at this time.

The succeeding Miocene floras from the Great Basin province in western Nevada range in age from 12–14 m.y. They include the Fallon, Purple Mountain and Chloropagus of the Carson Sink area, the Aldrich Station–Horsethief Canyon floras from the East Walker River drainage, and the Stewart Spring flora in the Cedar Mountain area. They all reveal a more sparsely forested region. Exotic deciduous hardwoods have largely disappeared. Sclerophyllous taxa are more common in the lower mixed conifer forest, and they increase in abundance and diversity southward. The alliances common to these floras are chiefly those of the present Sierran mixed conifer forest, represented by species of *Abies, Picea, Pinus, Chamaecyparis,* and *Sequoiadendron*. Associates include *Acer, Amelanchier,*

*Arbutus, Lithocarpus, Populus, Quercus,* and *Rosa.* Noteworthy are a few taxa whose nearest descendants are now confined either to the Klamath Mountain region *(Picea* cf. *breweriana)* or to that area and the southern Sierra *(Abies shastensis, Pinus balfouriana).* It is significant that the more southerly flora from Stewart Spring has more numerous sclerophylls that live in the southwestern U.S. and Mexico, including species of *Arbutus, Astronium, Cercocarpus, Colubrina, Garrya, Lyonothmnus, Populus, Sapindus,* and *Schinus.* Also present are taxa that contribute to the Great Basin juniper woodland, including *Juniperus, Peraphyllum,* and *Ribes,* as well as to sclerophyll vegetation in southern California, notably *Cercocarpus* and *Lyonothamnus.* The increasing number of sclerophylls in this more southerly flora is symptomatic of the major change that takes place a short distance to the south. They lived in warmer sites bordering an impoverished conifer–hardwood forest that reached down to the lake border from higher, cooler levels into a region where rainfall was now near 30 inches (762 mm) as compared with more than 35 inches (889+ mm) in the middle Miocene. Summer rainfall was reduced so that exotic deciduous hardwoods are quite rare; the taxa being represented by only 1 or 2 specimens in these floras.

Only a few younger floras are now known from the region, but they reveal a further restriction of forest at the expense of woodland as the trend to drier climate progressed. The small floras from the type Truckee Formation (6–8 m.y.) in the Carson Sink region represent liveoak–juniper woodland associated with *Ceanothus, Cercocarpus, Mahonia, Purshia,* and *Rhus* and with *Populus* and *Salix* along the lake and stream margins. The Verdi flora (5 m.y.) from the east front of the Sierra west of Reno represents a west slope lower Sierran forest composed of *Abies* (cf. *concolor), Pinus* (cf. *lambertiana, ponderosa),* and associates of *Arctostaphylos, Ceanothus, Prunus,* and *Ribes,* and with species of *Populus* and *Salix* along the stream margins. Oak woodland vegetation like that now on the lower western slope of the range is also present, including species of *Quercus* (cf. *lobata, wislizenii).* The abundant cottonwood is like the present variety along the outer coast from Santa Clara County (California) southward, indicating a mild climate like the oaks. Rainfall in the Verdi area was near 25 inches (635 mm). The Esmeralda flora south of Coaldale (about 8–9 m.y.) represents a dominant live oak woodland *(Quercus* cf. *arizonica)* with species of *Celtis, Populus,* and *Salix* along the lake border, and with *Arctostaphylos, Cercocarpus, Juniperus, Peraphyllum,* and *Sapindus* in the woodland.

These floras clearly reveal progressive desiccation southward and an increase in taxa of southwestern affinity (a relationship indicated also by the older Miocene floras of the region). To judge from the associated mammalian faunas which have numerous grazers, we may infer that grasslands were spreading at this time. This is consistent with the nature of the floras that show forests had by this time largely retreated into the bordering hills over the province and to the low Sierran rise to the west. Clearly, there is no evidence in this area of desert vegetation or arid climate in the period from 7 to 5 m.y.

Several pollen floras, variously dated at 3.5 to 2.5 m.y. and distributed from Wichman in western Nevada southward into Owens Valley of southeastern California, provide clear evidence for a pronounced rise in precipitation. This is demonstrated by the reappearance of a west-slope Sierran conifer forest over the region, with species of *Abies, Pinus, Sequoiadendron, Calocedrus*, among the conifers. Associates included *Acer, Ceanothus, Cornus, Corylus, Quercus, Ribes, Rhus*, and *Symphoricarpos*. The absence from the record of any of the common genera of the present desert at Wichman (which is in the upper *Artemisia* belt), or in the floras from the Coso area at the south margin of the present Great Basin Desert, must mean that these genera were not yet important constituents of the flora in the area. The floras show a progressive change southward, from a typical west-slope mid-Sierran forest at the north to one more nearly allied to the forest now in the San Gabriel Mountains and in the Panamint Valley region at the south margin of the area. Based on this record, the rise in precipitation in the Pliocene amounted to fully 15 inches (381 mm) or more. This corresponds in time to the formation of the first mountain glaciers in the Sierra which was then fully 4,000–6,000 feet (1,219–1,829 m) lower than at present in its central and southern sector. Clearly, the desert environment must be younger than 3.5 to 2.0 m.y.

Evidence from woodrat middens provides critical data regarding the nature of late glacial and post-glacial vegetation and climate over the present desert region (see Van Devender and Spaulding, this volume, 1979; Wells 1979). Most of the investigations have been in the Mohave and Sonoran provinces, not in the Great Basin. However, in the Sheep Range of southern Nevada, in the transition from the Great Basin to the Mohave province, there is evidence of the postglacial replacement of mesic juniper woodland by xeric juniper communities by 9,500 years B.P. The juniper woodland was in turn replaced by mixed scrub and blackbrush desert scrub by 7,500 years B.P. This was paralleled by the occurrence of late Wisconsin bristlecone pine–limber pine forest at an elevation of 6,230–6,890 feet (approximately 1,900–2,100 m) and its replacement by piñon–juniper woodland before 9,500 years B.P. This piñon–juniper still lives in this area. The early Holocene woodlands disappeared about 8,000 years B.P., following which the desert emerged. A generally similar sequence may be inferred for much of the Great Basin region.

*Origins of Taxa:* The Great Basin flora appears to have had two major sources. One is related to the east Asian deserts and semideserts as indicated by allied species of *Artemisia, Atriplex, Emplectocladus, Ephedra, Kochia, Suaeda*, and a number of grasses and herbs as well. There may have been interchange across the Beringian area during the later Tertiary (7 to 5 m.y.) and also during warm interglacials when climate was favorable. It is noteworthy that *Empletocladus andersonii* is allied to *E. mongolica* of the central Asian desert and steppes. Also, a small-leaved poplar in the late Tertiary of Nevada and Oregon is similar to *P. tremula* of Eurasia that ranges out into open grassland and steppe country along water courses. In addition, a cottonwood leaf similar to those of *P. euphratica* occurs in the later Tertiary of California and represents another link with the dry Asian flora. Past ties are also shown by the continuity of the *Artemisia frigida–Juniperus sibirica* community between the upper Yukon and the interior basins of Siberia, a link supported by distributional data presented by Yurtsev (1972). These taxa and closely related, presumably ancestral ones, enter the drier margins of taiga and adjacent conifer–hardwood forests. Under a climatic trend to drier conditions they would spread into the new open areas as forest slowly retreated.

The records of *Emplectocladus (andersonii), Purshia (tridentata)*, and *Peraphyllum (ramosissimum)* in the later Tertiary of Nevada imply that they probably contributed to the understory of the oak–juniper woodland and probably also occupied drier and warmer slopes over the region as an early Basin sage community. This community was presumably marginal to grassland which probably covered wide areas because there was still summer rain into the Pliocene.

The second group of plants that contribute to the Great Basin Desert and semidesert vegetation occur in the Mohave and most are also in Sonoran Desert region. These include soft-stemmed, highly branched shrubs distributed in *Chrysopsis, Chrysothamnus, Ericameria, Eriogonum, Haplopappus, Hazardia, Salvia, Stenotopsis*, and *Tetradymia*. Most of them form a shrubby sage matrix in the diverse oak–juniper–piñon woodlands marginal to all the western deserts where they are regularly associated with *Emplectocladus, Peraphyllum, Purshia*, and *Ribes (cereum)* which are recorded in the later Miocene of western Nevada. Since these shrubs are concentrated in the drier parts of southwestern North America, it is inferred that they probably originated in the understory of Madro–Tertiary vegetation, spreading north with it in the Miocene as climate became drier. They persisted over the interior lowlands as the more mesic woodland and grasslands retreated due to this drier climate. As grasslands were eliminated gradually from the lowlands, the open areas were now invaded by these drought resistant taxa, and a new type of vegetation quickly came into existence.

## Mohave

The Mohave province has a very different phytogeographic region. During the Miocene, the area was dominated by sclerophyllous oak–scrub woodland and subtropic thorn forest. Patches of oak–laurel forest lived in nearby moister, more equable sites. There are no records in the entire region of montane conifers or deciduous hardwoods such as those recorded a short distance to the north of Nevada where forests lived at a higher, colder level and under higher precipitation amounts. We have now descended into a lower, warmer region, into the Madrean province.

The Tehachapi flora (17 m.y.) northeast of Monolith represents a live-oak–piñon–cypress woodland composed of *Arbutus, Clethra, Persea, Quercus, Sabal,* and *Umbellularia*. Associates included diverse shrubs, notably *Arctostaphylos, Ceanothus, Cercocarpus, Heteromeles, Laurocerasus, Quercus* (scrub oak), and *Rhus*. Dry tropic scrub inhabited exposed parts of the basin as shown by *Acacia, Brahea, Celtis, Dodonaea, Euphorbia, Eysenhardtia, Ficus, Pithecellobium, Prosopis,* and *Randia*. Semidesert patches probably covered hot south slopes with shallow soil. Precipitation evidently did not exceed 25 inches (635 mm) in the middle Miocene, and during this time, temperatures were mild and frost absent. The small Ricardo flora (12 m.y.) from the El Paso Mountains, known chiefly from fossil wood, includes a dominant oak associated with piñon, cypress, palm (possibly *Sabal*), a legume (*Robinia* ?), buckbrush (*Ceanothus*), and a few leaves representing dry tropic scrub taxa (*Acacia, Lycium*). The small sample indicates that there were semidesert patches in the nearby area, and rainfall over the region probably was not less than 18 to 20 inches (457–508 mm).

The Anaverde flora near Palmdale is a woodland with *Persea* (avocado) abundant together with several live oaks, *Pinus* (cf. *sabiniana*), a palm, *Sapindus,* and several shrubs, notably *Ceanothus, Malosma, Peraphyllum, Quercus* (scrub oak), and *Rhamnus*. A few dry-tropic scrub taxa are present as relicts, notably species of *Colubrina, Dodonaea,* and *Eysenhardtia*. This flora, described above, occurs at the west margin of the present desert and indicates that elevations were not far above sea level, that climate was mild in winter and frostless, and summer rainfall was present. The abundance of *Persea* and the presence of *Malosma* imply that moderating influences from the west were operating; hence, the mountains that now separate the region from the coastal slope were not elevated appreciably.

Pollen floras from the Coso formation on the northern border of the Mohave Desert and at localities eastward to Panamint Valley indicate that this part of the province supported mixed conifer forest in the Pliocene (3.5 to 2.0 m.y.). The taxa are allied chiefly to those in the Sierran mixed-conifer forests. These include species of *Abies, Calocedrus, Pinus, Pseudotsuga, Sequoiadendron* and associates of *Alnus, Betula, Amelanchier, Ceanothus, Cornus, Garrya, Holodiscus, Quercus,* and *Ribes.* Floras farther to the east at Panamint Valley also have a component that is now in the San Gabriel Mountains of southern California. The floras of the Panamint Valley record a rise of 15–20 inches (381–508 mm) or more in precipitation, paralleling those conditions to the north in the Great Basin province where forests also replaced woodlands at this time.

The youthfulness of the Mohave Desert vegetation is indicated by the studies of numerous woodrat middens scattered across the region. These middens have radiocarbon dates of +40,000 to 9,000 years B.P. and show that piñon–juniper woodlands covered the lower slopes of the present desert ranges. Thus, these woodlands extended into many of the bordering basins that are presently low desert. The *Neotoma* middens often contain taxa that are no longer present in the mountains where the middens now occur, including the xeric juniper. Locally, below the conifer woodland belt in drier areas, there probably was a dense semidesert sage association much as there is today. It probably included some woody shrubs that are now confined farther south to the Sonoran region (see below). This implies that the lowest, drier parts of the desert basins probably received at least 10 inches (254 mm) rainfall and that the widely spaced shrubs of the present desert that live under 4–5 inches (102–127 mm) precipitation were not yet in existence as a regional feature 10,000 years B.P. Evidence from woodrat middens also shows that *Larrea* first invaded the Mohave province 9,000 years ago. It is evident that local deserts, if present, were confined to the driest sites scattered over the region, chiefly in the lee of high ranges and on south-facing slopes at the close of the last glacial period. The modern Mohave Desert as we now see it is certainly younger than 10,000 years.

The sources of the taxa in this region are considered below with the history of the Sonoran province. Like the Sonoran, the Mohave area was a part of the Madrean floristic province into the close of the Tertiary, but was segregated from it as a transitional desert during the Quaternary.

## Sonoran

The gradual development of the flora and vegetation of this region has been clarified by research on the history of the San Andreas fault system. It is now evident that fossil floras from southern California and Baja California west of the San Andreas fault system have been displaced fully 311 miles (500 km) northward to their present positions since the middle Miocene. This means that during the latest Cretaceous (70–65 m.y.), when *Araucaria* inhabited sites now at La Misión and Rosario in Baja California, it actually lived in the latitude of the present Viscaino Desert where rainfall is now 2 inches (51 mm) yearly. Also, the Paleocene Elsinore flora, composed of tree ferns (fronds over 5 feet (1.5 m) long), feather palm, and numerous large-leaved dicots of several genera, lived in the area of the present Sonoran desert near Rosario, Baja California. The reconstructed position of the Eocene Del Mar flora places it south of Rosario. As judged from pollen, it represents a dry tropic forest with species of *Bauhinia, Bombacopsis, Cercidium, Cuphea, Ficus, Foquieria, Guazuma,* and *Suriana,* with a woodland of *Celtis, Cissus, Forestiera, Fremontodendron, Ilex,* and *Quercus* in the bordering hills to the east (W. S. Ting MSS).

The Miocene Modelo and Puente floras of coastal southern California, which then were situated near the Mexican border, represent a rich evergreen oak–laurel woodland with *Annona, Juglans, Lyonothamnus, Persea, Pinus, Quercus,* and *Sabal* with shrubs in the understory, including *Cercocarpus, Fremontodendron,* and *Quercus* (scrub oak). They indicate that rainfall was near 30 inches (762 mm) at a minimum, winters were frostless, and summer rain was present in this region 14–15 m.y. ago. By contrast, the Mint Canyon flora (13 m.y.), now at a site several miles east of Newhall in southern California, was then in the Salton Sea area. The Mint Canyon flora is a rich woodland with numerous liveoaks associated with *Ilex, Juglans, Laurocerasus, Lyonothamnus, Persea,* and with *Ceanothus, Cercocarpus, Rhus,* and other sclerophylls in the understory. Drier sites supported species of *Acacia, Bursera, Caesalpinia, Cardiospermum, Dodonaea, Eysenhardtia, Fouquieria, Lysiloma, Pithecellobium,* and others that require frostless winters. They contributed to a dry scrub in the Mint Canyon basin. The drier aspect of this flora as compared with the Puente and Modelo in coastal California reflects its Miocene position in the lee of the low Peninsular ranges. The flora implies that the present desert area, with scarcely 2 inches (51 mm) annual rainfall, then had fully 20–25 inches (508–635 mm) distributed in summer and probably also in winter. The flora also implies winters were frostless. Clearly, the present desert environment in this area is much younger. This is shown also by woodrat middens from the Sonoran region in southern Arizona. They indicate piñon–juniper woodland occupied the present desert area during the time from 40,000 to 10,000 years ago. That generally similar conditions prevailed in the western part of the desert in California is consistent with the record of juniper woodland in *Neotoma* middens in the area near Catávina, in the Sonoran Desert of central Baja California.

The close similarity of the Mint Canyon flora, which was situated in the area of the Salton Sea in the late Miocene, to the Tehachapi–Ricardo–Anaverde floras of the Mohave region indicates that they contributed to the same phytogeographic province. In other words, whereas the Great

Basin area with its forests and woodlands was a distinct province in the middle Miocene, the differences between the Mohave and Sonoran regions have been established more recently. The marked change in the vegetation of the two provinces is attributed chiefly to a rise in elevation of about 2,400–2,600 feet (732–793 m), with a cooler, wetter climate to the north (Fig. 5.2). The boundary between these provinces was close to the present one. Segregation of the Mohave province resulted from the uplift of the Mohave block during the Late Pliocene and Quaternary. The Mohave was then transformed into a transitional or ecotonal desert, intermediate in climate, elevation, and composition with respect to the Great Basin to the north and the Sonoran Desert to the south. Thus, it is understandable that members of the Sonoran Desert flora reach northward in low basins (Salton, Blythe, and Needles troughs) to the Mohave province. It is in these basins that typically Sonoran Desert taxa as *Acacia, Burersa, Calliandra, Cercidium, Condalia, Dalea, Fouquieria, Lycium, Nolina, Olynea, Prosopis,* and *Washingtonia,* are within a few miles of the higher, colder Mohave province. They are not in that area today, though a number of their fossil relatives have records there in the Miocene. More numerous members of this group, distributed in *Acacia, Bursera, Euphorbia, Eysenhardtia, Ficus, Lysoloma, Pachycormus, Pithecellobium* and others that were in the northern part of the Miocene Madrean province now occur to the south and east in the Sonoran Desert and on its upper margins. There summer rain is more frequent in amount, and winters are frostless or nearly so. These plants, which give to the Sonoran Desert its arboreal character, were derived chiefly from thorn forest and dry-tropic scrub by gradual adaptation to drier climate during the later Tertiary. They were eliminated from the northern (Mohave) part of the province as summer rain decreased and especially as temperatures were lowered when the Mohave block was uplifted at the close of the Tertiary. This was the chief event that differentiated the Mohave from the Sonoran Desert flora (Fig. 5.2). A few hardier plants of this group still have relict sites in the Mohave region, including species of *Crossosoma, Dalea, Lycium,* and *Prosopis.*

*Origins of Taxa:* Most modern desert species in the Sonoran region appear to have originated from taxa that contributed to the drier margins of more mesic dry-tropic forest, thorn forest, and oak woodland that occupied the area during the Tertiary (Axelrod 1979a, Figs. 18–20). As aridity gradually increased, taxa that earlier were confined to dry sites in local areas spread out into the widening, progressively drier region. In attempting to understand the origins of its diverse taxa, it is important to note that all desert growth-forms occur also in oak woodland, grassland, thorn scrub, and dry tropic forest. Some of the adaptive types were already present

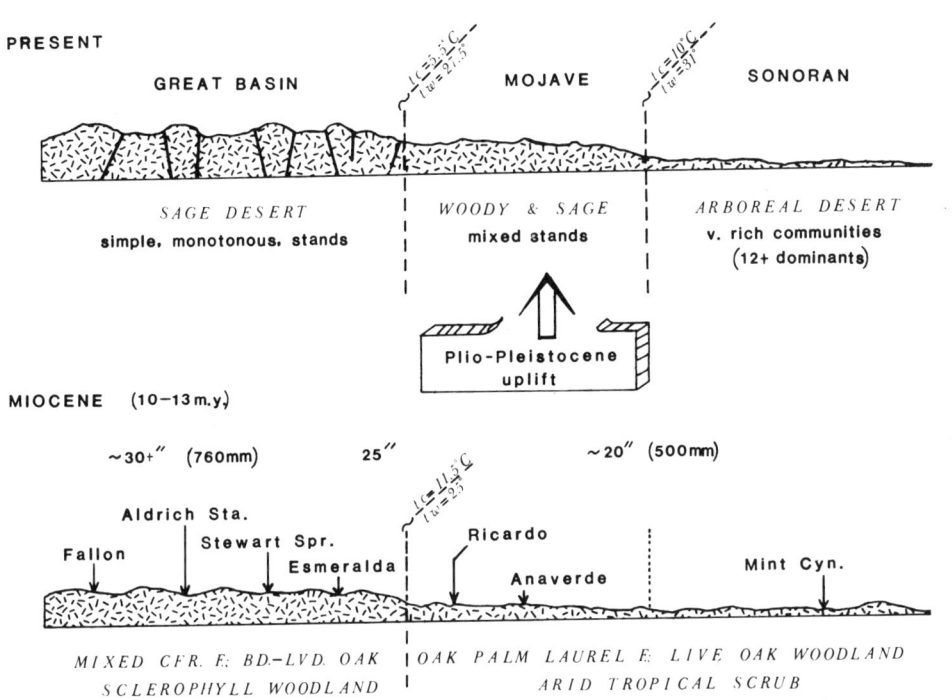

```
PRESENT
              GREAT BASIN                         MOJAVE              SONORAN
                                      Tc=5°C                Tc=10°C
                                      Tw=27.5              Tw=37

              SAGE DESERT          |  WOODY & SAGE  |   ARBOREAL DESERT
           simple, monotonous, stands |  mixed stands  |   v. rich communities
                                   |                |      (12+ dominants)
                                   |       ⇧        |
                                   |  Plio-Pleistocene |
                                   |      uplift    |

MIOCENE  (10–13 m.y.)

        ~30+" (760mm)           25"              ~20" (500mm)
                                    Tc=11.5°C
                                    Tw=23.5
           Aldrich Sta.              Ricardo
    Fallon   Stewart Spr.                              Mint Cyn.
              Esmeralda           Anaverde

   MIXED CFR. F; BD.-LVD. OAK  | OAK PALM LAUREL F; LIVE OAK WOODLAND
       SCLEROPHYLL WOODLAND    |      ARID TROPICAL SCRUB
```

Figure 5.2. Transect from western Nevada into southeastern California today (above) and in the Late Miocene (below). Uplift of the Mohave block brought to it a colder climate. This confined taxa southward to the warmer Sonoran province and enabled more temperate alliances from the north to invade the uplifted Mohave province. Uplift of the Sierra Nevada to the west brought a drier, colder climate to the lee and also blocked summer rain which had a source in the warm western sea. These factors restricted forest and oak woodland to the west and were also unsuited for species now in the summer-wet southwestern United States and adjacent Mexico that were represented by similar Neogene taxa in the present desert; from Axelrod 1979b, Fig. 13.

in the Middle Eocene when they lived under a dry (monsoon) season. For many taxa, a gradual change in the tempo of living would be the only requirement to adapt to a more arid environment. This would involve the gradual evolution of more rapid germination, growth, flowering, pollination, and seed setting, all of which could be induced by a general trend to increased aridity. However, on local outcrops of hard crystalline rocks (metamorphics, granitics, volcanics, and marble-limestones) on exposed (southern) slopes selection for greater drought would also take place. Adaptation to increased drought would be speeded up in local dry edaphic sites, as well as in local rainshadows in the lee of low ranges (Axelrod 1967 and 1972). Rate of evolution in these areas would greatly surpass that which was solely in response to a long gradual trend to aridity, to one spread over a period of fifty million years or more. Viewed in this manner, it seems probable that the diverse taxa in the Sonoran province have been adapting to drier areas since the Late Cretaceous at least, for this region was then a tropic savanna and dry-tropic forest as shown by the fossil floras recovered there (Fig. 5.3).

As reviewed above, the sequence of vegetation in the Sonoran region has been savanna ▶ dry tropic forest ▶ short tree forest ▶ thorn forest. And from the evergreen forests there has been a trend from oak–laurel forest ▶ live oak woodland ▶ chaparral ▶ sage (Axelrod 1979a, Fig. 20). From these vegetation zones have come the taxa that have adapted to the greater drought of the desert. They range from unique monotypic families to taxa similar to those on the borders of the desert today. On this basis, it seems probable that the isolated families that have no close allies, notably Crossomataceae, Fouquieriaceae, Koeberliniaceae, Simmondsiaceae, may be Late Cretaceous in age. Also, some families that were established in the Late Cretaceous–Paleocene have unique genera that may have been present in the developing dry area at this time, notably the Anacardiaceae *(Pachycormus)*, Arecaceae *(Brahea, Sabal, Washingtonia)*, Cactaceae (numerous types), Caesalpiniaceae *(Haematoxylon)*, Capparaceae *(Forchammeria)*, Rosaceae *(Vauquelinia)*, and others that then contributed to dry-tropic forest and scrub and to oak–laurel forest.

By Eocene time many genera were represented by species that form phylads that now extend from dry-tropic forest into thorn forest and tropical desert. Included here are such genera as *Acacia, Bauhinia, Bombax, Bumelia, Cardiospermum, Colubrina, Cordia, Ficus, Leucanea, Morus, Pithecellobium, Sapindus,* and *Zizyphus*, all of which were already present in the Eocene and adapting to drier climates.

During the Oligocene and Miocene there was a rapid spread of many typically western families, notably scores of genera in Apiaceae, Asteraceae, Bassicaceae, Hydrophyllaceae, Menthaceae, Poaceae, Polemoniaceae, and others that are largely authochthonous. Also, distinctive species

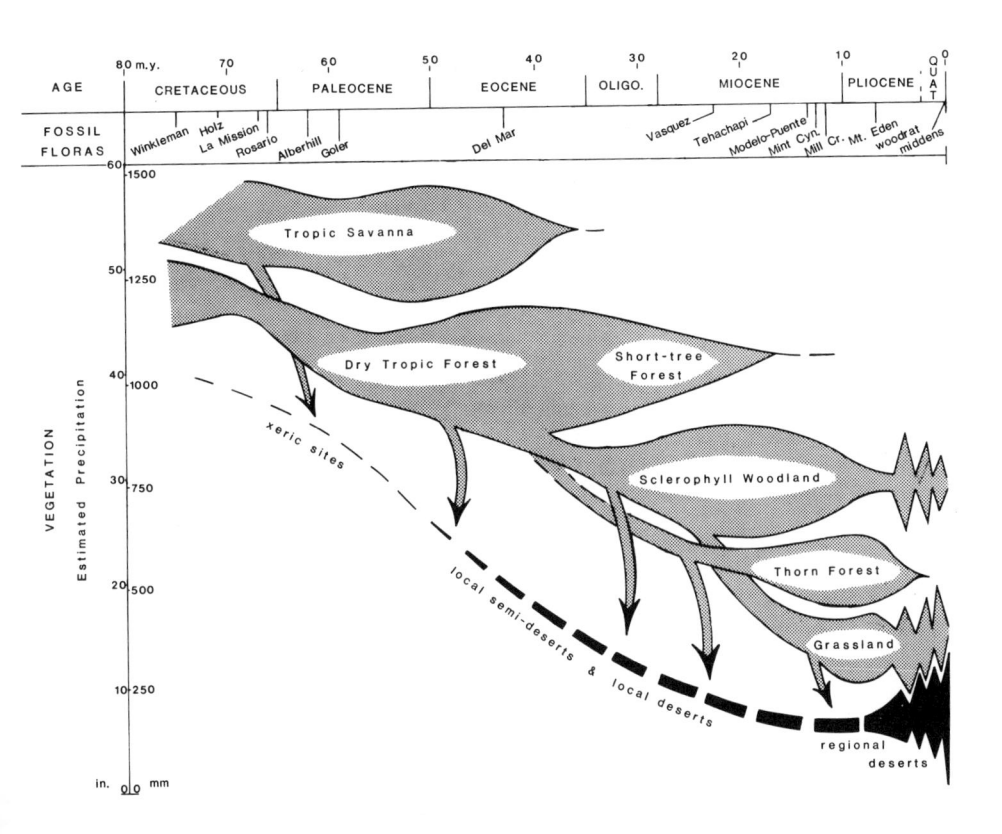

Figure 5.3. Sequence of vegetation in the Sonoran Desert region indicated by fossil floras from the Late Cretaceous into the close of the Pleistocene. Taxa have been invading dry sites as they appeared and spread, first in restricted dry edaphic sites and on local lee slopes, and then radiating more widely as the intensity and duration of drought increased following the Middle Eocene. The pattern accounts for the coexistence of ancient (Cretaceous) relicts (e.g., *Fouquieria*, *Koeberlinia*, and *Simmondsia*) that live side-by-side with new (Quaternary) annual species (e.g., *Clarkia*, *Gilia*, and *Layia*). In brief, the expanding dry area has been accumulating taxa for fully 70 million years; from Axelrod 1979b, Fig. 18.

of many older genera, such as *Abutilon, Agave, Atriplex, Bursera, Dalea, Dudleya, Eriogonum, Euphorbia, Ipomoea, Jatropha, Lycium,* and *Yucca,* are inferred to have originated at this time because some Miocene species are similar to them. In the Pliocene and Quaternary scores of herbaceous species from woodland and grassland communities ranged out into the spreading dry area and have persisted there as similar or related taxa. Others show only minor differences (races, subspecies, and varieties) and have survived invasions of moister communities and taxa during the wet pluvials. Included among these diverse alliances are numerous species of *Astragalus, Calochortus, Cryptantha, Eriogonum, Lupinus, Mentzelia, Oenothera, Penstemon, Senecio, Sphaeralcea,* and scores of others.

Viewed in this light, the flora of the Sonoran region is a repository for taxa that have been accumulating in a progressively drier, subtropic to tropic province during the past seventy million years. Many Sonoran Desert taxa have similar or allied species in woodland–chaparral and thorn forest vegetation that covered the area that is presently desert in the Miocene and later. Sonoran Desert taxa appear to have been preadapted structurally to the condition of increased drought and to have survived as aridity increased over the area as woodland and thorn scrub were eliminated. Thus, the Sonoran Desert history differs greatly from that of the Great Basin and also the Mohave Desert.

The modern taxa in the Sonoran Desert thus have widely divergent ages: monotypic families probably are Cretaceous, unique genera are Eocene, distinctive species are Miocene, and the others are younger. Herbaceous taxa have been added recently, even into the late Pleistocene. It was during the Quaternary that intense mountain building created many new subzones with novel biotic-climatic relations. Fluctuating glacial-pluvial and interglacial climates repeatedly brought together and then isolated interbreeding populations that created new, minor taxa. These new taxa were adapted to the present desert environment. As the Mohave block was uplifted during the Quaternary and was separated climatically from the Sonoran province, numerous alliances that earlier were common to both areas were eliminated from the Mohave province. This was in response to the colder climate at the higher elevations and to the colder climates of the glacial ages, because the Sonoran links are largely those of dry-tropical ancestry. Elevation of mountains to the west also blocked the ingress regular summer rains from the west coast of Mexico and this, no doubt, eliminated some taxa that germinate in the warm season. As the Mohave block was uplifted, taxa from the Great Basin province, which have interior Asian affinities, invaded the region and created a new transitional flora with respect to the desert areas north and south (Fig. 5.2).

## CONCLUSION

This brief summary review of paleobotanical evidence shows that regional (zonal) desert environments are not "earth-old features" as some would have us believe. There is not one shred of evidence to support such a notion. On the contrary, sequences of progressively younger fossil floras from areas presently desert—whether here or on other continents (Axelrod 1950, 1979b)—clearly show that these areas were earlier covered with rich forests and woodlands, and that desert vegetation gradually came into existence as progressively drier climate spread during the Late Cenozoic. Never in the history of the angiosperm phylum have desert taxa been more abundant, more widespread, or more diverse than at present. Our regional deserts represent new ecosystems: they have just been born! Unless we take better care of them nothing will remain but a barren terrain like the largely man-made desert that now stretches uninterruptedly for 4,200 miles (6,758 km) from the Atlantic shore of north Africa to the Thar desert of western India. The choice is yours.

## NOTES

1. Thanks are extended to the National Science Foundation for grants that have made it possible to collect and study Tertiary floras from the western desert region.

## REFERENCES

Axelrod, D. I. 1950. "Evolution of Desert Vegetation in Western North America." *Carnegie Inst. Wash. Pub.*, 590 VI:215–306.
———. 1967. "Drought Diastrophism and Quantum Evolution." *Evolution*, 21:201–209.
———. 1972. "Edaphic Aridity as a Factor in Angiosperm Evolution." *Amer. Naturalist*, 106:311–320.
———. 1979a. "Age and Origin of Sonoran Desert Vegetation." *Calif. Acad. Sci. Occas. Papers*, 132:1–72.
———. 1979b. "Desert Vegetation: Its Age and Origin," in J. R. Goodin and D. K. Northington (eds). *Arid Land Plant Resources*. Lubbock, Texas: Texas Tech. Univ., 1–72.
Shreve, F. 1942. "The Desert Vegetation of North America." *Bot. Review*, 8:195–246.
Van Devender, T. R., and W. G. Spaulding. 1979. "Development of Vegetation and Climate in the Southwestern United States." *Science*, 204:701–710 (see Chapter 6, this volume).
Wells, P. V. 1979. "An Equable Glaciopluvial in the West: Pleniglacial Evidence of Increased Precipitation on a Gradient from the Great Basin to the Sonoran and Chihuahuan Deserts." *Quaternary Research*, 12:311–325.
Yurtsev, B. A. 1972. "Phytogeography of Northeastern Asia and the Problem of Transberingian Floristic Interrelations," in A. Graham (ed). *Floristics and Paleofloristics of Asia and Eastern North America*. New York: Elsevier, 19–54.

> # 6

# DEVELOPMENT OF VEGETATION AND CLIMATE IN THE SOUTHWESTERN UNITED STATES*

Thomas R. Van Devender

*Arizona Natural Heritage Program
Tucson, Arizona*

and W. Geoffrey Spaulding

*University of Arizona
Tucson, Arizona*

## INTRODUCTION

In the past 15 years, analysis of packrat (*Neotoma* spp.) middens has provided several hundred radiocarbon-dated fossil plant assemblages from now arid and semiarid regions in the southwestern United States (Fig. 6.1). Packrats thoroughly sampled the vegetation on rocky slopes within 100 meters of the dry, protected shelters where middens are built and preserved. Many of the hundreds of plants in the fossil middens have been identified to species, allowing their distributions and autecologies to be used in paleoclimatic reconstructions. Fossil middens allow detailed paleoecological reconstructions of past communities in areas with few other sources of perishable organic materials. On the basis of the packrat midden record, we describe here the vegetational changes and inferred climates during the past 22,000 years in the warm deserts of the southwestern United States.

---

*Reprinted with permission from *Science*, 1979, 204:701–710; references and notes are in the format of the original *Science* article.

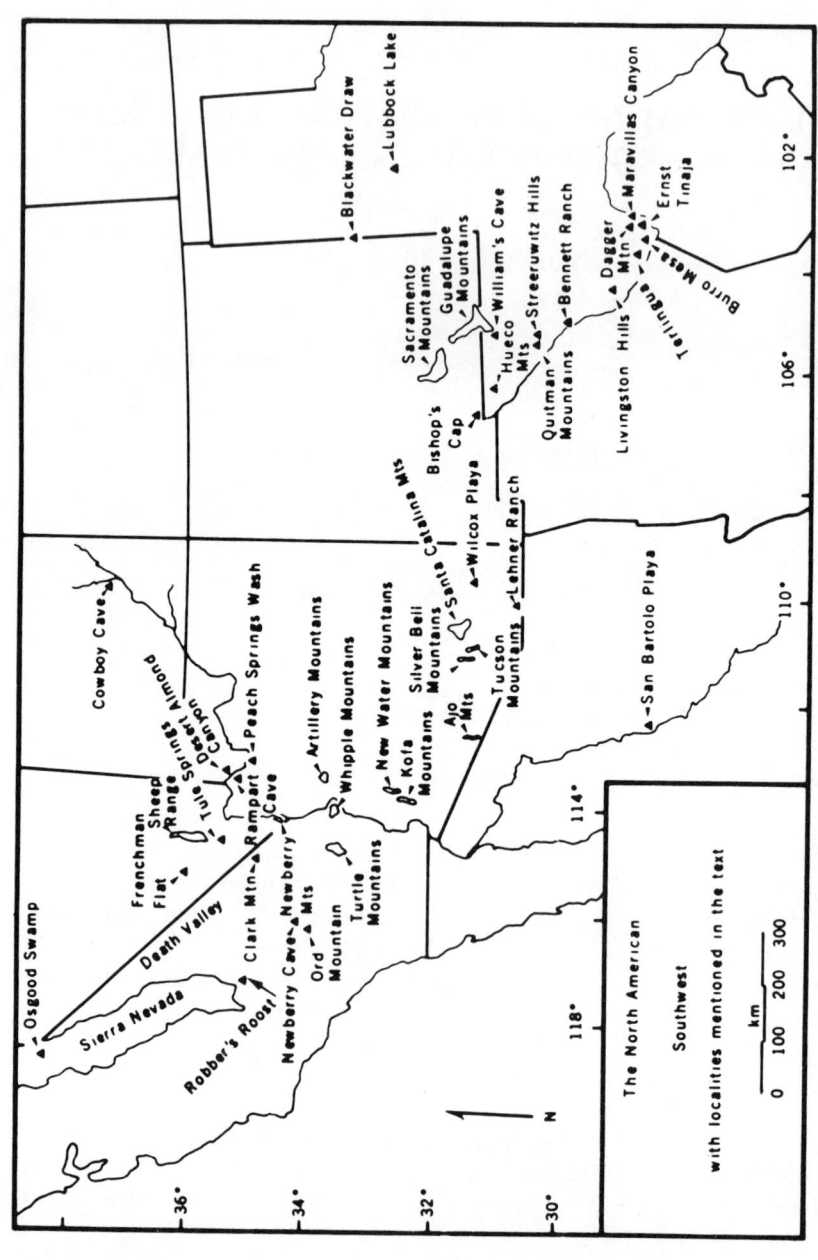

Figure 6.1. The southwestern United States with localities mentioned in the text.

## VEGETATION CHRONOLOGY

### Late Wisconsinan (22,000 to 11,000 years B.P.)

Packrat middens dating from the late Wisconsinan glacial maximum, 22,000 to 17,000 years B.P. (radiocarbon years before present), to about 11,000 years B.P. document the occurrence of pinyon–juniper woodlands at middle elevations of 1525 to 550 m in areas now occupied by desertscrub communities. Time series of midden assemblages from single sites or several sites in a small area show few important changes in composition, suggesting that the pinyon–juniper woodlands were relatively stable throughout this 11,000-year period.

The species of pinyon in the midden samples are Colorado pinyon (*Pinus edulis* Engelm.) and Mexican pinyon (*P. cembroides* Zucc. var. *remota* Little) in the Chihuahuan Desert and border pinyon (*P. cembroides* var. *bicolor* Little) and single-needle pinyon (*P. monophylla* Torr. & Frém.) in the Sonoran and Mohave deserts (Fig. 6.2). Middens recording this pinyon–juniper woodland extend from Ord Mountain, San Bernardino County *(1)*, and Robber's Roost, Kern County *(2)*, California, on the western side of the Mohave Desert (116°W), to the Guadalupe Mountains, Culberson County *(3)*, and Maravillas Canyon, Brewster County *(4)*, Texas (103°W). In the present Chihuahuan Desert, pinyon–juniper midden records extend from the Big Bend to the Guadalupe Mountains in Texas, and to Bishop's Cap, Doña Ana County, New Mexico (29° to 32°N) *(5)*. In Arizona, pinyon–juniper middens have been found from Montezuma's Head, Ajo Mountains, Pima County, to Desert Almond Canyon and Peach Springs Wash, Grand Canyon, Mohave County (32° to 36°N) *(6)*. The midden sample from Kern County at 35°35'N is the northernmost late Wisconsinan pinyon–juniper midden in California *(1, 2, 7, 8)*. In Nevada and California north of 36°N, single-needle pinyon may have been restricted to elevations above 1585 m and absent from middle elevation juniper woodlands. Table 6.1 is a summary of data on pinyon–juniper middens from the Southwest.

The lowest late Wisconsinan pinyon record in the Southwest is from a midden sample dated at 12,960 ± 210 years B.P. from an elevation of 510 m in the Whipple Mountains, San Bernardino County, California *(7)*. Other late Wisconsinan midden samples from about 600 to 280 m along the Colorado River in Arizona and California contain juniper woodland assemblages without pinyon *(9, 10)*. A similar juniper woodland at 645 to 425 m is documented by a large series of middens from the Rampart Cave area in the lower Grand Canyon of Arizona *(6)*. Desert-scrub communities probably persisted along the Colorado River at elevations below about 400 to 300 m, but middens older than 11,000 years B.P. with desertscrub assemblages have yet to be discovered. Nonetheless, important dominants in the present Mohave and Great Basin deserts have been found in late

134    *Origin and Evolution of Deserts*

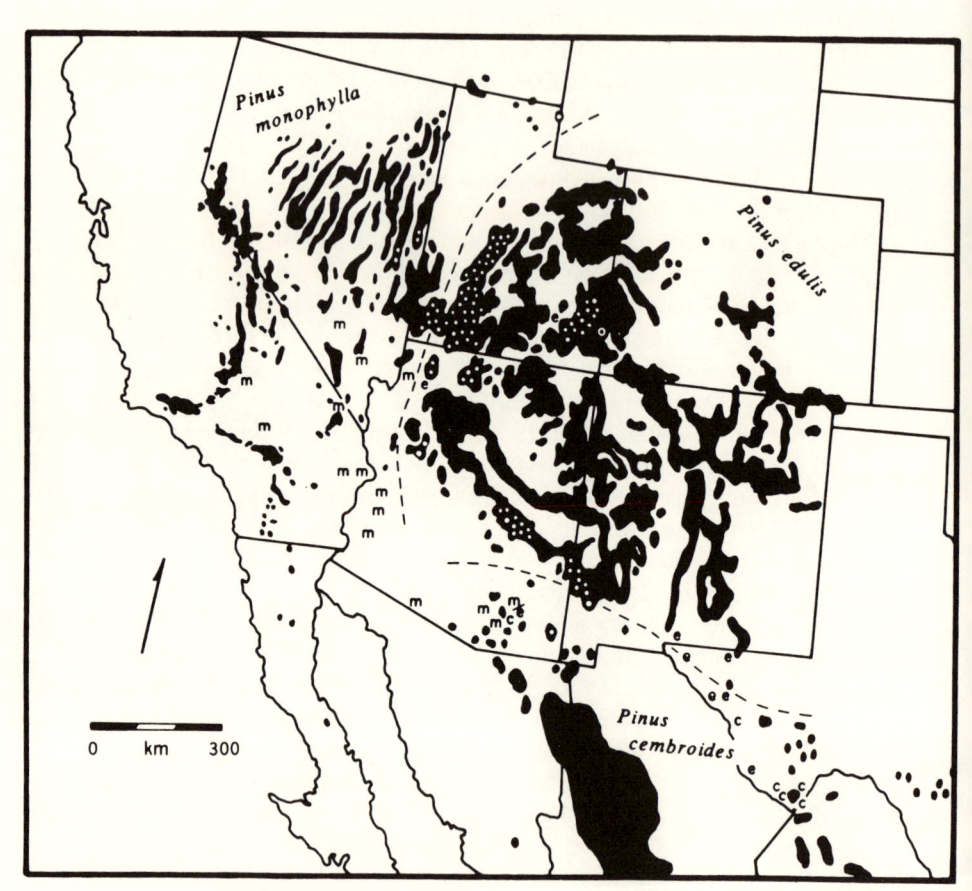

Figure 6.2. Map of pinyon species in the Southwest.

Wisconsinan woodland middens from sites at lower elevations and farther south than they occur today *(6, 7, 9, 11, 12)*. These include big sagebrush *(Artemisia tridentata* Nutt.), shadscale *(Atriplex confertifolia* Wats.), blackbrush *(Coleogyne ramosissima* Torr.), mountain mahogany *(Cercocarpus intricatus* Wats.), Joshua tree *(Yucca brevifolia* Engelm.), Whipple yucca *(Y. whipplei* Torr.), and creosote bush *(Larrea divaricata* Cov.). Few characteristic Sonoran Desert plants have been found in late Wisconsinan packrat midden samples.

Packrat middens from higher elevations document past montane conifer communities in some areas. Approximately 13,000 years ago a community of spruce *(Picea* sp.), Douglas fir *(Pseudotsuga menziesii* Franco), southwestern white pine *(Pinus strobiformis* Engelm.), and dwarf juniper *(Juniperus communis* L.) with some Colorado pinyon was at an elevation of 2000 m in an area now in the desert–grassland and woodland ecotone in the Guadalupe Mountains of Texas *(3)*. Spruce and dwarf juniper no longer occur in Texas. In southeastern Utah, at Cowboy Cave, Wayne County, spruce and Douglas fir grew at an elevation of 1710 m in a present pinyon–juniper area at 11,000 years B.P. *(13)*. In the Santa Catalina Mountains, Pima County, Arizona, Arizona cypress *(Cupressus arizonica* Greene) and Douglas fir grew at 1555 m near the present upper limit of the Sonoran Desert palo verde *(Cercidium microphyllum* Rose & Jtn.)–saguaro *(Cereus giganteus* Engelm.) community at 13,850 ± 220 years B.P. and 14,450 ± 150 years B.P. (laboratory numbers WK-162 and WK-163, on *Cupressus arizonica*). Both border pinyon and hybrids between Colorado and single-needle pinyons are in the latter samples. On Clark Mountain, San Bernardino County, California, limber pine *(Pinus flexilis* James), and white fir *(Abies concolor* Lindl.) occurred with single-needle pinyon as low as 1910 m in a present pinyon–juniper woodland at 12,460 ± 190 years B.P. *(14)*. Great Basin bristlecone pine *(Pinus longaeva* Bailey, as *P. aristata* Engelm.) was associated with these species in two other samples from the same site at 23,600 ± 950 and 28,720 ± 1800 years B.P. In the Sheep Range, southern Nevada, woodland communities dominated by Utah juniper *(Juniperus osteosperma* Little) and often containing single-needle pinyon, limber pine and, occasionally, white fir, occupied areas that are now blackbrush desertscrub at 1585 to 1860 m, during the late Wisconsinan. Higher in the Sheep Range, subalpine bristlecone pine–limber pine forest extended from 1900 to 2400 m between 22,000 and 12,000 years B.P. *(9)*.

### Early Holocene (11,000 to 8000 years B.P.)

The end of the late Wisconsinan pinyon–juniper woodlands is recorded by the youngest dated woodland middens with pinyon at about 11,000 years B.P. in the Chihuahuan, Sonoran, and Mohave deserts (Table 6.1).

Table 6.1. Late Wisconsinan packrat middens from North America containing pinyon pine. Abbreviations: C, *Cupressus arizonica*; J, *Juniperus* sp.; N, *Neotoma* dung; Picebi, *Pinus cembroides* var. *bicolor*; Picere, *Pinus cembroides* var. *remota*; Pied, *P. edulis*; Pifl, *P. flexilis*; Pilo, *P. longaeva*; Pimo, *P. monophylla*; Pisp, *Picea* sp.; S, *Nothrotheriops shastense* dung; TR, this report; U, uriniferous material.

| Latitude and longitude | Site | Elevation (m) | Age | Material dated | Associates | Pinyon species | Reference |
|---|---|---|---|---|---|---|---|
| A Chihuahuan Desert | | | | | | | |
| | | | Big Bend, Brewster County, Texas | | | | |
| 29°16′N, 103°01′W | Ernst Tinaja No. 1 | 760 | 15,300 ± 670 (WK-174) | J | *Koeberlinia spinosa*, *Quercus hinckleyi*, *Yucca* cf. *rostrata* | Picere | TR |
| 29°16′N, 103°23′W | Burro Mesa No. 1 | 1200 | 18,750 ± 360 (not given) | U | *Agave lecheguilla*, *Berberis trifoliolata*, *Quercus grisea* | Picere | (4) |
| 29°18′N, 103°41′W | Terlingua No. 1 | 915 | 15,000 ± 440 (WK-175) | J | *Cercocarpus montanus*, *Cowania eriacefolia*, *Yucca* cf. *rostrata* | Picere | TR |
| 29°32′N, 103°06′W | Dagger Mountain No. 1 | 880 | 20,000 ± 390 (not given) | U | *Agave lecheguilla*, *Berberis trifoliolata*, *Quercus grisea* | Picere | (4) |
| 29°32′N, 103°06′W | Dagger Mountain No. 3 | 850 | 16,250 ± 240 (not given) | U | *Agave lecheguilla*, *Celtis reticulata*, *Quercus pungens* | Picere | (4) |
| 29°32′N, 102°49′W | Maravillas Canyon No. 1A | 600 | 11,560 ± 140 (not given) | U | *Agave lecheguilla*, *Quercus pungens*, *Yucca rostrata* | Picere | (4) |
| 29°32′N, 102°49′W | Maravillas Canyon No. 1C | 600 | 12,550 ± 130 (not given) | U | *Agave lecheguilla*, *Juglans microcarpa*, *Quercus pungens* | Picere | (4) |
| 29°32′N, 102°49′W | Maravillas Canyon No. 2 | 600 | 13,350 ± 170 (not given) | U | *Berberis trifoliolata*, *Quercus pungens*, *Yucca rostrata* | Picere | (4) |
| 29°32′N, 102°49′W | Maravillas Canyon No. 3 | 600 | 14,800 ± 180 (not given) | U | *Berberis trifoliolata*, *Celtis reticulata*, *Quercus pungens* | Picere | (4) |
| 29°32′N, 102°49′W | Maravillas Canyon No. 1B | 600 | 12,000 ± 150 (not given) | U | *Agave lecheguilla*, *Quercus pungens*, *Yucca rostrata* | Picere | (4) |

| | | | | | | |
|---|---|---|---|---|---|---|
| 29°33'N, 102°49'W | Maravillas Canyon TRV No. 3 | 600 | 16,160 ± 330 (A-1842) | J | *Berberis* cf. *trifoliolata*, *Quercus* sp., *Yucca* cf. *torreyi* | Picere | TR |

Livingston Hills, Presidio County, Texas

| | | | | | | |
|---|---|---|---|---|---|---|
| 29°47'N, 104°22'W | Shafter No. 1B | 1310 | 15,695 ± 230 (A-1581) | J | *Quercus hinckleyi*, *Q. pungens*, *Yucca* cf. *rostrata* | Pied | (24) |

Rio Grande, Presidio County, Texas

| | | | | | | |
|---|---|---|---|---|---|---|
| 30°37'N, 104°59'W | Bennett Ranch No. 1 | 1035 | 18,190 ± 380 (A-1831) | N | *Berberis haematocarpa*, *Juniperus* sp., *Prosopis glandulosa* | Picere | TR |
| 30°37'N, 104°59'W | Bennett Ranch No. 3 | 1035 | 11,000 ± 320 (A-1801) | J | *Agave* sp., *Nolina* sp., *Opuntia imbricata* | Picere | TR |
| 30°37'N, 104°59'W | Bennett Ranch No. 4 | 1035 | 12,030 ± 170 (A-1836) | J | *Agave* cf. *neomexicana*, *Forsellesia spinescens*, *Nolina* sp. | Picere | TR |

Sierra Diablo, Hudspeth County, Texas

| | | | | | | |
|---|---|---|---|---|---|---|
| 31°07'N, 105°09'W | Streeruwitz Hills No. 1 (P3U) | 1430 | 14,290 ± 290 (A-1843) | J | *Agave* cf., *neomexicana*, *Berberis trifoliolata*, *Yucca elata* | Pied | TR |
| 31°07'N, 105°09'W | Streeruwitz Hills No. 1 (P4) | 1430 | 18,060 ± 1320 (A-1623) | J | *Atriplex canescens*, *Berberis haematocarpa*, *Celtis reticulata* | Pied | TR |

Quitman Mountains, Hudspeth County, Texas

| | | | | | | |
|---|---|---|---|---|---|---|
| 31°08'N, 105°24'W | Quitman Mountains No. 1 | 1430 | 10,910 ± 170 (A-1612) | J | *Cercocarpus montanus*, *Quercus pungens*, *Symphoricarpos* sp. | Pied | (7, 44) |
| 31°08'N, 105°24'W | Quitman Mountains No. 2 | 1430 | 12,040 ± 470 (A-1843) | J | *Berberis haematocarpa*, *Cercocarpus montanus*, *Quercus pungens* | Pied | TR |

Hueco Mountains, El Paso County, Texas

| | | | | | | |
|---|---|---|---|---|---|---|
| 31°53'N, 106°09'W | Picture Cave No. 1D | 1430 | 12,030 ± 210 (A-1699) | J | *Berberis haematocarpa*, *Cercocarpus montanus*, *Quercus pungens* | Pied | (17) |
| 31°54'N, 106°09'W | Tank Trap Wash No. 1 (5) | 1340 | 19,610 ± 1150 (A-1710) | Pied | *Cercocarpus montanus*, *Mortonia scabrella* var. *scabrella*, *Quercus pungens* | Pied | TR |

Table 6.1 continued.

| Latitude and longitude | Site | Elevation (m) | Age | Material dated | Associates | Pinyon species | Reference |
|---|---|---|---|---|---|---|---|
| *Hueco Mountains, El Paso County, Texas (continued)* |
| 31°54′N, 106°09′W | Tank Trap Wash No. 2 | 1340 | 21,200 ± 990 (A-1772) | J | *Cercocarpus montanus, Forsellesia spinescens, Quercus pungens* | Pied | TR |
| 31°54′N, 106°09′W | Navar Ranch No. 3B | 1370 | 16,240 ± 430 (A-1645) | J | *Berberis trifoliolata, Forsellesia spinescens, Opuntia imbricata* | Pied | TR |
| 31°55′N, 106°03′W | Hueco Tanks St. Park No. 1 | 1420 | 13,500 ± 250 (A-1624) | J | *Quercus toumeyi, Ribes* sp., *Symphoricarpos* sp. | Pied | (17) |
| *Guadalupe Mountains, Culberson County, Texas* |
| 31°55′N, 104°50′W | Cave C-08 midden | 2000 | 13,060 ± 280 (A-1549) | Pisp | *Juniperus communis, Pinus strobiformis, Pseudotsuga menziesii* | Pied | (3) |
| 31°54′N, 104°50′W | William's Cave No. 2 | 1500 | 12,040 ± 210 (A-1540) | J | *Prunus serotina, Quercus* sp., *Robinia neomexicana* | Pied | TR |
| *Bishop's Cap, Doña Ana County, New Mexico* |
| 32°11′N, 106°36′W | Shelter Cave Sloth No. 1 | 1400 | 11,330 ± 370 (A-1878) | S | *Juniperus* sp., *Opuntia imbricata, Sphaeralcea* sp. | Pied | TR |
| **B Sonoran Desert** |
| *Ajo Mountains, Pima County, Arizona* |
| 32°07′N, 112°42′W | Montezuma Head No. 1A | 975 | 20,490 ± 510 (A-1695) | J | *Artemisia tridentata, Quercus turbinella* ssp. *ajoensis, Yucca brevifolia* | Pimo | (7) |
| 32°07′N, 112°42′W | Montezuma Head No. 1B | 975 | 21,840 ± 650 (A-1696) | Pimo | *Artemisia tridentata, Opuntia chlorotica, Yucca brevifolia* | Pimo | (7) |
| 32°07′N, 112°42′W | Montezuma Head No. 1C | 975 | 17,830 ± 870 (A-1697) | J and Pimo | *Artemisia tridentata, Berberis harrisoniana, Yucca brevifolia* | Pimo | (7) |
| 32°07′N, 112°42′W | Montezuma Head No. 1D | 975 | 13,500 ± 390 (A-1698) | J | *Agave deserti, Artemisia tridentata, Yucca brevifolia* | Pimo | (7) |

| | | | | | | |
|---|---|---|---|---|---|---|
| | | | *Tucson Mountains, Pima County, Arizona* | | | |
| 32°19′N, 111°12′W | Tucson Mountains No. 3 | 740 | 21,000 ± 700 (A-994) | J | *Agave* sp., *Dasylirion wheeleri*, *Opuntia chlorotica* | Pimo | (27, 44) |
| | | | *Santa Catalina Mountains, Pima County, Arizona* | | | |
| 32°21′N, 110°53′W | Pontatoc Ridge No. 2 | 1555 | 13,850 ± 220 (WK-162) | C | *Arctostaphylos* sp., *Pseudotsuga menziesii* | Picebi, Pimo × Pied | TR |
| 32°21′N, 110°53′W | Pontatoc Ridge No. 4A | 1555 | 14,450 ± 150 (WK-163) | C | *Arctostaphylos* sp., *Cupressus arizonica*, *Juniperus* sp., *Pseudotsuga menziesii* | Picebi, Pimo × Pied | TR |
| | | | *Silver Bell Mountains, Pima County, Arizona* | | | |
| 32°27′N, 111°28′W | Wolcott Peak No. 2 | 860 | 14,550 ± 800 (A-1286) | J | *Celtis pallida*, *Opuntia phaeacantha*, *Prosopis juliflora* | Pimo | (27, 48) |
| 32°27′N, 111°28′W | Wolcott Peak No. 5 | 860 | 12,130 ± 500 (A-1287) | J | *Agave* sp., *Opuntia chlorotica*, *Quercus turbinella* | Pimo | (27, 48) |
| | | | *Picacho Mountains, Pinal County, Arizona* | | | |
| 32°38′N, 111°24′W | Picacho Peak No. 1B | 655 | 11,100 ± 300 (A-1835) | J | *Berberis trifoliolata*, *Ferocactus acanthodes*, *Quercus* cf. *turbinella* | Pimo | TR |
| 32°38′N, 111°24′W | Picacho Peak No. 1A | 655 | 13,170 ± 200 (A-1827) | J | *Artemisia* cf. *tridentata*, *Ferocactus acanthodes*, *Opuntia chlorotica* | Pimo | TR |
| | | | *Kofa Mountains, Yuma County, Arizona* | | | |
| 33°24′N, 114°01′W | Burro Canyon No. 1 (6) | 860 | 13,400 ± 350 (A-1357) | J | *Artiplex confertifolia*, *Encelia farinosa*, *Rhus aromatica* | Pimo | (27, 48) |
| 33°24′N, 114°01′W | Burro Canyon No. 1 (1) | 860 | 14,400 ± 330 (A-1315) | J | *Atriplex canescens*, *Opuntia chlorotica*, *Quercus turbinella* | Pimo | (27, 48) |
| | | | *New Water Mountains, Yuma County, Arizona* | | | |
| 33°36′N, 113°55′W | New Water Mountains No. 4 | 615 | 10,880 ± 390 (A-1285) | J | *Acacia greggii*, *Ferocactus acanthodes*, *Larrea divaricata*, *Quercus turbinella* | Pimo | (27, 48) |

Table 6.1 continued.

| Latitude and longitude | Site | Elevation (m) | Age | Material dated | Associates | Pinyon species | Reference |
|---|---|---|---|---|---|---|---|
| *Whipple Mountains, San Bernardino County, California* ||||||||
| 34°16'N, 114°25'W | Redtail Peak No. 5 | 510 | 12,960 ± 210 (A-1666) | Pimo | *Cercocarpus intricatus, Nolina bigelovii, Yucca whipplei* | Pimo | (48) |
| *Artillery Mountains, Mohave County, Arizona* ||||||||
| 34°20'N, 113°35'W | Artillery Mountains No. 2 | 725 | 18,320 ± 400 (A-1101) | J | *Arctostaphylos pungens, Ferocactus acanthodes, Quercus turbinella* | Pimo | (27, 48) |
| 34°23'N, 113°28'W | Artillery Mountains No. 3 | 725 | 21,000 ± 400 (USGS-196) | J | *Acacia greggii, Artemisia tridentata, Larrea divaricata, Quercus dunnii* | Pimo | (27, 48) |
| C Mohave Desert ||||||||
| *Turtle Mountains, San Bernardino County, California* ||||||||
| 32°20'N, 114°50'W | Turtle Mountains No. 1 | 850 | 19,500 ± 380 (not given) | (ng) | *Opuntia erinacea, Ribes* cf. *velutinum* | Pimo | (8) |
| 34°20'N, 114°50'W | Turtle Mountains No. 2 | 730 | 13,900 ± 200 (not given) | (ng) | *Cercocarpus intricatus, Opuntia erinacea, Ribes* cf. *velutinum* | Pimo | (8) |
| *Ord Mountain, San Bernardino County, California* ||||||||
| 34°40'N, 116°50'W | Ord Mountain | 1220 | 11,850 ± 550 (UCR-149) | J | *Ephedra* sp., *Opuntia* sp., *Purshia glandulosa* | Pimo | (1) |
| *Newberry Mountains, Clark County, Nevada* ||||||||
| 35°15'N, 114°37'W | Sacatone Wash | 730 | 19,620 ± 600 (I-3659) | (ng) | *Quercus dunnii* | Pimo | (49) |
| 35°16'N, 114°37'W | Newberry Mountains No. 1 | 850 | 13,380 ± 300 (Gak-1988) | Pimo | *Quercus chrysolepis, Q. dunnii, Purshia glandulosa* | Pimo | (49) |

| | | | | | | |
|---|---|---|---|---|---|---|
| | | | *Peach Springs Wash, Mohave County, Arizona* | | | |
| 35°43'N, 113°23'W | Cave of the Early Morning Light No. 1 | 1300 | 16,580 ± 460 (A-1718) | J | *Artemisia tridentata, Cercocarpus intricatus* | Pied | (6), TR |
| | | | *Scodie Mountains, Kern County, California* | | | |
| 35°36'N, 117°57'W | Robber's Roost No. 1C | 1130 | 13,800 ± 400 (A-1763) | J | *Artemisia tridentata, Ceanothus* sp., *Opuntia basilaris* | Pimo | (2) |
| 35°36'N, 117°57'W | Robber's Roost No. 1D | 1130 | 12,820 ± 400 (A-1762) | J | *Artemisia tridentata, Purshia glandulosa, Quercus turbinella* | Pimo | (2) |
| 35°36'N, 117°57'W | Robber's Roost No. 2A | 1130 | 12,960 ± 270 (A-1761) | J | *Artemisia tridentata, Purshia glandulosa, Yucca brevifolia* | Pimo | (2) |
| | | | *Spring Range, Clark County, Nevada* | | | |
| 36°02'N, 115°23'W | Blue Diamond Road No. 3 | 1050 | 15,040 ± 650 (UCR-725) | J | *Atriplex canescens, Mortonia scabrella* var. *utahensis* | Pimo | TR |
| 36°02'N, 115°23'W | Blue Diamond Road No. 5 | 1110 | 15,800 ± 680 (UCR-726) | J | *Agave utahensis, Artemisia tridentata, Forsellesia nevadensis* | Pimo | TR |
| | | | *Grand Canyon, Mohave County, Arizona* | | | |
| 36°06'N, 113°56'W | Rampart Cave, Unit B | 535 | 14,810 ± 220 (A-1570) | J | *Artiplex confertifolia, Fraxinus anomala, Ribes montigenum* | Pimo | (6) |
| 36°07'N, 113°54'W | Desert Almond No. 10 | 635 | 12,650 ± 380 (A-1720) | J | *Cercocarpus intricatus, Nolina microcarpa, Symphoricarpos* sp. | Pimo and Pied | (6) |
| | | | *Sheep Range, Clark County, Nevada* | | | |
| 36°28'N, 115°15'W | Penthouse No. 2 | 1580 | 11,550 ± 150 (A-1774) | J | *Ceanothus greggii, Forsellesia nevadensis, Symphoricarpos* sp. | Pimo | TR |
| 36°28'N, 115°15'W | Penthouse No. 1 | 1600 | 19,400 ± 300 (A-1772) | J | *Ceanothus greggii, Forsellesia nevadensis, Symphoricarpos* sp. | Pimo | TR |
| 36°28'N, 115°15'W | Willow Wash No. 4A | 1585 | 21,350 ± 440 (WSU-1858) | J | *Artiplex confertifolia, Pinus flexilis, Ribes montigenum* | Pimo | TR |

Table 6.1 continued.

| Latitude and longitude | Site | Elevation (m) | Age | Material dated | Associates | Pinyon species | Reference |
|---|---|---|---|---|---|---|---|
| *Sheep Range, Clark County, Nevada (continued)* ||||||||
| 36°29′N, 115°15′W | South Crest No. 1 (4)$_2$ | 1990 | 21,700 ± 500 (LJ-2840) | Pilo/Pifl | Abies concolor, Cercocarpus intricatus, Philadelphus microphyllus | Pimo | TR |
| 36°29′N, 115°15′W | Flaherty Mesa No. 1 | 1770 | 20,380 ± 340 (WSU-1862) | J | Ephedra viridis, Pinus flexilis, Ribes montigenum | Pimo | TR |
| 36°34′N, 115°18′W | Spires No. 2 | 2040 | 18,800 ± 130 (USGS-198) | Debris | Artemisia tridentata, Cercocarpus intricatus, Jamesia americana | Pimo | TR |
| 36°37′N, 115°17′W | Deadman No. 1 (1) | 1970 | 17,420 ± 250 (LJ-3707) | Pilo/Pifl | Chamaebatiaria millefolium, Fallugia paradoxa, Juniperus osteosperma | Pimo | TR |
| 36°37′N, 115°17′W | Deadman No. 1 (4) | 1970 | 18,680 ± 280 (WSU-1857) | J | Atriplex confertifolia, Pinus flexilis, Pinus longaeva | Pimo | TR |
| 36°37′N, 115°17′W | Deadman No. 1 (2) | 1970 | 16,800 ± 245 (WSU-1860) | J | Jamesia americana, Opuntia polyacantha, Salvia dorrii | Pimo | TR |
| 36°38′N, 115°17′W | Eyrie No. 3 (1) | 1855 | 16,490 ± 220 (WSU-1853) | J | Ephedra viridis, Opuntia polyacantha, Pinus flexilis | Pimo | TR |

The single-needle pinyon record reported from the Whipple Mountains, San Bernardino County, California, is not directly associated with the radiocarbon age of 8910 ± 380 years B.P. *(9)*. A new age of 12,960 ± 210 years B.P. on single-needle pinyon wood is from Redtail Peaks No. 5, a separate midden from the same site.

Xeric, middle-elevation juniper, or juniper–oak woodlands developed synchronously with the disappearance of pinyons in the Southwest. Early Holocene woodlands in the southwestern deserts between 10,000 and 8000 years B.P. have been discussed *(7)*. Similar xeric woodland midden assemblages with radiocarbon ages between 11,000 and 10,000 years B.P. have also been found in all of the warm desert areas in the Southwest *(5, 8, 13)*. The early Holocene xeric woodland period in the Southwest was from 11,000 to 8000 years B.P.

The late Wisconsinan juniper woodlands of Arizona and California below 600 m persisted into the early Holocene with little change. Most xeric woodland species were present in these areas until about 8000 years B.P. *(7)*. Big sagebrush and shadscale appear to have retreated from more southern woodlands by 11,000 years B.P. Blackbrush may have survived until about 10,000 years B.P. and mountain mahogany, Joshua tree, and Whipple yucca until 8000 years B.P. Creosote bush was present in the juniper woodlands. California juniper (*Juniperus californica* Carr.) is a xeric-adapted species that usually occurs below Utah juniper. California juniper may have displaced Utah juniper in the early Holocene woodlands. Unfortunately, the species of the fossil juniper materials are not easily identified, and changes in juniper species have not been well documented.

In the northern Mohave Desert, the late Wisconsinan juniper woodlands below about 1600 m persisted into the Holocene. Several important changes in other taxa occurred during the early Holocene, however. Joshua tree appears to have expanded its range into Death Valley, Inyo County, California, and to the Frenchman Flat area, Clark County, Nevada *(8, 15)*. Creosote bush probably entered the northern part of its present range in Nevada at this time. The oldest radiocarbon age reliably associated with creosote bush in the Sheep Range is 8100 ± 120 years B.P. (Penthouse 1, 1:A-1771, on *Neotoma* fecal pellets). This sample is a midden containing juniper found at an elevation of 1560 m on a southeast-facing slope, 100 m above the local limit of creosote bush, and 400 m below the present lower limit of Utah juniper. As modern pinyon–juniper woodlands displaced the earlier bristlecone–limber pine forests in southern Nevada in the early Holocene, single-needle pinyon also may have expanded into lower areas such as the Spotted Range *(8)*, or even into the Great Basin to the north *(16)*.

Early Holocene creosote bush–white bursage (*Ambrosia dumosa* Payne) communities were well developed below about 300 m. Middens with this assemblage from the Wellton Hills, Yuma County, Arizona, at 175 to 160 m were radiocarbon dated at 10,750 ± 400 to 8150 ± 260 years B.P. *(7)*. A similar assemblage from Picacho Peak, Imperial County, California, at 245 m was dated at 8650 ± 280 years B.P. (A-1876, on *Opuntia basilaris*) *(12)*. Creosote bush–white bursage communities are characteristic of low-elevation areas in the Lower Colorado Valley section of the Sonoran Desert and the Mohave Desert.

Packrat middens at elevations higher than about 1800 m document a transition from late Wisconsinan forests to essentially modern communities in the early Holocene. In the Guadalupe Mountains of Texas, a Douglas fir–southwestern white pine forest at 2000 m was replaced by a juniper grassland community after 11,500 years B.P. *(3)*. The disappearance of spruce and dwarf juniper from this site between 13,000 and 11,500 years B.P. probably records an earlier climatic event. Macrofossils of two species of sedge (*Carex* sp.) and horsetail (*Equisetum* sp.), and pollen of spruce, Douglas fir, and birch (probably *Betula fontinalis* Sarg., water birch) suggest that relatively mesic conditions may have persisted in the dry canyon at Cowboy Cave, Utah, until 8700 years B.P. *(13)*.

In the Sheep Range of Nevada, mesic juniper communities from 1585 to 1860 m were replaced by xeric juniper woodland before 9500 years B.P. The juniper woodlands were in turn replaced by mixed scrub and blackbrush desertscrub by 7500 years B.P. Late Wisconsinan bristlecone–limber pine forests from 1900 to 2100 m disappeared before 9500 years B.P. and were replaced by the pinyon–juniper woodland that still exists at these sites. In a mesic canyon at 2400 m, a midden with an age of 10,600 ± 130 years B.P. (LJ-3729, on bristlecone and limber pine needles) contains bristlecone, limber, ponderosa (*Pinus ponderosa* Laws.), and pinyon pine, Rocky Mountain juniper (*Juniperus scopulorum* Sarg.), and white fir. Ponderosa pine, Rocky Mountain juniper, and white fir are dominant species in the present community. Older late Wisconsinan middens from the same site contain bristlecone and limber pines and dwarf juniper, but lack ponderosa pine, Rocky Mountain juniper, and white fir *(11)*.

## Middle and late Holocene (8000 years B.P. to present)

The youngest records of displaced woodland plants in present deserts are about 8000 years old in the Chihuahuan Desert in Texas, the Sonoran Desert in Arizona and California, and the Mohave Desert in Arizona, California, and Nevada *(7, 8)*. The end of the early Holocene woodlands in these now warm deserts appears to have been a rapid, widespread, synchronous event about 8000 years B.P. Packrat middens indicative of modern desert vegetation younger than 8000 years B.P. are common, but few have been dated by carbon-14 analysis. The oldest creosote bush middens are dated at 5800 ± 250 years B.P. (UCR-135, on *Larrea divaricata*) and 5880 ± 250 years B.P. (URC-134, on miscellaneous twigs) from the Lucerne Valley *(1)*, and 7400 ± 150 years B.P. (UCLA-560, on uriniferous material) from Newberry Cave *(8)*, both from San Bernardino County, California. Similar early Holocene creosote bush middens were mentioned earlier. King's *(1)* Lucerne Valley study documented a continuation of the creosote bush community into the late Holocene.

At the beginning of the middle Holocene, woodland species migrated northward, retreated to higher elevations in the mountains, and disappeared in the lowlands. Desert-adapted species increased in abundance and dispersed into new areas. Creosote bush–white bursage communities expanded greatly into the lowlands of the Sonoran and Mohave deserts. Joshua tree was restricted to higher elevations to the north on the edges of the Mohave Desert. It was associated more often with creosote bush and blackbrush than with pinyon and juniper *(15)*. As rocky slopes became more xeric, catclaw (*Acacia greggii* Gray) became a riparian species in the washes of the Sonoran and Mohave deserts. Important dominant species, such as foothills palo verde, saguaro, and ironwood (*Olneya tesota* Gray), apparently moved into the United States from the Mexican lowlands around the head of the Gulf of California. Ocotillo (*Fouquieria splendens* Engelm.) is a widespread, distinctive, southwestern species that has not been found in any late Wisconsinan or early Holocene middens despite its frequent occurrence at fairly high (up to 1350 m) elevations today. It may have invaded most of the Southwest during the middle Holocene. Later fluctuations in the structure and composition of the plant communities in the Sonoran and Mohave deserts were of small magnitude and were relatively minor events within the present vegetational regime.

In the Chihuahuan Desert in New Mexico and Texas, a middle Holocene grassland community probably preceded the formation of the present, diverse, succulent desertscrub communities at elevations of 1200 to 2000 m. Important perennials in the latter communities, such as creosote bush, lechuguilla (*Agave lecheguilla* Torr.), mariola (*Parthenium incanum* H.B.K.), Big Bend silver leaf (*Leucophyllum minus* Gray), white thorn (*Acacia neovernicosa* Isely), and many others may have been present in small edaphic microhabitats in middle Holocene grasslands. The establishment of desertscrub communities in the northern Chihuahuan Desert is probably the last major vegetational change in the Southwest (excluding historic changes). Midden samples from an elevation of 1430 m from Picture Cave, Hueco Mountains, El Paso County, Texas, record modern desertscrub communities at 1530 ± 120 and 1700 ± 100 years B.P. (A-1706 and A-1726, on *Opuntia phaeacantha*-type) *(17)*. A series of seven middens from 1130 to 1310 m from Rocky Arroyo and Last Chance Canyon, Eddy County, New Mexico, document modern desertscrub communities between 4000 years B.P. and the present *(18)*.

## LATE WISCONSINAN CLIMATE

Evidence from deep sea cores, the Greenland ice sheet, and pollen-stratigraphic sites document the cyclic nature of Quaternary climates. The durations of glacial periods have been on the order of 100,000 years and interglacial periods only on the order of 10,000 to 20,000 years *(19, 20)*. Therefore, the woodlands and forests recorded by packrat midden materials at low elevations in the Southwest probably represent typical environments throughout much of the Quaternary. The present Holocene deserts do not represent general conditions during this period.

The nature of the late Wisconsinan climate in the Southwest is controversial and deserves discussion. The term "pluvial climate" is used in the Southwest, where continental glaciation did not occur. The most noticeable effect of "glacial climates" beside vegetation changes was the filling of now dry playa lakes when the continental ice sheets were well developed *(21)*. The term "pluvial" climates carries a connotation of wetter climate due to an actual increase in precipitation. However, in most geological and biological systems it is difficult to separate the effects of precipitation and temperature. Inferences of the late Wisconsinan climate in the Southwest have ranged from a model of lower winter temperature or annual temperatures *(22, 23)* to a model of mild winters and cool summers *(24)*, and from a model of decreased precipitation with maintenance of the present seasonal distribution of precipitation *(25)* to a model of greatly increased winter precipitation *(7, 25)*. Many of these models have been generated to satisfy pluvial lake water budgets or have been based on the distributions of solifluction deposits that are assumed to imply lowered snowlines in the past.

The species and composition of fossil assemblages from packrat middens provide insight into paleoclimates. The number of species living in comparable habitats decreases with increasing latitude or elevation. This is commonly attributed to the limiting effects of lower winter temperatures and shorter growing seasons with increasing altitude and latitude. Colder and longer winters during the late Wisconsinan may be expected to have resulted in less diverse woodland and forest assemblages and a lack of desert species in the packrat middens. Instead, most fossil assemblages are equally or more diverse than their modern counterparts. In most instances they are mixtures of woodland and warm desert species. Middens in the Sonoran and Mohave deserts do contain important Great

Basin species such as big sagebrush and shadscale, but simple cold steppe or steppe desert assemblages have not been found south of 36°N.

Galloway (22) provided a strong case for acceptance of the cold-dry model of late Wisconsinan climate in the Southwest. He postulated a 1300- to 1400-m lowering of timberline due to a temperature decrease of 10° to 11°C for all seasons and a 10 to 20 percent reduction in precipitation. His thesis was based on cursory observations of undated solifluction deposits in New Mexico (22). More recently, after a literature review of similar deposits, Brakenridge (23) inferred a 1000-m snowline depression, 7° to 8°C cooling in all seasons, and a precipitation somewhat less than today. If an environmental lapse rate of 6°C per 1000 m is applied to the data used by Galloway and Brakenridge, the implied magnitudes of lowering of vegetational zones are 1750 m and 1250 m, respectively. Cooling of lesser magnitude would not be enough to fill the playa lakes without increased precipitation.

Plant macrofossils in middens and cave fills in the Guadalupe Mountains of Texas, 175 km south of Galloway's Sacramento Mountains study area, provide a test of these inferences. Macrofossil assemblages at an elevation of 2000 m contained species of subalpine (spruce and dwarf juniper), montane (Douglas fir and southwestern white pine), and woodland (Colorado pinyon and juniper) affinities about 13,000 years B.P. (3). The association of subalpine plants with more xerophytic species suggests that this site was near the lower limit of the spruce forest. The lower limit of modern conifer forest with spruce is about 2430 m of elevation, 110 km to the northwest in the massive Sacramento Mountains. Spruce and dwarf juniper no longer occur in the Guadalupe Mountains and a modern analog with a physiographic setting comparable to the paleocommunity is not available. Earlier full-glacial communities at this site were probably a little more mesic.

A midden from William's Cave at 1500 m in the Guadalupe Mountains records a pinyon–juniper woodland at 12,040 ± 210 years B.P. Middens from other Trans-Pecos Texas sites, including Maravillas Canyon, Brewster County (4) (Table 1), Bennett Ranch, Presidio County, and the Hueco Mountains, El Paso County, record few changes in local pinyon–juniper woodland communities from elevations of 600 to 1350 m between 16,000 to 18,000 years B.P. and 11,000 years B.P. Late Wisconsinan pinyon–juniper middens from other Trans-Pecos sites document similar woodlands throughout this period. The full-glacial vegetation at William's Cave was probably little if any more mesic than the 12,000 years B.P. pinyon–juniper woodland. Even the most modest inference of 1000-m vegetational lowering in the Galloway–Brakenridge models would predict a mixed conifer forest with Douglas fir, southwestern white pine, ponderosa pine, or even spruce at William's Cave. If the timberline was depressed 1000 m then the subalpine forest was greatly compressed, and inferred paleotemperatures of Galloway and Brakenridge only relate to elevations above 2000 m and not to the Southwest in general.

Many of the fossils in packrat middens contain species that are indicators of winter temperatures. Beaked yucca (*Yucca rostrata* Engelm.) and crucifixion thorn (*Castela stewartii* C.H. Mull.) are now restricted to Chihuahuan desertscrub communities in the Big Bend region in Texas and south into Mexico. They were in a pinyon–juniper woodland at 1310 m in the Livingston Hills, Presidio County, Texas, well north of their present range at 15,695 ± 230 years B.P. *(26)*. A related crucifixion thorn (*C. emoryi* Gray) was in a juniper–Joshua tree community at 550 m at 11,450 ± 400 years B.P. (A-1328 on *Yucca brevifolia* Engelm.) on Brass Cap Point, Kofa Mountains, Yuma County, Arizona; now it is restricted to low-elevation desertscrub communities *(27)*. In the Sheep Range of Nevada, shadscale is now restricted to desert communities below 1600 m. It was present at elevations up to 2150 m in mixed conifer and bristlecone–limber pine communities from more than 48,000 to at least 15,000 years B.P. *(11)*. Big sagebrush grew as far south as Montezuma's Head, in the Ajo Mountains of southwestern Arizona *(7)*, and Shelter Cave, in south-central New Mexico, in the late Wisconsinan. In southern Nevada big sagebrush is now dominant in areas with cooler summers and more winter precipitation than in areas with blackbrush or creosote bush *(28)*. All of these associations suggest that late Wisconsinan winters were mild.

The faunal record does not support an interpretation that late Wisconsinan winter temperatures were cooler than present winter temperatures. Late Wisconsinan faunal assemblages from many sites in the central and eastern United States contain mixtures of northern and southern forms that suggest equable climates with mild winters and cool summers *(24)*. Late Pleistocene cave faunas from the Southwest are mixtures of forest, woodland, and grassland animals. Southwestern packrat middens of late Pleistocene and early Holocene age contain remains of animals now restricted to desertscrub habitats in woodland assemblages *(29)*. The desert tortoise (*Gopherus agassizi* Cooper) is now restricted to desertscrub habitats west of the Continental Divide in the Sonoran and Mohave deserts. During the late Wisconsinan it inhabited pinyon–juniper woodlands in the northern Chihuahuan Desert in New Mexico and Texas.

The coldest winter temperatures in the midcontinent and the Great Basin occur when Arctic or polar continental air masses move to the south. "Northers" or "nortes" bring cold air and freezing temperatures south of the Tropic of Cancer in Mexico including all areas in the Chihuahuan Desert. Bryson and Wendland *(30)* suggested that 3500-m-high continental ice sheets prevented cold Arctic air from entering the midcontinent. Moreover, the air above the ice sheets was warmed adiabatically as it descended and they postulated that between 13,000 and 10,000 years B.P. winter temperatures were relatively mild. Elimination of northers would result in warmer winter temperatures in a huge area as far south as Mexico City.

Moisture deficits appear to control the present lower elevational and southern geographical limits of many southwestern plants. Upper elevational and northern limits may be governed by temperature or competition with other species (31). Cooler global climates and the inference of mild winters during the late Wisconsinan suggest that summer temperatures in the Southwest were much cooler than today, resulting in reduced evaporation, water retention in playa lakes, and reduced water stress for plants at the lower limits of their ranges. However, lowered summer temperatures alone are not sufficient to explain most of the fossil plant records. Without greatly lowered annual temperatures, the high water levels in the playa lakes suggest a real increase in precipitation (21, 32). The San Bartolo Playa in the Sonoran Desert, 30 km north of Bahia Kino, Sonora, Mexico, is at 29°N and just slightly above sea level (33). San Bartolo Playa was a large freshwater lake in the late Wisconsinan when the sea level was lowered. The present annual precipitation is about 130 mm. Temperatures and potential evaporation are high. Moisture was surely imported to San Bartolo in the late Wisconsinan to fill the playa unless a cooling of unreasonable magnitude is postulated.

Middens in Arizona, California, and Nevada record a dramatic expansion of woodland, chaparral, and cold desert plants during the late Wisconsinan. Many of the species in the middens now occur in areas to the north or west with greater percentages and absolute amounts of winter rainfall than the midden sites (8). Late Wisconsinan records of woodland species now associated with high summer rainfall are meager. Most annual plants in packrat middens from the western Sonoran and Mohave deserts are species that respond to winter rainfall. The few annuals in the middens that now respond to summer precipitation also germinate, grow, and reproduce in response to fall precipitation and warm temperatures. Increased winter precipitation and reduced summer temperatures can account for most of the observed late Wisconsinan plant distributions in the Southwest. The apparent stability of late Wisconsinan pinyon–juniper woodlands for 11,000 years suggests that the vegetation was not very sensitive to global temperature fluctuations, but was recording a general climate dominated by moisture.

The presence of the Cordilleran ice sheet, lowered eustatic sea level, colder sea-surface temperatures, and possible cold air drainage from the frozen Arctic Ocean across the Bering Strait, all probably contributed to intensification of the Aleutian Low at lower latitudes than today. This may have resulted in increased frontal storms south of the crest of the Sierra

Nevada (36°N) and as far east as Trans-Pecos Texas. Pacific frontal storms usually lose much of their moisture by the time they reach the Chihuahuan Desert, but often cause precipitation as they meet moist air masses from the Gulf of Mexico. Late Wisconsinan winter frontal storms may have begun earlier in the fall than today and lasted later in the spring. Colder sea surface temperatures probably moved the late summer–early fall hurricanes farther south and eliminated this source of precipitation from the Southwest.

Today the Southwest is divided into regions with predominantly winter precipitation in the west and predominantly summer precipitation in the east. We infer a more uniform winter precipitation dominance in both areas in the late Wisconsinan. The xeric juniper woodlands at middle elevations and the bristlecone–limber pine forests at higher elevations in the northern Mohave Desert suggest that southern Nevada was relatively drier than areas south of 36°N *(3, 7, 8, 11, 13, 14)*. This apparent anomaly may be attributed to the Sierra Nevada rainshadow.

## EARLY HOLOCENE CLIMATE

The documented persistence of woodland until about 8000 years B.P. in the middle-elevation deserts of the Southwest appears to contradict earlier chronologies based on fossil pollen. Essentially modern climate and vegetation after 12,000 to 11,000 years ago have been inferred on the basis of pollen studies *(7, 34)*. The pollen record from Osgood Swamp, in the Sierra Nevada of California, indicates that a shift to modern pine forest began about 11,000 years B.P. and was completed by 10,000 years B.P. *(35)*. Fossil pollen from Tule Springs, Clark County, Nevada, records a major vegetational change about 12,000 years B.P. However, spectra characteristic of the present Mohave Desert communities did not appear until about 7500 years B.P. *(34)*. The pollen record from Lehner Ranch Arroyo, Cochise County, Arizona, indicates that a major vegetational change marking the beginning of the Holocene occurred 11,200 years B.P. *(36)*. Changes in montane conifer distributions appear to be well reflected in lowland sedimentary pollen records. Midden records can provide a calibration of the pollen records and help separate local pollen from that transported from the nearest mountains.

The midden record confirms the loss of pinyon and other mesic species as well as big sagebrush and shadscale from middle-elevation woodlands by 11,000 years B.P. At higher elevations the transition from late Wisconsinan subalpine communities to woodland and montane communities approaching modern composition also occurred at this time. Thus, the midden record and the pollen stratigraphic records are complementary and not in opposition. For the packrat midden record and stratigraphic pollen record in the Southwest, we suggest that a climatically defined Pleistocene–Holocene boundary be placed at 11,000 years ago, a time of consistent, widespread, contemporaneous vegetational change throughout the Southwest. Environmental changes at about 11,000 years B.P. are also reflected by the upper boundaries of sedimentary deposits at Tule Springs, Nevada *(34,)* the Lehner Ranch Arroyo, Arizona *(36)*, Blackwater Draw, New Mexico *(37)*, and the Lubbock Lake Site, Texas *(38)*. The youngest records of extinct large mammals are in the same units at these sites.

The climate of the early Holocene appears to have been characterized by a continuation of the late Wisconsinan winter precipitation regime. Its persistence for 3000 years into the Holocene implies that "glacial" and "pluvial" climates were not synchronous and the "pluvial" climates are the result of "glacial" climates. As the Cordilleran ice sheet dissipated, the Aleutian Low and the winter storm track assumed their present position. The persistence of the Laurentide ice sheet probably delayed development of the Bermuda High and summer monsoonal rain west of the Continental Divide. Early Holocene middens from the Sonoran Desert lack many characteristic Sonoran Desert species and suggest that summer rains had not begun.

If the late Wisconsinan winters were mild and were caused by the blocking effect of the Cordilleran and Laurentide ice sheets, colder winters may have begun after about 11,500 years B.P. *(30)* as the ice-free corridor opened between the two ice sheets in western Alberta *(39)*. The same corridor that allowed Paleoindians to enter the mid-continent would have allowed northers south of the Laurentide ice sheets in the winter. Lower winter temperatures probably caused range changes in many plants and animals by 11,000 years B.P. *(24)*. Early Holocene northers have been suggested as a causal factor in the extinction of some late Pleistocene megafauna. However, we consider this unlikely because: (i) megafaunal extinctions occurred in many different climatic regimes throughout the Western Hemisphere; (ii) the magnitude of the difference between the climate of the late Wisconsinan and that of today in the Southwest was small compared to the ecological amplitudes of most large herbivores *(40)*; and (iii) similar climatic events at the end of earlier glacial stages were not marked by similar extinctions.

## MIDDLE AND LATE HOLOCENE CLIMATES

The present climatic and vegetational regimes were established after about 8000 years B.P. Winter precipitation was reduced in or withdrawn from much of the Southwest. The summer monsoon expanded, resulting in the present geographic difference in seasonality of rainfall and the related segregation of the biota. The middle Holocene warm period has been termed the Altithermal, the Xerothermic, and the Hypsithermal *(41, 42)*. The term Altithermal connotes a dry climate as well as a warm period. It has been uncritically extended from the Great Basin, characterized by winter rainfall, to areas in the Southwest that have predominantly summer precipitation. Atmospheric circulation patterns that would result in dry conditions in the Great Basin are unlikely to cause summer droughts in the Chihuahuan Desert. The term Altithermal should be discarded or should be restricted to the northern Mohave Desert and Great Basin, where a warm and dry middle Holocene climate is documented *(11, 16, 43)*. Summer rainfall in areas now characterized by summer monsoons probably was greater than at present because warmer global temperatures favor the development of the Bermuda High *(28, 44)*. The present northern Chihuahuan Desert is relatively high in elevation and the present climate is marginal for desert-grassland or succulent desertscrub communities. Middle Holocene wet climates probably favored development of grassland. Widespread loss of well-developed, mature soils on bedrock during the middle and late Holocene probably augmented the development of xeric microhabitats and desert vegetation *(45)*. The establishment of northern Chihuahuan desertscrub communities in the late Holocene is the most recent major vegetational change in the Southwest induced by climate.

## VEGETATIONAL DYNAMICS

The ecological impact of Quaternary climatic changes in the Southwest traditionally has been expressed in terms of the elevational displacement of vegetation zones, with modern analogs being used to interpret fossil pollen spectra and macrofossil assemblages *(4, 8, 46)*. Estimates of lowering of vegetation zones range from about 350 to 1000 m, with larger estimates at higher elevations and latitudes *(7)*. However, simple vertical displacements are unrealistic because plant species responded differentially to climatic changes and not as community units. Modern analog communities with compositions similar to the fossil assemblages in middens are often difficult to find. Warm desert species such as catclaw, barrel cacti (*Echinocactus polycephalus* Engelm. & Bigel., *Ferocactus acanthodes* Brit. & Rose), and brittlebush (*Encelia farinosa* Gray, *E. frutescens* Gray) were common associates of late Wisconsinan woodland dominants in the Mohave and Sonoran deserts. Other xerophytes such as creosote bush and white bursage that now are common associates of the above desert species were uncommon or absent from these woodland assemblages. In southern Nevada and the Grand Canyon in Arizona, pinyon–juniper woodland now occurs below forest in the vegetational gradient. In the late Wisconsinan, juniper expanded much more than pinyon, and a pinyon–juniper zone may not have been present at all. In the Chihuahuan Desert, juniper woodlands and juniper grasslands are important communities on the upper peripheries of the desert. In the late Wisconsinan, pinyon–juniper woodlands were present at all elevations between 1500 m and the Rio Grande at 600 m, and xeric juniper communities have not been found.

In Davis' *(19)* recent summaries of the late Quaternary history of the eastern deciduous forest, she concluded that the plant communities have not yet reached equilibrium in response to postglacial climates. Lag times of differing durations have been observed for the establishment of several important tree species. Migration rates were differentially affected by successional processes such as dispersal capability, soil development, and biotic competition. In contrast, we conclude that new communities with relatively stable composition were established soon after climatic changes occurred in the Southwest. The most important difference between the Southwest and the Appalachian, New England, and mid-continent areas discussed by Davis is the low precipitation in the Southwest.

The vegetation zones in the Southwest are arranged vertically in an altitudinal moisture gradient, with drier desert communities below woodlands and with forests on the mountain tops. Mountains modify the local climate through orographically induced precipitation and adiabatically cooled temperatures. Mountains serve as both source areas and refugia for mesophytic plants in fluctuating environments. Most woodland species found in late Wisconsinan or early Holocene packrat middens in present desert areas are now living on mountains within 100 to 200 km of the site (Fig. 6.2). The forests of the Southwest are often restricted to montane islands of small areal extent and are potentially vulnerable to local extinctions. Dispersal of forest species can be expected to have occurred in the past when vegetation zones were lowered sufficiently for intermountain connections or when larger target areas increased the chances of long-distance dispersal. Brown's *(47)* work on the montane mammals of isolated mountains in the Great Basin suggests that dispersals of boreal species occurred in the late Wisconsinan and extinctions in the Holocene.

Changes in composition of montane plant communities during the Holocene were relatively minor because these communities adjusted quickly to climatic changes. Desert species persisted at low elevations in the southern Mohave Desert and around the Gulf of California, and at higher elevations in woodlands in the late Wisconsinan and early Holocene. Changes in abundance and dispersals of desert species, in some cases over fairly long distances, appear to have been rapid. We suggest that the rapid responses to climatic changes exhibited by desert and woodland species are related to an observation that their present distribution is highly dependent on precipitation. The present distributions of forest species apparently reflect differences in regional temperature regimes, as well as precipitation. Competition exists in all of these communities, but competitive advantages are strongly related to local climatic regimes. The biota of the Southwest is far more stressed by the current climatic regimes than it was by the "rigors" of the late Wisconsinan climate.

## REFERENCES AND NOTES

1. T. J. King, Jr., *Great Basin Nat.* 36, 227 (1976).
2. N. F. McCarten, unpublished data. Three macrofossil assemblages ranging in age from about 13,800 to 12,800 years B.P. record a pinyon–juniper woodland in present creosote bush desert at 1125 m of elevation.
3. T. R. Van Devender, P. S. Martin, A. M. Phillips III, W. G. Spaulding, in *Transactions: Symposium on the Biological Resources of the Chihuahuan Desert, United States and Mexico*, R. H. Wauer and D. H. Riskind, Eds. (National Park Service, Washington, D.C., 1977), pp. 107–113; T. R. Van Devender, W. G. Spaulding, A. M. Phillips III, in *Biological Investigations in the Guadalupe Mountains National Park*, H. H. Genoways and R. J. Baker, Eds. (National Park Service, Washington, D.C., in press).
4. P. V. Wells, *Science* 153, 970 (1966); in *Transactions Symposium on the Biological Resources of the Chihuahuan Desert, United States and Mexico*, R. H. Wauer and D. H. Riskind, Eds. (National Park Service, Washington, D.C., 1977), pp. 67–83.
5. T. R. Van Devender and B. L. Everitt, *Southwest. Nat.* 22, 337 (1977). Additional midden samples from Shelter Cave, Bishop's Cap, Doña Ana County, New Mexico, are dated at >26,000 years B.P. (SC No. 2A, A-1753, on *Juniperus* sp.) and at >28,000 years B.P. (SC No. 2B, A-1759, on *Juniperus* sp.).
6. T. R. Van Devender and J. I. Mead, *J. Ariz. Acad. Sci.* 12, 3 (1976); A. M. Phillips III, thesis, University of Arizona, Tucson (1977).
7. T. R. Van Devender, *Science* 198, 189 (1977).
8. P. V. Wells and R. Berger, *ibid.* 155, 1640 (1967).
9. J. E. King and T. R. Van Devender, *Quat. Res. (N.Y.)* 8, 191 (1977).
10. P.V. Wells, *ibid.* 6, 223 (1976).
11. W. G. Spaulding, *J. Ariz. Acad. Sci.* 12, 3 (1977). Research in the Sheep Range of southern Nevada produced an additional 60 radiocarbon-dated midden assemblages from 1500 to 2400 m.
12. T. R. Van Devender and K. L. Cole, unpublished observation. Fourteen late Wisconsinan and early Holocene woodland middens from the Whipple Mountains, San Bernardino County, California, range from 13,900 to 8910 years B.P. and are from elevations of 520 to 320 m.
13. W. G. Spaulding and T. R. Van Devender, *Southwest. Nat.* 22, 260 (1977); W. G. Spaulding and K. L. Petersen, in *Cowboy Cave*, J. D. Jennings, Ed. (Univ. of Utah Anthropological Papers, Salt Lake City, in press).
14. P. J. Mehringer, Jr., and C. W. Ferguson, *J. Ariz. Acad. Sci.* 5, 284 (1969).
15. P. G. Rowlands, T. R. Van Devender, W. G. Spaulding, unpublished data.
16. P. J. Mehringer, Jr., in *Models and Great Basin Prehistory: A Symposium*, D. D.

Fowler, Ed. (Univ. of Nevada, Desert Research Institute Publications in Social Sciences No. 12, Reno, 1977), p. 134.

17. T. R. Van Devender and D. H. Riskind, *Southwest. Nat.*, in press.

18. T. R. Van Devender, D. H. Wiseman, J. G. Gallagher, unpublished data.

19. M. B. Davis, *Am. Quat. Assoc. Abstr.* (No. 13) (1974); *Geosci. Man* 13, 13 (1976).

20. C. Emiliani, *Quat. Res. (N.Y.)* 2, 270 (1972); G. J. Kukla, R. K. Matthews, J. M. Mitchell, Jr., *ibid.*, p. 261; H. E. Wright, Jr., *ibid.*, p. 274.

21. R. B. Morrison, in *The Quaternary of the United States*, H. E. Wright, Jr., and D. G. Frey, Eds. (Princeton Univ. Press, Princeton, N.J., 1965), pp. 265–268; G. I. Smith, in *Means of Correlation of Quaternary Successions*, R. B. Morrison and H. E. Wright, Jr., Eds. (Univ. of Utah Press, Salt Lake City, 1968), pp. 293–310; L. B. Leopold, *Am. J. Sci.* 249, 152 (1951); E. Antevs, *Am. Antiq.* 20, 317 (1955).

22. R. W. Galloway, *Ann. Assoc. Am. Geogr.* 60, 245 (1970).

23. G. R. Brakenridge, *Quat. Res. (N.Y.)* 9, 22 (1978).

24. A. H. Harris, *Tex. J. Sci.* 22, 3 (1970); in *Transactions: Symposium on Biological Resources of the Chihuahuan Desert Region, United States and Mexico*, R. H. Wauer and D. H. Riskind, Eds. (National Park Service, Washington, D.C., 1977), pp. 23–52.

25. D. L. Johnson, *Quat. Res. (N.Y.)* 8, 154 (1977).

26. T. R. Van Devender, C. E. Freeman, R. D. Worthington, *Southwest. Nat.* 23, 289 (1978).

27. T. R. Van Devender, thesis, Univ. of Arizona, Tucson (1973).

28. J. C. Beatley, *Am. Midl. Nat.* 93, 53 (1975).

29. T. R. Van Devender, K. B. Moodie, A. H. Harris, *Herpetologica* 32, 298 (1976); T. R. Van Devender, A. M. Phillips III, J. I. Mead, *Southwest. Nat.* 22, 49 (1977); K. B. Moodie and T. R. Van Devender, *Herpetologica*, in press.

30. R. A. Bryson and W. M. Wendland, in *Life, Land and Water*, W. J. Mayer-Oakes, Ed. (Univ. of Manitoba Press, Winnipeg, 1967), pp. 271–298.

31. F. Shreve, *Ecology* 5, 128 (1924).

32. C. T. Snyder and W. B. Langbein, *J. Geophys. Res.* 67, 2385 (1962).

33. J. Lecolle, M. Lancin, A. C. del Rio, *Univ. of Nac. Auton. Mex. Inst. Geol. Rev.* 1, 204 (1977); N. Petit-Maire and L. Casta, in *Recherches Francaises sur le Quaternaire* (International Quaternary Association, Brussels, 1977), pp. 303–322.

34. P. S. Martin and P. J. Mehringer, Jr., in *The Quaternary of the United States*, H. E. Wright, Jr., and D. G. Frey, Eds. (Princeton Univ. Press, Princeton, N.J., 1965), pp. 433–451; P. J. Mehringer, Jr., in *Pleistocene Studies in Southern Nevada*, H. M. Wormington and D. Ellis, Eds. (Nevada State Museum, Anthropological Papers No. 13, Reno, 1967), pp. 129–200.

35. D. P. Adam, in *Quaternary Paleoecology*, E. H. Cushing and H. E. Wright, Jr., Eds. (Yale Univ. Press, New Haven, Conn., 1967), pp. 275–301.

36. P. J. Mehringer, Jr. and C. V. Haynes, *Am. Antiq.* 31, 17 (1965).

37. C. V. Haynes, in *Late Pleistocene Environments of the Southern High Plains*, F. Wendorf and J. J. Hester, Eds. (Publications of the Fort Burgwin Research Center, No. 9, Taos, N.M., 1975), pp. 57–96.

38. V. T. Holliday, H. Haas, R. Stuckenrath, in *Lubbock Lake: Late Quaternary Studies on the Southern High Plains*, E. Johnson, Ed. (Academic Press, New York, in press); T. W. Stafford, *Am. Antiq.*, in press.

39. P. S. Martin, *Science* 179, 969 (1973); see abstracts by L. E. Jackson, Jr., W. H. Mathews, N. W. Rutter, A. Mac Stalker, *Am. Quat. Assoc. Abstr.*, 5th meeting (1978), pp. 1–22.

40. W. G. Spaulding and P. S. Martin, in *Biological Investigations in the Guadalupe Mountains National Park*, H. H. Genoways and R. J. Baker, Eds. (National Park Service,

Washington, D.C., in press). The Shasta ground sloth (*Nothrotheriops shastense* Hofstetter) ranged from Joshua tree–juniper communities of Gypsum Cave, Nevada, at 600 m, to mixed-conifer forests with Douglas fir near the High Caves in the Guadalupe Mountains of Texas, at 2000 m. Other large herbivores in the late Pleistocene of the Southwest probably had similar wide ranges.

41. E. Antevs, *Univ. Utah Bull.* 38, 168 (1948).
42. P. B. Sears, *Bot. Rev.* 8, 708 (1942); E. S. Deevey and R. F. Flint, *Science* 125, 182 (1957).
43. V. C. LaMarche, Jr., *Quat. Res. (N.Y.)* 3, 632 (1973).
44. T. R. Van Devender and F. M. Wiseman, in *Paleoindian Lifeways*, E. Johnson, Ed. (West Texas Museum Association, Lubbock, 1977), pp. 13–27.
45. C. H. Muller, *Ecology* 21, 206 (1940).
46. P. S. Martin, *ibid.* 44, 436 (1963); P. J. Mehringer, Jr., *J. Ariz. Acad. Sci.* 3, 172 (1965); H. E. Wright, Jr., A. M. Bent, B. S. Hansen, L. J. Maher, Jr., *Geol. Soc. Am. Bull.* 84, 115 (1973).
47. J. H. Brown, in "Intermountain biogeography: A symposium," K. T. Harper and J. L. Reveal, Eds., *Gt. Basin Nat. Mem. No. 2* (Brigham Young Univ., Salt Lake City, 1978), pp. 209–228.
48. R. M. Lanner and T. R. Van Devender, *Forest Sci.* 20, 207 (1974).
49. P. H. Leskinen, *Madroño* 23, 234 (1975).
50. E. L. Little, Jr., "Atlas of United States trees," *U.S. Dep. Agric. Vol. I Misc. Publ. No. 1146* (1971).
51. R. M. Lanner, *Silvae Genet.* 23, 108 (1974).
52. This research was accomplished with the aid of NSF grants DEB 76-19784 to T.R.V.D., DEB 75-13944 to P.S. Martin, and DEB 77-20802 to W.G.S. A. Long, J. Sheppard, S. Robinson, and W. Ferguson provided radiocarbon ages. P. Mehringer supplied samples for study. V. Markgraf and P. S. Martin, University of Arizona, and D. Fullerton, U.S. Geological Survey, reviewed this manuscript. J. Lekawa, S. Spaulding, and D. Gaines typed the manuscript.

# Part II

**1981 Symposium**

# PREFACE

Donald R. Haragan

Texas Tech University
Lubbock, Texas

There is abundant evidence that reflects the human tendency to exploit the natural environment. This exploitation tends to be most severe in marginal areas such as the transition zone between two climatic regions. Additional stress placed upon these areas as a result of agricultural production and grazing can be devastating.

Desert climates are more variable than those of any other ecosystem, particularly at the interface with the fragile transition zone at the desert boundary. The recent five-year drought (1969–73) in the African Sahel focused attention on this border area adjacent to the Sahara where apparent expansion of the desert was taking place. Were the changes which occurred in surface vegetation and subsequent erosion of top soil a reflection of long-term climatic change or a result of increased stress imposed by agricultural production and grazing at a time when the natural environment was least able to withstand it? Certainly the answer is a complicated one which must consider both direct effects as well as the feedback processes that are initiated as a result.

Climatic change refers to a change in long-term mean values or the variability about the mean. It is a quasi-permanent change that is irreversible over a significantly long time period. Periodic drought, on the other hand, is an isolated event which represents an infrequent but expected (in a probabilistic sense) occurrence. Whereas extended drought could reflect the onset of a major and permanent change in climate, it is more likely a temporary occurrence indicative of the natural variability of precipitation and thus, atmospheric circulation.

The African Sahel is an example of a regime subject to recurrent drought. Its annual precipitation results from rains associated with the summer monsoon. When the monsoon is weak, the result is a dry year. It is during these drought years that the human contribution to desert encroachment can become dominant as the environment attempts to withstand the increased stress imposed by man and his activities.

In March 1981, the committee on Desert and Arid Zone Research (CODAZR) of the Southwestern and Rocky Mountain Section of the American Association for the Advancement of Science sponsored a symposium on deserts and desertification. Two major papers were presented by Farouk El-Baz and Derek Winstanley. These are reprinted in this volume along with an invited essay by Michael M. Verstraete, who focuses on the ambiguity that continues to cloud the meaning of desertification and its interpretation by various investigators.

# Deserts and Desertification: Geological and Climatological Perspectives

# 7

# A GEOLOGICAL PERSPECTIVE OF THE DESERT

Farouk El-Baz

ITEC Optical Systems
Lexington, Massachusetts

## INTRODUCTION

The terms desertification and desertization have been used either interchangeably or to signify man-made and natural processes, respectively. Their use has helped support the incorrect belief that the desert is manmade. However, geological and archaeological evidence indicate that the desert is a natural environment caused by the scarcity or total lack of rain. The Sahara, largest of the terrestrial deserts, has evolved through alternation of wet and dry climatic periods from 200,000 B.P. until the last drought set in 5,000 years ago. It is important to understand the effects of previous climates and today's weather conditions on the desert environment. It is also important to understand the physical medium of desert formation and expansion to comprehend what occurs at the desert fringe. Space photographs allow the study of regional characteristics of desert areas and the comparisons between the deserts of Earth and Mars.

The term *desertification* is defined as "the impoverishment of arid, and semi-arid and some subhumid ecosystems by the impact of man's activities. It is . . . the result of land abuse" (UNEP, 1977, p. 1). This definition is the most commonly used to define the term. However, Le Houérou (1977, p. 17) states that "The word *desertization* is preferred to the term *desertification* for several reasons. Desertization has been defined (Le Houérou, 1962, 1968) as the extension of typical desert landscapes and landforms to areas where they did not occur in the recent past. This process takes place in arid zones bordering the deserts under average annual rainfalls of 100 to 200 mm with outside limits of 50 to 300 mm. The word desertification has been—and still is—used by many authors to describe degradation of various types and forms of vegetation, including the subhumid and humid forest areas, which have nothing to do with deserts either physically or biologically."

Considering Le Houérou's geographic limitations, Rapp (1974) expanded the definition of desertization to "the spread of desert-like conditions in arid and semiarid areas up to 600 mm due to man's influence or to climatic change." He also noted that this definition conformed with that of desertification, as defined by Sherbrooke and Paylor (1973). Thus, the two terms have been used by different authors sometimes to describe different processes and sometimes the same process (Glantz, 1977). Rapp's definition was adopted by the United Nations Environment Program (UNEP, 1975) to describe the original term, desertification, with the understanding that "the scientific community frequently uses 'desertification' to mean a process caused by man, and 'desertization' a process regardless of cause."

The use of both ungainly terms continued to flourish during the past decade, and resulted in much confusion. Many workers preferred the use of "desertification" for man-made processes and "desertization" for the results of physical ones. This complicated the question of causes of desertification. Many authors appeared to agree with Novikoff (1975) that "the main agent for desertization is actually man." To emphasize this point a new term was coined at a conference held in 1975 in Tehran by UNEP and the Iranian Government on "de-desertization."

The result of all this is the unfortunate popular belief that the desert is man-made, and furthermore, that if our ancestors created the desert, then with our new technological capabilities we can undo it. Both concepts are incorrect. Furthermore, it is my opinion that these new terms are all unnecessary. Easily understood terms with precise meanings exist to describe land degradation by such processes as soil erosion, salinization, and dune encroachment. The term "desert" itself needed no modifications. It is as ancient as written language itself. It came to us from the ancient Egyptian hieroglyph pronounced *Teśret* (Budge, 1966, p. 172), via the Latin verb *desero*, to abandon. From the latter came *desertum*, a waste place or wilderness and *desertus* meaning abandoned, relinquished or forsaken.

The term desert, which denotes areas that receive less than 250 mm of rain per year, is thus a very suitably descriptive one. There is numerous evidence that today's deserts once hosted great numbers and varieties of flora and fauna. When weather conditions changed, these tracts of land were forsaken by the biota for other regions where life-sustaining water was more plentiful. The North African Sahara is an example of this, where archaeological evidence indicates wetter climatic conditions between 5,000 and at least 10,000 years ago (see, for example, Wendorf and Schild, 1980).

Aridity is also a matter of degree. The most commonly used climatic classification was established by Meigs (1953) in which the degrees of aridity are identified: semiarid, arid, and extremely arid (Fig. 7.1). On the basis of this classification the area of semiarid lands includes 21,243,000 km$^2$; that of arid lands encompasses 21,803,000 km$^2$; and the extremely arid lands cover 5,812,000 km$^2$ of the land area of the Earth (Shantz, 1956). This climatic aridity is due to three general conditions occurring individually or in combination: separation by topography or distance from major moisture sources, existence of dry stable air masses, and the lack of storm systems (Dregne, 1976, p. 7).

## THE EASTERN SAHARA

Consideration of the eastern part of the Sahara sheds light on the evolution of desert landscapes in space and time. This region is the largest dry tract of land on Earth. It falls within the largest dry area in the aridity index map of Henning and Flohn (1977). The Budyko ratio that is the basis for this map is known as the "radiational index of dryness." It expresses the relationship between net radiation and precipitation at the surface. Both quantities are taken in energy units and applied to long-term yearly mean values. This ratio thus expresses the number of times the annual net radiation could evaporate the precipitation at a given place. The eastern Sahara has a Budyko ratio of 200, which means that the received solar radiation is capable of evaporating 200-times the amount of rainfall.

In this hyperarid desert, lack of rain and persistent wind erosion create a landscape that is reminiscent of that peculiarly flat terrain, in which vehicles may move in most directions at will. During journeys into the Western Desert of Egypt, tracts are crossed that may have not been crossed by humans in thousands of years. However, in numerous places one encounters tangible evidence of past human habitation (El-Baz et al., 1980).

Along mountain slopes and scarps there are petroglyphs with colored paintings of animals that must have flourished in a savanna-like environment. In ancient dry valleys there are habitation sites strewn with hand-axes and knives chipped from quartzite and flint. These implements must have been used by hunters in the geological past. Often one encounters ostrich eggshell fragments, in some cases close to the carbon remains of the fire on which the eggs may have been cooked thousands of years ago.

These objects bring to mind a picture of the eastern Sahara that is vastly different from the way it looks today. Thousands of years ago nature was

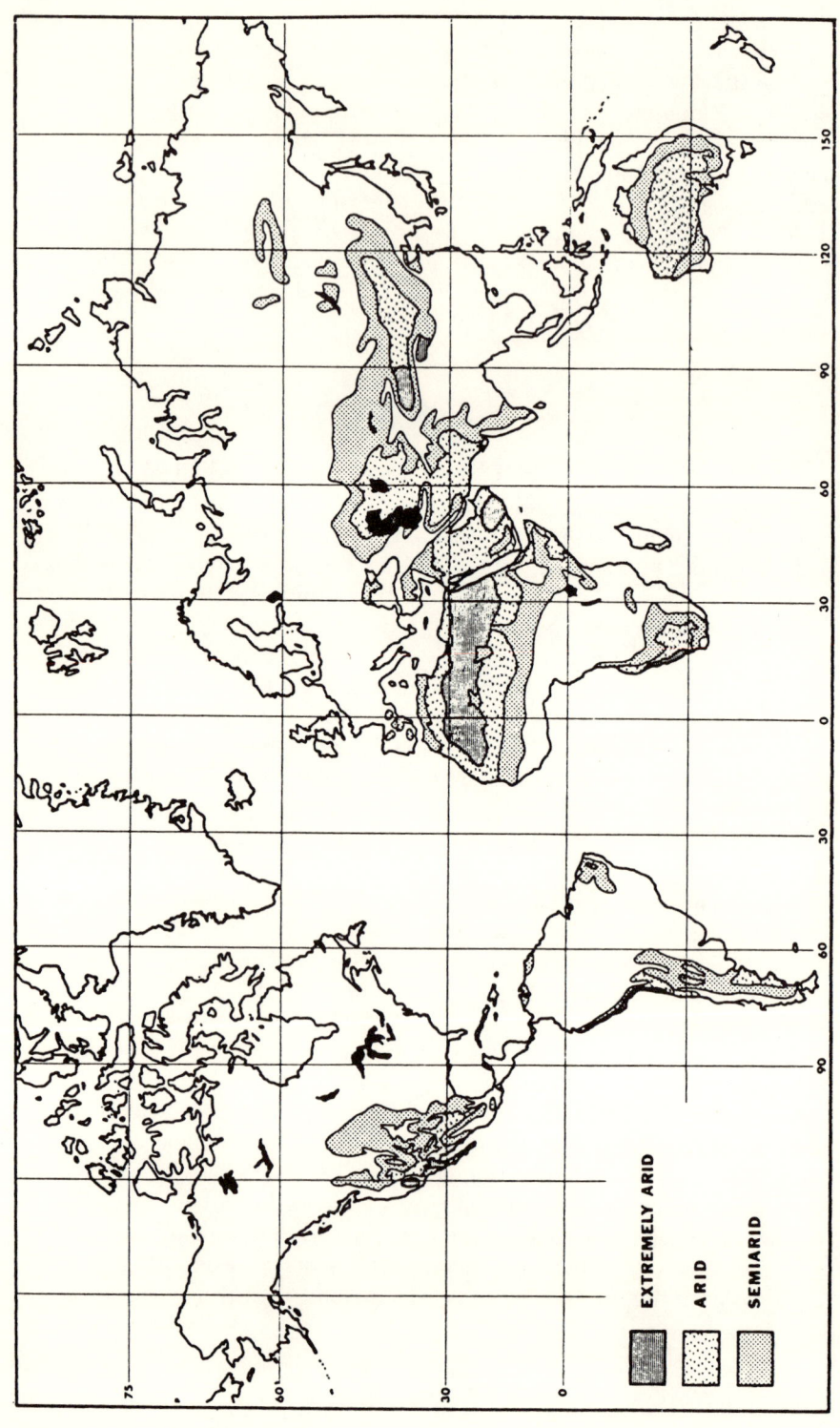

Figure 7.1. Arid regions of the world (modified from Meigs 1953). Polar arid regions not shown; after Dregne 1976.

much kinder and rain-fed vegetation covered large tracts of land around lakes with thriving fish populations. Then, the climate started changing and the rain clouds gradually disappeared. The land was forsaken by the vegetation, animals and man.

It appears that such a development was not a one time event, but happened in cycles. Haynes (1981) established such cycles in the southern part of the Western Desert of Egypt which he called Arba'in Desert. Working with geological and archaeological evidence, Haynes was able to decipher numerous alternations of dry and wet climates during the Quaternary Period, the past 1,000,000 years of Earth's history. Most significant are indications that the great depressions in the desert existed in essentially their present configuration 200,000 years ago. This is indicated by remains of Late Acheulean people who must have used artesian springs in the depression floors.

Starting about 100,000 years ago, a dry period ensued and the water table dropped. Humans and animals disappeared. Wind erosion set in and the depressions were deepened by deflation that continued for tens of thousands of years. Sometime after 60,000 years ago, a relatively wet climate returned and the water table rose. Ponds filled the desert depressions and man and animals appeared again. The human settlers of this Mousterian time were hunters of big game animals, for handaxes and rock knives pepper their occupation sites.

Occupation of the desert basins oscillated between 60,000 years ago and the start of the Recent Epoch, 25,000 years ago. Wet periods brought life to the desert, and alternating dry climates forced the desertion of all biota. After these, a relatively long dry period endured for 15,000 years. Not until 10,000 years ago did plants, animals and man, in that sequence, return to the Arba'in Desert. At this time, Late Paleolithic and Neolithic peoples brought domesticated animals with them, probably from the central Sudan, as Haynes and fellow researchers believe. These prehistoric settlers practiced agriculture around the shores of lakes, which filled and dried up three times, before the final drought set in over 5,000 years ago.

Such alternations of wet and dry periods appear to have occurred in the earlier geologic history of the Sahara. Although most contemporary deserts are probably no older than five million years old, the Sahara shows signs of aridity that go back to mid-Tertiary times. Mainguet et al. (1979) studied oscillations of the boundary between the Sahara and the Sahel (a name from the Arabic word for shoreline). Migrations of this boundary to the north and south, which are triggered mainly by climatic changes, are shown in Fig. 7.2. The latter clearly shows that the southern boundary of the Sahara was once farther south by at least 5°, than it is today.

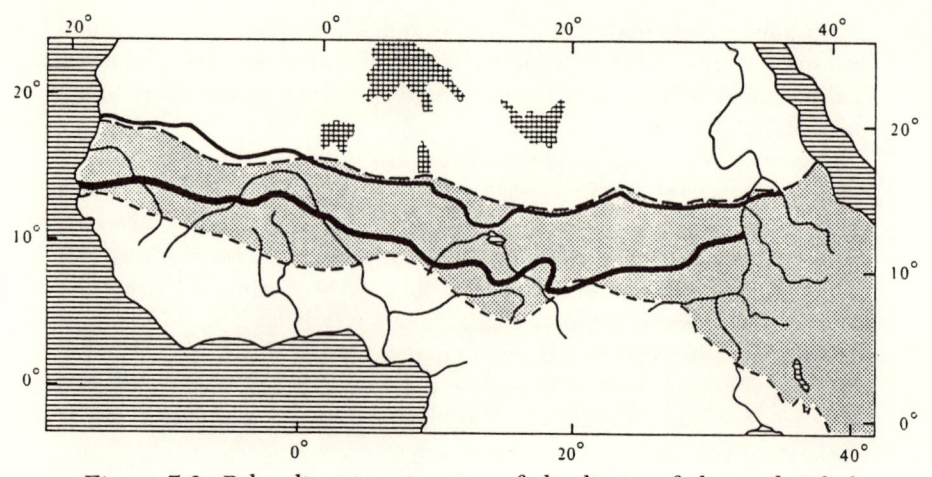

Figure 7.2. Paleoclimatic migration of the limits of the arid Sahel. Upper and lower dashed lines mark the zone of migration and represent the 150 mm and 1,000 mm isohyets respectively; after Mainguet and Callot 1978.

## THE SPACE PERSPECTIVE

The space age has opened a new era in desert research. Photographs taken from space provide a new tool that allows the study of regional patterns of wind erosion and sand deposition. Because of their large areal coverage, Earth-orbital photographs and images are especially helpful in mapping regional patterns of sand distribution, in studying large dune masses and in determining the direction of sand movement (McKee et al., 1977; El-Baz, 1977; McKee, 1979; Mainguet and Callot, 1978; and El-Baz et al., 1980).

Because of the repetitive coverage, space photographs allow the monitoring of changes to the terrain, which indicate natural improvement or degradation of the environment over a period of years or decades. Thus, they are used to monitor reclamation projects at the desert fringe, and point to areas that may be more suitable than others. For example, in the late 1950s the Egyptian Government started "The Liberation Province," a major reclamation effort just west of the Nile Delta. The project was met with many difficulties during the early years, but as reclamation proceeded northward, the project began to bear fruit. The reason for this became evident after comparing two photographs of the area taken by the astronauts of Gemini 5 in 1965 and Apollo-Soyuz in 1975 (Slezak and

El-Baz, 1979). The reclaimed area totaled 1,100 km² in the ten year period. The photographs showed that the southern part of the project extended into a zone of active sand, which should have been avoided. The northern extension of the project was in more suitable, fertile soil.

More importantly, photographs taken from space clearly depict color variations of desert surfaces, which are indicative of changes in surface composition. These photographs have been used in the past to confirm field observations of the red color in desert sands. For example, in the Namib Desert of Southwest Africa, where linear dunes have migrated from west to east along the coast of Namibia, the sands farthest inland are much redder in color and are of greater age (Logan, 1960). Skylab 4 photographs of the same region show color zones in the dune sand. In these photographs, younger sands near the coast appear brighter than the redder zones farther inland (McKee et al., 1977). Furthermore, Apollo-Soyuz photographs of southern Australia were used to illustrate dune reddening as a function of increasing distance from the source. Photographs of the Lake Blanche area in the Sturt Desert and of the Lake Eyre region in the southern Simpson Desert show an increase in red color as the distance from the sand source increases (El-Baz, 1978).

The red color in desert sands has been attributed to the presence of hematite coatings on individual grains (see, for example, Walker, 1967), although the origin of such reddening remains controversial. The variation in grain coating is significant because of its effects on the spectral signature of the sands on space images and photographs. Recent studies indicate that the coating on sand grains is composed of kaolinite with powdery hematite, thus linking such reddening to desert varnish as described by Potter and Rossman (1977). Kaolinite in the coating is believed to originate as dust that percolates through the sand and adheres to the surfaces of the grains. Thus, the processes that result in the darkening of rock surfaces with time through the formation of desert varnish also act upon individual sand grains (El-Baz and Prestel, 1980).

Sand samples studied from the Western Desert of Egypt show that the coating on quartz grains in samples from three locations increases in thickness from about 0.5 microns in the north to about 1.5 microns in the middle to between 2 and 5 microns in the south (McCay et al., 1980). These results not only confirm the observation of reddening of the sands as the transport distance increases, but also suggest that the quartz grains acquire the coatings during eolian transport. Therefore, the reddening property can be used to determine the relative ages of color zones in the same sand field, and thus can be indicative of the transport direction of the sand.

It is anticipated that additional color, high-resolution photographs of desert regions will be obtained from the Space Shuttle. This will be done by the use of the large format camera (LFC) to acquire mapping quality, stereo, 10–20 m resolution photographs on color and/or black-and-white film. The camera derives its name from the size of individual frames: 23 cm × 46 cm. Its 305 mm, f/6 lens has a 40 × 70° field-of-view (El-Baz and Ondrejka, 1978). The camera is to be placed on a palate in the Shuttle's cargo bay. In this mode of deployment it operates in Earth orbit, returns with the Shuttle, and provides the photographs more rapidly and cost effectively than any other planned system. From the Shuttle altitudes of 200–400 km the coverage of this camera will allow the study of up to 87,000 km$^2$ in one photograph. Such photographs are ideal for studies relating to the regional distribution patterns of desert surfaces, and particularly dune orientation and relative color of desert sands.

## WIND EROSION AND DEPOSITION

In the hyperarid desert, running water no longer plays a significant role in the transportation and deposition of sediments. The desert is dominated by an eolian environment, in which wind is the main agent of erosion, transportation and sedimentation. In this environment, particulate material originates from the disintegration of rock by both mechanical and chemical weathering (Fig. 7.3). The disintegration exposes the particles to the agents of erosion, which in turn cause more loosening of particles from the rock. Depending on their size these particles are either carried in suspension as dust, saltate to accumulate as dune, or lag behind with larger fragments of rock.

Thus, wind deposits are discretely zoned in response to the capacity of the wind to sort out and segregate particles by grain size. The finest particles (clay and silt particles, up to 0.05 mm in size) are winnowed out wherever they are exposed and whirled away into the atmosphere as dust, settling out of suspension beyond the zones of high wind energy (Breed et al., 1980). Saharan dust storms, for example, carry such fine dust particles concentrated at altitudes of 1.5 km and 3.7 km in the atmosphere. It was estimated that 25 to 37 million tons of dust are transported through the 60°W longitude each year, which is equivalent to the present rate of pelagic sedimentation for the entire north equatorial region of the Atlantic Ocean (Prospero and Carson, 1972). Similarly, in temperate regions the wind picks up particles of glacial silt and clay and deposits them as loess. A buff colored deposit of loess up to 100 meters thick scoured from the Mongolian Plateau covers most of northern China.

Fine and medium sized sand grains saltate readily in strong desert winds. By the saltation process, the wind segregates particles of 0.05 to 0.5 mm sizes from the clays, silts and gravels and shepherds them into

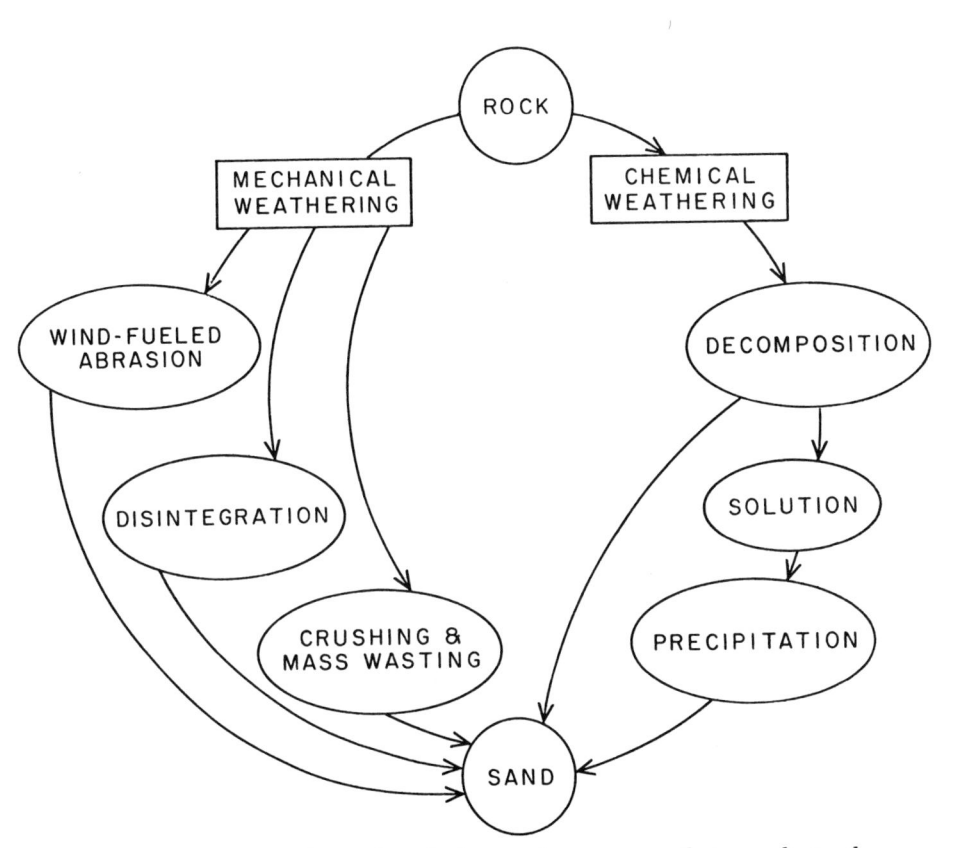

Figure 7.3. The physical and chemical processes that result in the formation of sand-sized particulate material from solid rock.

dunes. The movement of sand by saltation depends on the nature of the surface. The sand particles jump to higher levels if they saltate on gravel rather than on a sandy surface.

In contrast, particles too large (0.5 to 2 mm in diameter) to be lifted off the surface by the bombardment of saltating grains may gradually and erratically move or roll along the surface. With high winds the whole surface covered by such grains appears to be creeping slowly along the wind direction.

Segregation of particles by the wind into varying sizes usually results in the formation of vast flat plains that are veneered with a surface of granules or pebbles, commonly well-sorted and usually one grain thick. This lag forms an armor that is apparently in equilibrium with the strongest winds. The process of surface creep, by which the wind distributes the coarse materials, seems imperceptible except under rare high-velocity wind conditions. Removal of the coarse lag results in immediate deflation of the suddenly unprotected, underlying silts and sands, which produces lasting scars (Breed et al., 1980).

Saltating sand grains usually result in accumulations in a large number of forms. Generally speaking, sand-sized grains accumulate in the form of sand sheets with rippled, undulated surfaces or as free dunes and obstacle-related dunes. Free dunes, which are by far the most abundant, can be isolated simple forms, coalesced compound groups, or complex accumulations. The basic geometric shapes of dunes are straight (linear, transverse and longitudinal dunes), crescentic (barchan and parabolic dunes), and domical (including dome, pyramid and star dunes). All types of dunes may be active, semifixed or fixed by vegetation. Dune shapes vary considerably in different areas and often within the same locality (El-Baz, 1980).

Dunes usually group in bundles (Fig. 7.4), and a larger number of dunes form a dune field. Huge accumulations of sand dunes are known as sand seas. As previously stated, detailed knowledge of the texture and morphology of these sand seas was made possible through the interpretation of photographs and images taken from space. For example, data from Meteosat allow the recognition of general sand movement patterns in all of the Sahara. Similarly, Landsat images and photographs taken on manned space missions allow the mapping of dune accumulations of the Great Sand Sea in the Western Desert and of the Taklimakan Desert in northwestern China.

Prolonged wind erosion creates isolated hills. Also corrasion features, shaped solely by the wind can be 100 km in length (Mainguet and Callot, 1978). Yardangs, the smaller wind sculpted features that resemble in-

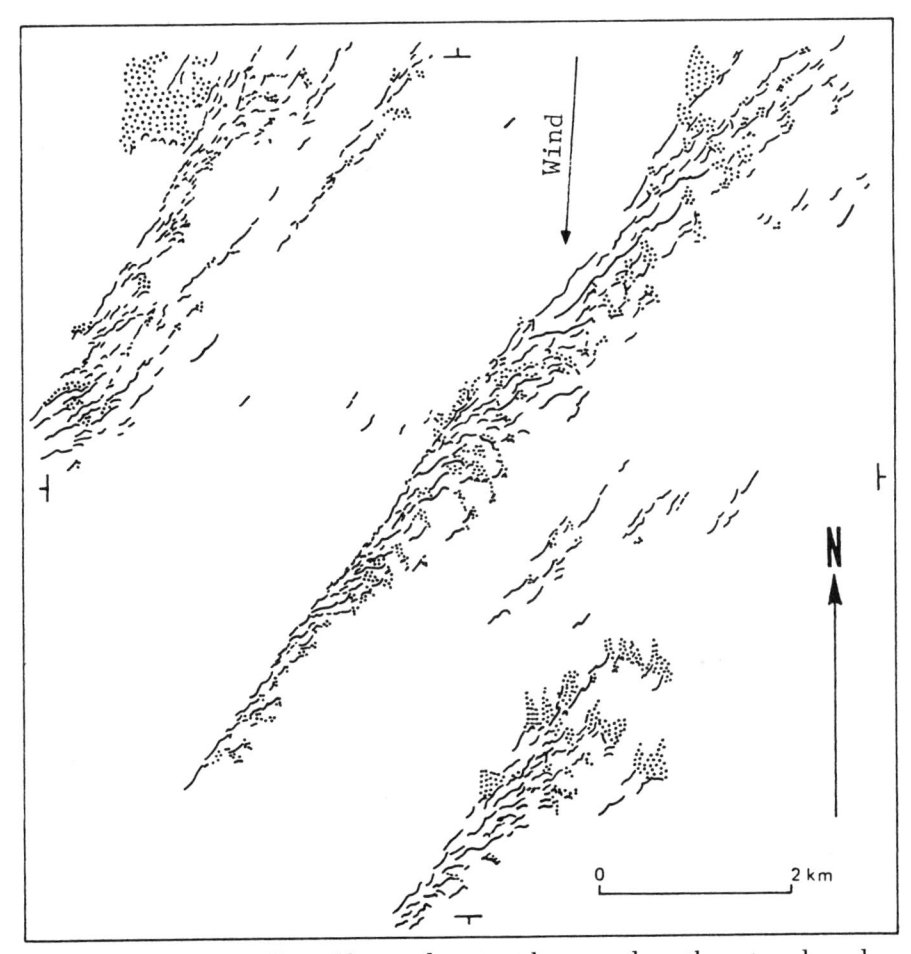

Figure 7.4. Bundles of linear dunes with tapered southwest ends and open northeast sides. Note the asymmetry in the lower (downwind) parts; after Mainguet and Callot 1978.

verted boat hulls, occur in numerous localities, indicating windformed features. However, the role of vorticity in developing lineations by wind erosion was only recently established by Whitney (1978).

## COMPARISONS WITH MARS

Wind action in the hyperarid desert creates a landscape that is reminiscent of that on Mars. For example, features in the eastern Sahara have been compared to those of the Cerberus region of Mars (El-Baz, 1980). In the Western Desert of Egypt, the present eolian episode has greatly modified, but not obliterated, products of previous climates. Because a similar evolutionary history may have occurred on the surface of Mars, even on a larger scale, it is important to consider the Martian features in light of their Saharan counterparts.

The Western Desert of Egypt is characterized by remnants of pluvial-interpluvial cycles including lacustrine deposits, inverted wadis, and terrace deposits along escarpments. Most prominent among the pluvial features are the dry channels in the Gilf Kebir plateau, which is capped by wind-resistant silicified sandstone. Incised into the 300 m-high cliffs of the Gilf are 10 to 30 km-long channels that end abruptly as box canyons. The lack of significant catchments on the plateau surface suggests that the channels were formed by ground water sapping at the base of cliffs. Another possibility is that former catchment areas were present in softer beds that have been deflated by eolian action. In both cases, analogies could be drawn to cliff-related channels on Mars.

It is significant that in the open parts of the Western Desert, linear dunes predominate singly, as dune bundles, or in the vast Great Sand Sea. However, crescent dunes occur basically in depressions, particularly along escarpments. Crescentic dune accumulations are analogous to the larger dune mass in the north polar region of Mars, which may be similarly confined in a low area bounded by a plateau. The rate of motion of dunes in one of the Western Desert depressions, the Kharga depression, varies between 20 m and 100 m per year; the smaller the dune, the faster it moves (Embabi, 1981). This may give us a basis for estimating the rate of motion of Martian crescentic dunes, with considerations of the differences in the two wind regimes.

As discussed by El-Baz (1981), a circular crater, 4 km in diameter, among the dunes of the Great Sand Sea displays dark colored material in the southern part of the crater interior. More importantly there is a distinct dark patch in the lee of the crater. This crater appears to have modified the patterns of material transport by the wind in exactly the same way as do craters in the Cerberus region of Mars.

El-Baz and Maxwell (1979) describe dark streaks in the wind shadow of mountains and hills in the Western Desert with streamlined patterns that are similar to those in the lee of craters on Mars. The spindle-shaped streaks in the Egyptian desert change boundaries in response to changes in the depositional pattern of sand on either side. Alterations of the deposition of sand occur due to changes in wind direction.

Unlike shadow streaks which form due to the lack of deposition in the lee of large topographic prominences, knob streaks develop from the deposition of eolian material downwind of gaps between knobs (El-Baz and Maxwell, 1979). In the Sahara as on Mars these streaks are usually lighter in color than the surrounding surfaces. Study of the shape parameter in both cases shows a higher degree of streamlining of the terrestrial streaks, indicating a more efficient eolian regime.

As on the equatorial region of Mars, the Western Desert of Egypt displays large fields of parallel corrasion features and numerous yardangs (El-Baz et al., 1980). In addition, remnants of scarps in the Western Desert are usually in the shape of inselbergs or knobs. Similarly, knobby terrain on Mars occurs near boundaries between plains and plateau units. The length to width ratios for measured knobs in Farafra (Egypt) and in Cerberus (Mars) are 0.63 and 0.65 respectively, even though the Martian knobs are 100-times larger than those in the Western Desert.

A further analogy relates to the blocks of varying sizes, which litter the surface of the Western Desert. Such areas resemble the block-strewn surfaces in the Viking lander sites. Two block fields in the southwestern part of the Egyptian desert were studied and compared to Martian block fields (Garvin et al., 1981). One of the block fields surrounded a basaltic hill of Quaternary age with angular blocks 20–40 cm in diameter. In this field blocks are equidimensional, angular, with planar fractures, and slightly embedded in the sandy substrate, with few fillets, moats or wind tails. The other field consists of blocks, 20–50 cm across, which appear to have been placed there by floods during infrequent fluvial episodes. In this field the rocks are elongate, subangular, and usually with bimodal surface texture. The two block fields correlate well with the Viking lander sites in overall rock elongation form, rock roundness, and the presence of facets. From this correlation, it is plausible that the blocks in the Martian sites are made of massive basalt like those in the Western Desert. Also the blocks in both cases appear to have been emplaced by cataclysmic events such as occasional floods (Egypt) or meteorite impacts (Mars).

The blocks in the Egyptian desert discussed above exhibit pitted and fluted surfaces. The pits occur singly or in rows. Often a row of elongated pits forms a flute, and some of the flutes have pits in them (Garvin et al., 1981). Wind tunnel studies of air flow over and around non-streamlined hand specimens show that windward abrasion coupled with negative air flow, secondary flow, and vorticity in a unidirectional wind explain the complex array of pits and flutes (McCauley et al., 1979). These pits and flutes bear a striking resemblance to the pits and flutes in Martian rocks photographed at the Viking landers. This suggests that the blocks in the lander sites may have also been pitted and fluted by the wind.

## METEOROLOGICAL MONITORING

Because the desert environment is dominated by the wind, it is very important to understand the wind patterns of any desert region under investigation. The problem is complex because the wind tends to often change directions. Field observations indicate that, on small scales, the wind often changes directions and forms vortices that cause air to flow in the reverse direction. Where furrows exist in the terrain, the wind is funneled through them with an increase in velocity, and thus in erosive power. On larger scales the wind tends to intimately follow the contours of slopes and faces of scarps and cliffs.

The situation is further complicated by the fact that in most countries meteorological stations are limited to locations in and around cities. In desert areas particularly, meteorological stations are widely spaced and are placed in oases which are located in depressions, where surrounding cliffs exert a great deal of influence on the wind. These facts have to be taken into account when analyzing wind data from any desert region.

This situation is illustrated by one of the oases depressions in the Western Desert of Egypt. In this desert the general dune orientations change from N–NW in the northern part to N–NE in the southwest (Bagnold, 1933). The Farafra depression is centrally located in this desert. It is bounded by three scarps creating a roughly triangular shape. It is enclosed on the northern side by a low scarp and on its eastern and western sides by higher scarps; the width of the depression continually increases to the south where it meets the Dakhla depression 200 km away. The distance between the east and west cliffs at the latitude of the Farafra Oasis, N27°, is about 90 km. The El-Quss Abu-Said plateau west of the oasis is oriented N45°E with its long axis about 63 km in length, and its width about 29 km (Fig. 7.5).

The Great Sand sea west of the Farafra depression is composed of whaleback dunes with longitudinal dunes superimposed on top (Bagnold, 1933). The dunes vary in orientation, between N–S to N26°W, with an average orientation of N13°W (Manent and El-Baz, 1980). The average length of the dunes is 70 km and the average width is 2.5 km. East of the Great Sand Sea in the Farafra region is a smaller dunefield between El-Quss Abu-Said plateau and the northern escarpment (A in Fig. 7.5).

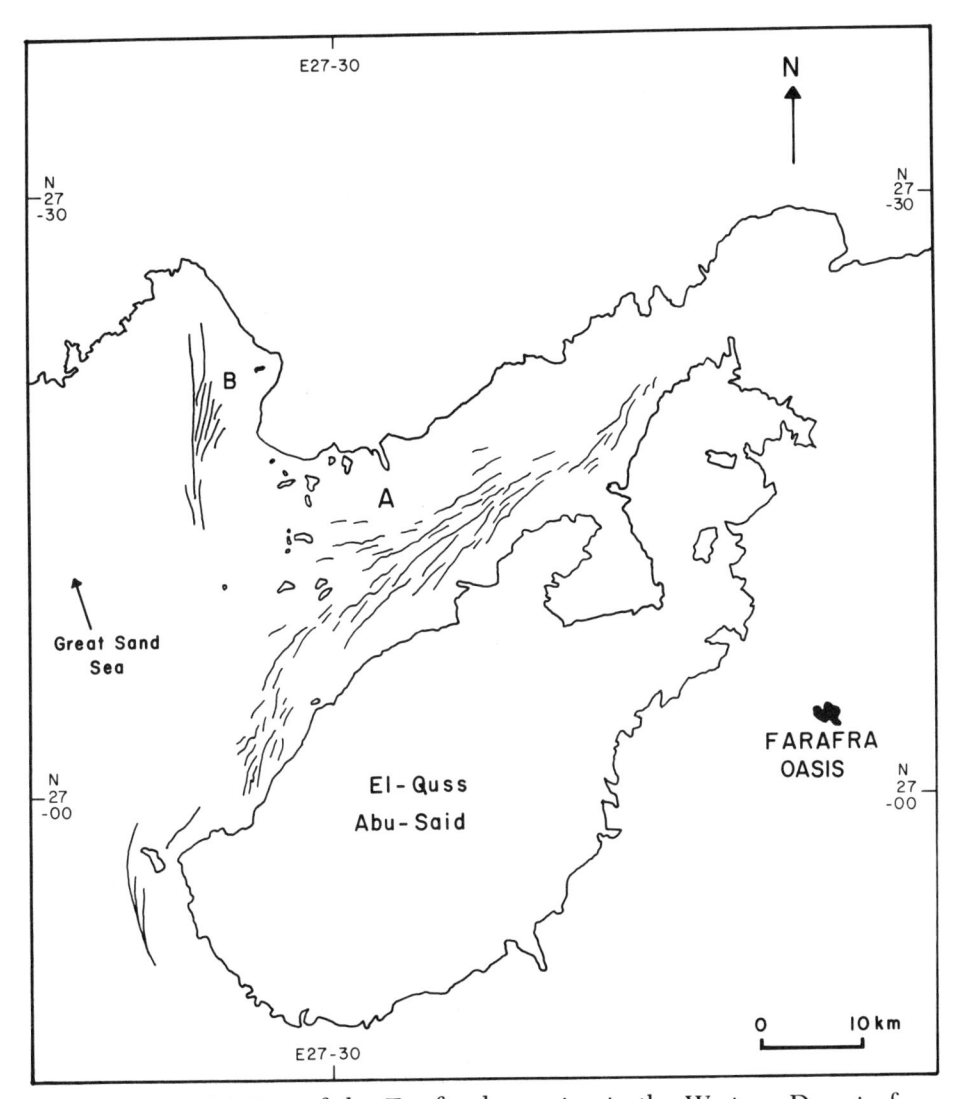

Figure 7.5. Part of the Farafra depression in the Western Desert of Egypt. the El-Quss Abu-Said plateau west of Farafra Oasis deflects the southerly winds and controls the orientation of dunes in fields A and B; after Manent and El-Baz 1980.

Within this dunefield, the size and orientation of dunes are different from those of the Great Sand Sea. Here, the dunes are smaller, with an average length of 7 km and an average width of 0.2 km. They converge and taper to the northeast and are more widely spaced to the southwest. The orientation of the northern scarp is N58°E and of Abu-Said plateau N45°E. The resultant direction of these two scarps is N52°E, which is close to the orientation of the dunes, which is N50°E.

West of this area is another smaller dunefield that is oriented N6°E (B in Fig. 7.5). It is surrounded by two scarps, one oriented N50°E and the other N38°W. The resultant direction of these two scarps is N6°E, which is parallel to the orientation of the dunefield. Comparison of the size and orientation of the Great Sand Sea dunes and those in the Farafra depression dunefields suggests that the topography is affecting the direction and strength of the wind in the formation of dunes within the depression.

The available wind data were studied to correlate them with the dunes in the Farafra region. These data were derived from surface wind N-summaries recorded in the Farafra oasis between 1958 and 1966, and were compiled and prepared by the Environmental Technical Applications Center of the U.S. Air Force. The wind speed was recorded in knots to the nearest 10° of direction at three to six hour intervals. During this nine year period, a total of 11,844 observations were recorded, of which 2,683 were calm winds (less than 1 knot). The rest were calculated into percentages of the total amount of wind and then organized by month. Each month was broken up into sixteen directional sources which were grouped into five categories of velocity.

The annual summary when plotted for sand-moving winds gives a northerly direction (Fig. 7.6). This can be misleading. When sand-moving winds are plotted by season and month (Fig. 7.6), changes in wind direction are apparent throughout the year, and agree with the dune patterns in the Great Sand Sea. However, there is not a single month with wind blowing in the direction of the dunes within the Farafra depression. Therefore, the scarps must affect the orientation of the dunes by deflecting the wind. The resultant directions of the scarps that bound the two smaller dunefields are nearly the same as the orientations of the enclosed dunes (Manent and El-Baz, 1980).

This example illustrates the need to obtain wind data in numerous localities in the open desert. Space-age technology has paved the way for the utilization of automated stations that can gather meteorological data in remote desert regions. Data collected by such means can be transmitted to orbiting satellites, which then retransmit the data to ground receiving stations for processing, distribution and analysis. There are three basic elements to such a scheme: (1) a data collection platform connected to

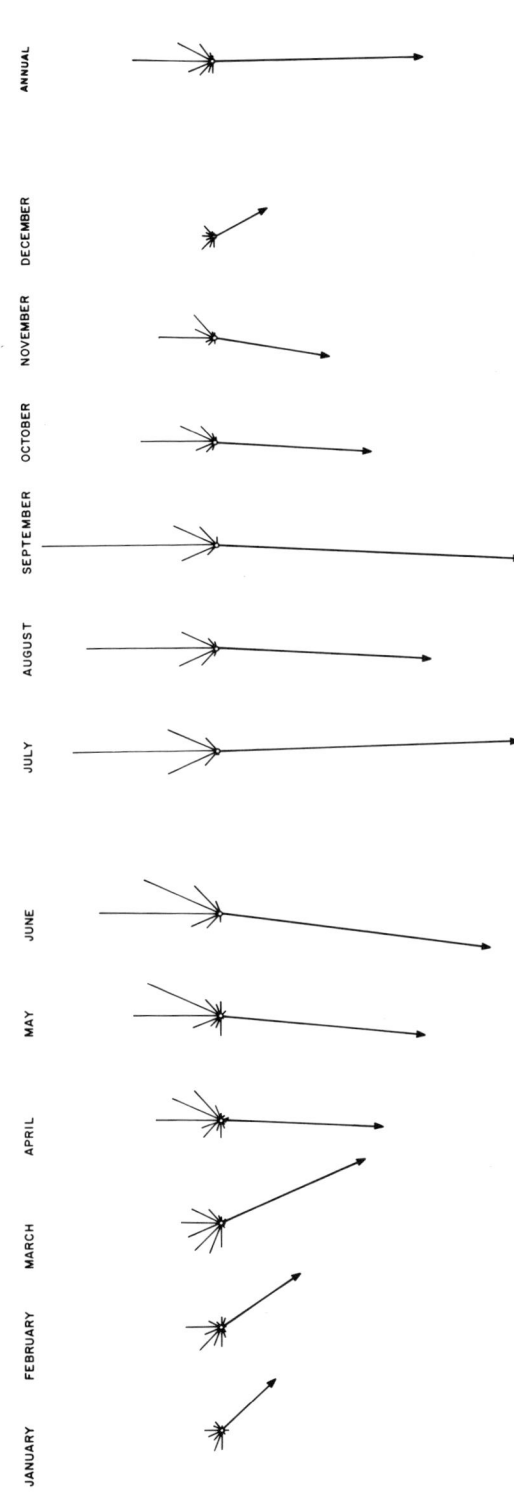

Figure 7.6. Directions of sand moving potential as computed from Farafra Oasis wind data; after Manent and El-Baz 1980.

the sensor recorders; (2) a radio transponder with receiving and transmitting capabilities on board a satellite; and (3) a data receiving station for retrieval, processing, and dissemination of the collected data.

## CONCLUSIONS

1. The terms *desertification* and *desertization* are both vague and unnecessary. Clearly defined and more specific terms exist to describe the various processes and causes of land degradation.

2. Contrary to popular belief, the desert is a natural type of landform that results from the scarcity or lack of rain. The belief that the desert is man-made is scientifically invalid.

3. The eastern Sahara, the driest large expanse of desert, was formed by alternation of wet and dry climates from 200,000 to 5,000 years ago. Human habitation in this desert followed the wet periods, and ceased during dry periods.

4. Space photographs provide a new tool to study the desert, particularly because of the large aerial coverage and the clear depiction of color changes. Because of the repeated coverage of the same area these photographs are very useful in monitoring changes with the passage of time.

5. Color photographs obtained from Earth orbit are important in establishing the degree of reddening of desert sands. These sands become redder as the transport distance increases, thus allowing the mapping of relative age zones within large sand fields.

6. The wind is the main force of erosion in the hyperarid desert environment. The wind creates deep grooves in the surface rocks resulting in the formation of corrasion features and yardangs.

7. The wind is also an effective agent of transportation and deposition of particulate materials. The finest particles are carried as dust, medium-sized grains accumulate in the form of dunes, and the larger and heavier particles remain to form an armored surface.

8. Features of the hyperarid deserts such as the eastern Sahara resemble wind-blown features on Mars. Similarities are not limited to the view from orbit, such as streaks in the lee of topographic barriers, but also to detailed surface features, such as block distributions and pitting in rocks by the wind.

9. Desert winds are strongly affected by local topography. In the Western Desert of Egypt scarps within oases depressions deflect the winds and control the orientation of dunes. Thus, the wind data collected in these depressions do not represent the wind patterns in the open desert.

10. Meteorological monitoring by automated stations is recommended for remote desert regions. Collected data may be transmitted to satellites for retransmission to centers for data analysis and interpretation.

## REFERENCES

Bagnold, R. A. 1933. "A Further Journey Through the Libyan Desert." *Geogr. J.* 82:103–129.
Breed, C. S., N. S. Embabi, H. A. El-Etr, and M. J. Grolier. 1980. "Wind Deposits in the Western Desert." *Geogr. J.* 146:88–90.
Budge, E. A. W. 1966. *Egyptian Language*. Routledge and Kegan Paul Ltd., London.
Dregne, H. E. 1976. *Soils of Arid Regions*. Elsevier Scientific Publishing Co., New York.
El-Baz, F. 1977. *Astronaut Observations from the Apollo-Soyuz Mission*. Smithsonian Institution Press, Washington, D.C.
El-Baz, F. 1978. "The Meaning of Desert Color in Earth Orbital Photographs." *Photogram. Eng. Rem. Sens.* 44:69–75.
El-Baz, F. 1980. "Space-Age Developments in Desert Research." *Episodes* 1980 (4):12–17.
El-Baz, F. 1981. "Circular Feature Among Dunes of the Great Sand Sea." *Science* 213:439–440.
El-Baz, F. et al. 1980. "Journey to the Gilf Kebir and Uweinat, Southwest Egypt, 1978." *Geogr. J.* 146:51–93.
El-Baz, F., and T. A. Maxwell. 1979. "Eolian Streaks in Southwestern Egypt and Similar Features on Mars." p. 3017–3030 in *Proceedings of the Tenth Lunar and Planetary Science Conference*. Pergamon Press, New York.
El-Baz, F., and D. J. Prestel. 1980. "Desert Varnish on Sand Grains from the Western Desert of Egypt: Importance of the Clay Component and Implications to Mars." p. 254–256 in *Lunar and Planetary Science XI*. Lunar and Planetary Institute, Houston, Texas.
El-Baz, F. and R. J. Ondrejka. 1978. "Earth Orbital Photography by the Large Format Camera." p. 703–718 in *Proceedings of the Twelfth International Symposium on Remote Sensing of Environment*. Environmental Research Institute of Michigan, Ann Arbor, Michigan.
Embabi, N.S. "Barchans of the Kharga Depression." in El-Baz, F., and T. A. Maxwell (eds.) *Desert Landforms of Southwestern Egypt* (in press).
Garvin, J. B., J. W. Head and F. El-Baz. 1981. "Rock Morphology of Basalts in the Western Desert of Egypt: Implications for Viking Lander Sites on Mars." p. 326–329 in *Lunar and Planetary Science XII*. Lunar and Planetary Institute, Houston, Texas.
Glantz, M. H. 1977. "The U.N. and Desertification: Dealing with a Global Problem." p. 1–15 in Glantz, M. H. (ed.) *Desertification—Environmental Degradation in and Around Arid Lands*. Westview Press, Boulder, Colorado.
Haynes, C. V. "The Darb El Arba'in Desert: A Product of Quaternary Climatic Change." in El-Baz, F., and T. A. Maxwell (eds.) *Desert Landforms of Southwestern Egypt* (in press).
Henning, D. and F. Flohn. 1977. "Climate Aridity Index Map." U.N. Conference on Desertification, Nairobi, Kenya.
Le Houérou, H. N. 1962. *Les pâturages naturels de la Tunisie aride et désertique*. Inst. Sces. Econ. Appl. Tunis, Paris.
Le Houérou, H. N. 1968. "La désertisation du Sahara septentrional et des steppes limitrophes." *Ann. Alger. de Geogr.* (Alger), 6:2–27.

Le Houérou, H. N. 1977. "The Nature and Causes of Desertization." p. 18–38 in Glantz, M. H. (ed.) *Desertification–Environmental Degradation in and Around Arid Lands.* Westview Press, Boulder, Colorado.

Logan, R. F. 1960. *The Central Namib Desert.* National Research Council Publication 785. National Academy of Sciences, Washington, D.C.

Mainguet, M. and Y. Callot. 1978. *L'Erg de Fachi—Bilma, Chad—Niger.* Centre Nat. Res. Sci., Paris.

Mainguet, M., L. Cannon-Cossus and M. C. Chemin. 1979. "Dégradation dans les régions centrales de la République du Niger." *Trav. Inst. Géogr. Reims,* 39–40:61–73.

Manent, L. S., and F. El-Baz. 1980. "Effects of Topography on Dune Orientation in the Farafra Region, Western Desert of Egypt, and Implications to Mars." p. 298–300 in *Reports of Planetary Geology Program—1980.* NASA Tech. Mem. 82385. National Aeronautics and Space Administration, Washington, D.C.

McCauley, J. F., C. S. Breed, F. El-Baz, M. I. Whitney, M. J. Grolier, and A. W. Ward. 1979. "Pitted and Fluted Rocks in the Western Desert of Egypt: Viking Comparisons." *J. Geophys. Res.* 84:8222–8232.

McCay, D., C. Constantopoulos, D. J. Prestel, and F. El-Baz. 1980. "Thickness of Coatings on Quartz Grains From the Great Sand Sea, Egypt." p. 304–306 in *Reports of Planetary Geology Program—1980.* NASA Tech. Mem. 82385. National Aeronautics and Space Administration, Washington, D.C.

McKee, E. D. 1979. *A Study of Global Sand Seas.* Geol. Surv. Prof. Pap. 1052, U.S. Gov. Printing Office, Washington, D.C.

McKee, E. D., C. S. Breed and S. G. Fryberger. 1977. "Desert Sand Seas." p. 5–47 in *Skylab Explores the Earth.* NASA SP-380. National Aeronautics and Space Administration, Washington, D.C.

Meigs, P. 1953. "World Distribution of Arid and Semi-Arid Homoclimates." p. 203–210 in *Review of Research in Arid Zone Hydrology, Arid Zone. Res.,* I. UNESCO, Paris.

Novikoff, G. 1975. "The Desertisation of Range Lands and Cereal Cultivated Lands in Presaharan Tunisia." p. 163 in Novikoff, G., F. H. Wagner and P. S. Kouri (eds.) *Tunisian Presaharan Project Progress Report #3.* Utah State University, Logan, Utah.

Potter, R. M., and J. R. Rossman. 1977. "Desert Varnish: The Importance of Clay Minerals." *Science* 196:1446–1448.

Prospero, J. M. and T. N. Carson. 1972. "Vertical and Areal Distribution of Saharan Dust Over the Western Equatorial North Atlantic Ocean." *J. Geophys. Res.* 77:5255–5265.

Rapp, A. 1974. *A Review of Desertization in Africa: Water, Vegetation and Man.* Secretariat for International Ecology, Stockholm, Sweden.

Shantz, H. L. 1956. "History and Problems of Arid Lands Development." p. 3–25 in White, G. F. (ed.) *The Future of Arid Lands.* Amer. Assoc. Adv. Sci. Pub. 43.

Sherbrooke, W. C., and P. Paylor. 1973. *World Desertification: Causes and Effect.* Office of Arid Lands Studies: Information Paper #3, University of Arizona, Tucson, Arizona.

Slezak, M. H., and F. El-Baz. 1979. "Temporal Changes as Depicted on Orbital Photographs of Arid Regions in North Africa." p. 26–272 in El-Baz, F., and D. M. Warner (eds.) *Apollo-Soyuz Test Project Summary Science Report. Volume II: Earth Observations and Photography.* NASA SP-412. National Aeronautics and Space Administration, Washington, D.C.

United Nations Environment Program. 1975. *International Cooperation to Combat Desertification.* UNEP Liaison Office. Ad Hoc Interagency Task Force, 26–28 June 1975. Geneva, Switzerland.

United Nations Environment Program. 1977. *Technology and Desertification.* United Nations Conference on Desertification, August 29–September 9, 1977, Nairobi, Kenya.

Walker, T. R. 1967. "Formation of Red Beds in Modern and Ancient Deserts." *Geol. Soc. Amer. Bull.* 78:353–368.

Wendorf, F., and R. Schild. 1980. *Prehistory of the Eastern Sahara.* Academic Press, New York.

Whitney, M. I. 1978. "The Role of Vorticity in Developing Lineation by Wind Erosion." *Geol. Soc. Amer. Bull.* 89:1–18.

# 8

# DESERTIFICATION: A CLIMATOLOGICAL PERSPECTIVE

Derek Winstanley

*National Center for Atmospheric Research*
*Boulder, Colorado*

## INTRODUCTION

*Desertification* is a horrible word, the use of which has probably created more problems than it has helped to solve. The problems and issues associated with desertification became apparent in the 1970s, largely as a result of the widespread publicity given to the droughts in tropical Africa, particularly in the Sahelian zone, Ethiopia and the Horn of Africa. In the late 1960s and the early 1970s there was increasing concern over the problems associated with continued growth on a finite planet (see, for example, Meadows *et al.*, 1972). This concept led to concerns of overpopulation, shortages in food supply, scarcity and overexploitation of resources, and environmental degradation, including desertification. In that these problems affected many peoples in many countries, they were perceived to be global in nature. One method of seeking solutions to these problems was the convening of world conferences held under the auspices of the United Nations. The Conference on Desertification, held in Nairobi in 1977, was one such conference.

The problems associated with desertification are complex and involve interactions and feedbacks between man and his environment. One of the physical components is climate. It is known that variations in climate affect both the environment and human activities, but there are also concerns that human activities might be changing the climate. As human population is expected to increase to nearly six billion by the year 2000, and maybe to ten billion next century, concern over the impacts of human activity on the environment and the effects of environmental change on man is well justified.

The subject I address—a climatological perspective of desertification—is very broad and it is important that I start by outlining what aspects I shall cover and the approach I shall take. Let me make it clear that I will not attempt to cover all the aspects of desertification, or even all the climatological aspects. For comprehensive reviews on these subjects I suggest reading "Desertification: Its Causes and Consequences" (U.N., 1977) and "Desertification" (Glantz, 1977). Although desertification is a global problem, and it has been estimated that some eighteen million square miles, or 30 percent of the world's land surface, are threatened by desertification (U.N., 1977), I shall restrict my examples largely to the continent of Africa, with which I am most familiar. I do not propose to attempt to clarify the definition of the word *desertification,* but rather to give some examples of climatic variability and its effects on biological productivity in arid and semiarid areas. As the loss of biological productivity is characteristic of the process of desertification, I therefore view variations in climate, and particularly protracted droughts, as an important cause of desertification. I also believe that man plays an important role in the process of desertification.

Deserts themselves are characterized by extremely low rainfall and natural aridity. It is in semiarid areas that variations in rainfall are an important factor in the process of desertification; the lower and more uncertain the rainfall, the greater is the potential for desertification. However, rainfall in semiarid areas is not the only source of water in these areas; vast quantities of water are transported into these regions by rivers that originate in more humid areas. It is this water and, hence, the rainfall in the more humid areas that provides the potential for hydroelectric and irrigation schemes in the semiarid areas affected by desertification. Considered here is variation in water availability in Africa, and particularly the reduced availability during drought periods. My perspective is that major fluctuations in rainfall that are associated with droughts and the process of desertification in semiarid areas are often part of much larger, coherent patterns of variations in rainfall that also encompass more humid areas. I believe that understanding the nature of these climatic variations is extremely important in developing resource management strategies, including strategies to combat desertification.

Over large parts of Africa a high percentage of the population is engaged in agriculture and directly dependent upon the rains for both food and cash crops. It is this economic structure, combined with the high interannual variability of water resources, that makes societies particularly vulnerable to variations in climate and to desertification.

This essay is based largely on the results of my own research and on my experiences in Africa. Some of the results, I suggest, call for reevaluation of the role of climate variations in the process of desertification and have important implications for development planning.

I start by making some general comments on desertification and then present some examples to illustrate the significance of variations in rainfall in the population dynamics of locusts, birds and fish that inhabit areas subject to desertification. Desertification, however, is also a human problem, with the most important aspect lying in the impacts of desertification on man himself (U.N., 1978; Hare, 1977; Le Houérou, 1977). Therefore, I shall look also at the impacts of variations in rainfall on agricultural production in West Africa and at the significance of these variations for water resource development projects. I believe that the process of desertification has both social and physical causes. I therefore consider it important to take a broad, multidisciplinary perspective on the fundamental importance of climatic variations in ecology, development, and desertification.

## DESERTIFICATION AND THE ROLE OF RAINFALL VARIATIONS

At the U.N. Conference, desertification was defined as the diminution or destruction of the biological potential of the land that can lead ultimately to desert-like conditions (U.N., 1978). Le Houérou (1977) uses the word *desertization* rather than *desertification* to describe the extension of typical desert landscapes and landforms to areas where they did not occur in the recent past. According to Le Houérou, this process takes place in arid zones bordering the deserts under average annual rainfalls of 100 to 200 mm, with outside limits of 50 to 300 mm. Rapp (1974) considers desertification as the spread of desert-like conditions in arid or semiarid areas with up to 600 mm of rainfall.

While I accept the diminution or destruction of the biological potential of the land as being an essential feature of desertification, I do not restrict my analysis to areas receiving less than 600 mm of rainfall. I shall show that the same variations in climate which contribute to the process of desertification, or desertization, in low rainfall areas along the desert fringe also extend into the humid areas receiving over 3,000 mm of rain annually. However, changes in annual rainfall of several hundred millimeters are likely to have less direct ecological and social impact in areas that receive over 3,000 mm of rain than in areas that receive, say, only 600 mm. What I am concerned with are changes in ecological conditions and biological productivity associated with regional variations in climate. Rather than restrict my analysis to rigidly delineated zones or regions, my aim is to attempt to understand the nature of the variations in rainfall in both space and time and then to look at some of the impacts.

I do not intend to describe in detail what happens when desertification occurs. The precise nature of the degradation depends upon local soil and vegetation conditions and landforms. Some of the more general changes that are typical of desertification include: reduction in biomass production; breakdown of soil structure; more rapid run-off; loss of top soil; and fall in groundwater level. When the equilibrium is delicate, as under water stress, even a small change in one component can have repercussions throughout the entire ecosystem; sometimes the system is disrupted beyond a critical threshold whence natural recovery will not normally occur.

While considerable controversy exists concerning the causes of desertification, the general consensus is that man is the main agent. It is the overexploitation and degradation by man of vegetation, soil, and water—three main elements that serve as foundations for life—that is viewed as the main cause of desertification. Above all, liability to desertification is a function of pressure of land use, as reflected in density of population of livestock or the extent to which agriculture is mechanized (U.N., 1977).

Drought in semiarid areas, associated with a decrease in rainfall, is recognized as a recurrent menace in many parts of the world. It is further recognized that desertification usually breaks out at times of drought stress. Parts of Colorado, for example, are semiarid and it is during drought years such as 1977 and 1980 that the stressed environment is most susceptible to degradation. It is the inability of many dryland communities to respond to succeeding droughts, particularly in the low-income developing countries, that represents the human aspect of desertification. Desertification can feed on itself and become self-accelerating and is thus a dynamic process.

As regards longer-term variations in climate, or climatic change, the consensus is that there is no evidence of climatic deterioration as a general explanation to the phenomenon of desertification (Roche, 1973; Mason, 1976; Bunting, Dennet, Elston and Milford, 1976; Kidson, 1977; U.N., 1977; Le Houérou, 1977; Hare, Kates and Warren, 1977). The view is that desert conditions are formed, largely by the actions of man, in areas that, from a strictly climatic point of view, should not be entirely desert. The prevailing climatic conditions are thought to remain constant while biological productivity decreases. As the patchwork of desertification grows and links up, however, it can eventually join with the climatic desert, and the final result will look exactly as if the desert had spread.

At the same time, it is acknowledged that the question of climatic change as a cause of desertification cannot be answered with confidence and it would be unwise to rule out the possibility of change. Furthermore, it is acknowledged that the question has great significance for strategies to combat desertification.

Currently, however, national and international plans to combat the process of desertification (U.N., 1978) concentrate on the modification of human activities. The view expressed at the U.N. Conference was that man already has adequate knowledge and the economic and technical means to bring the advance of desertification to a halt. The strategies recommended to combat desertification include: improved land management; the adoption of insurance schemes against the risk and effects of drought; and the strengthening of science and technology.

Preliminary results of my research, however, indicate that in parts of tropical Africa subject to desertification there is indeed evidence of longer-term climatic deterioration. An implication of this is the possibility that longer-term natural changes in climate have indeed contributed, and continue to contribute, to the degradation of ecological conditions and the reduction in biological potential in these regions. Furthermore, there exists the possibility that since the climatic change already has a long history of evolution it could continue in the future and be a major constraint on development prospects in the affected regions. I should emphasize, however, that this evidence of climatic deterioration applies only to parts of the continent of Africa. Although desertification is a global problem, the question of climatic change and its significance in the process of desertification should be investigated on a regional basis.

## RAINFALL IN TROPICAL AFRICA

Let us start with some basics. Climate can be defined as the fluctuating aggregate of atmospheric conditions characterized by the states and developments at a particular site or over a given area (W.M.O., 1966). There are a number of climatic elements, but I shall deal only with rainfall.

It is important to note that inherent in the above definition of climate is a degree of variability of atmospheric conditions over time: mean values of the elements—the prevailing climate—can remain the same over a period of thirty years, but a degree of variability in the values of the climatic elements from month to month and year to year is quite "normal." Climate is said to change when the statistical characteristics of the parameters that are used to describe climate are inconsistent from one thirty-year period to another. This can take the form of a change in the mean value or in the frequency distribution of the values, or both. It can include fluctuations, trends or discontinuities.

Rainfall varies both spatially and temporally, and there are some fundamentally important relationships between rainfall variations, vegetation types and agricultural crops. It is evident from Figure 8.1, which shows the geographical distribution of mean annual rainfall over Africa for the period 1931–1960, that large variations in rainfall occur over short dis-

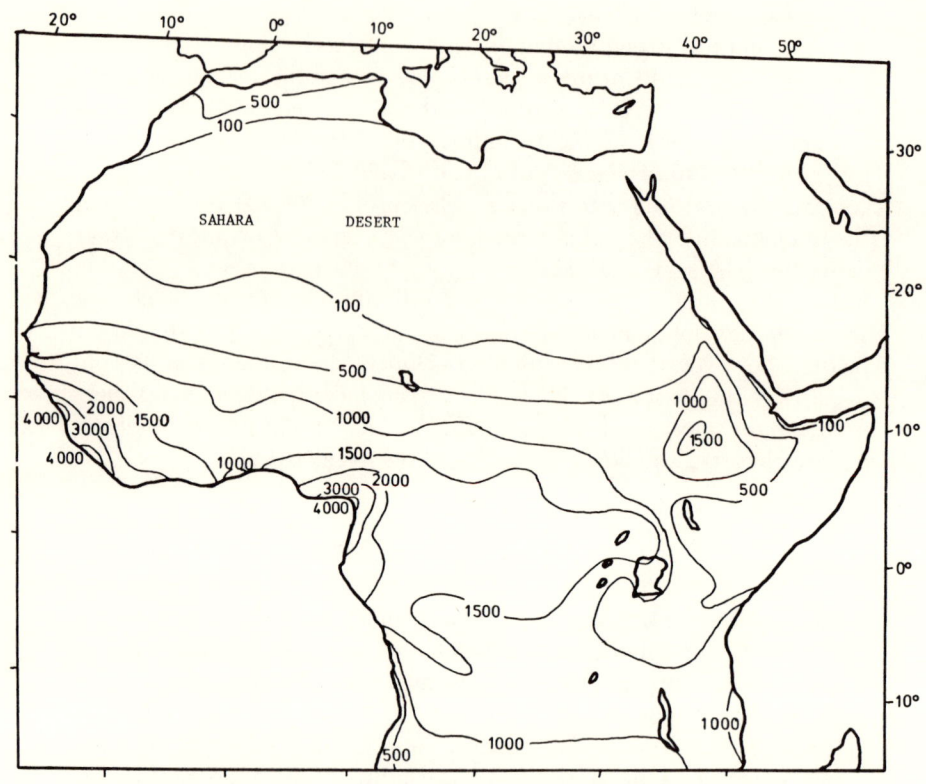

Figure 8.1. Distribution of mean annual rainfall (mm) in Africa (1931–1960).

tances. The Sahara Desert is an extensive area of extremely arid conditions, where mean annual rainfall averages less than about 100 mm. In areas that are characterized by natural desert conditions we do not speak of the process of desertification as being at work. However, it does occasionally rain in these arid areas and then, as I shall show, locusts breed and migrate outwards to less arid areas, where they do degrade the environment.

The amount of annual rainfall is an important factor determining the natural vegetation and the type of crops that can be grown in each region. Each crop has specific water requirements for optimum growth and maximum yield; the geographical distribution of each crop is thus limited by climatic factors. Only about 600 miles to the south of the Sahara Desert mean annual rainfall in West Africa is in excess of 3,000 mm. Clearly, such a steep rainfall gradient must be accompanied by rapid changes in vegetation conditions over short distances. It is these geographical variations in rainfall amounts that also provide the opportunity for regional diversity in crop production; they also impose constraints on expanding the area of production of each crop. The main crops along the southern fringe of the Sahara are sorghum, millet, maize, peanuts, cotton, and rice. It is the variations in rainfall over time that largely determine the interannual variations in crop yield and production.

It is not only annual rainfall that is important in determining ecological conditions and crop yields, but also the seasonal distribution of rainfall. Along the Mediterranean coast of Africa, for example, the wet season is in the cooler months from September through April. As these rains are ending the tropical rains begin to spread northwards and they reach the southern fringe of the Sahara Desert in August. In the equatorial regions there are two seasonal rainfall maxima in April–June and September–October.

This distribution of rainfall is closely related to the global patterns of air circulation and their seasonal changes. In the northern hemisphere winter the mid-latitude westerlies are strong and extend southwards over the Mediterranean and North Africa. Rainfall in these regions is typically associated with eastward moving depressions at the surface, and with the eastward or leading edges of troughs at higher levels in the atmosphere. These winter rains extend as far south as northern Mauritania in the west and the Red Sea and the Horn of Africa in the east.

The rains further south are associated with the seasonally migrating wind belts in the tropics and with the Inter-Tropical Convergence Zone (ITCZ), which separates the dry north-easterlies from the humid equatorial westerlies. Rainfall to the south of the ITCZ is also associated with mobile disturbances in the pressure and wind fields, but in this case the disturbances tend to move from east to west.

These patterns of air circulation in the tropics and in mid-latitudes are linked together dynamically in complex ways that we do not fully understand. It is probably accurate to say that what is happening over tropical Africa is related to what is happening further north over Europe and Asia, and probably also further south over the southern oceans. These regional linkages in atmospheric conditions we call teleconnections, and I shall illustrate some of these and their ecological significance.

In the periods June through August and November through March the rainfall belts in mid-latitudes and in the tropics are quite separate from each other. Even if we look at synoptic weather charts on a day-to-day basis, there is little evidence of direct linkages between the two zones. However, in the transition months of April–May and particularly September–October, direct links between tropical and extra-tropical circulation and rainfall distribution patterns become more evident (Fig. 8.2).

If we look at surface synoptic charts, or at satellite photographs, we can sometimes see bands of cloud and rain extending from West Africa to the Mediterranean coast, or from the Horn of Africa northwards over Ethiopia and Saudi Arabia into the Middle East. It is these situations, when moist tropical air is drawn northwards and feeds into the leading edge of a pressure trough in the mid-latitude westerlies, that rain can occur in the heart of the almost rainless Sahara and Arabian Deserts, and along the desert fringes. Understanding the nature of these rainfall patterns and the linkages between the tropics and the mid-latitudes is of importance in studying the process of desertification in a regional setting.

There is a general consensus that over periods of thousands of years climates do change and the climatic margins of the deserts do shift. Figure 8.3 shows qualitatively the major climatic shifts over the past 25,000 years in the zone to the south of the Sahara Desert. It is evident that climatic conditions have been both wetter and drier than the present day climates. Four or five thousand years ago the Sahara was much greener and more fertile than it is today. Rock carvings and paintings in the central Sahara depict hippopotamus, elephant, giraffe, rhinoceros, antelope and ostrich. Fossilized grain seeds from the edible jujube tree and the southern nettle tree have been found in the same area, and the latter only flourish today where annual rainfall is more than 300 mm (Gerster, 1961).

There is general agreement about the broad features of these major climatic shifts and the fact that they must have been due to natural causes. There are conflicting views, however, as to whether the climatic deterioration about 4,000 years ago took the form of an abrupt step-like transition, or whether there has been progressive desiccation over the past 4,000 years, which might be continuing today. As I indicated earlier, the consensus is that the climates of tropical Africa over at least the past few

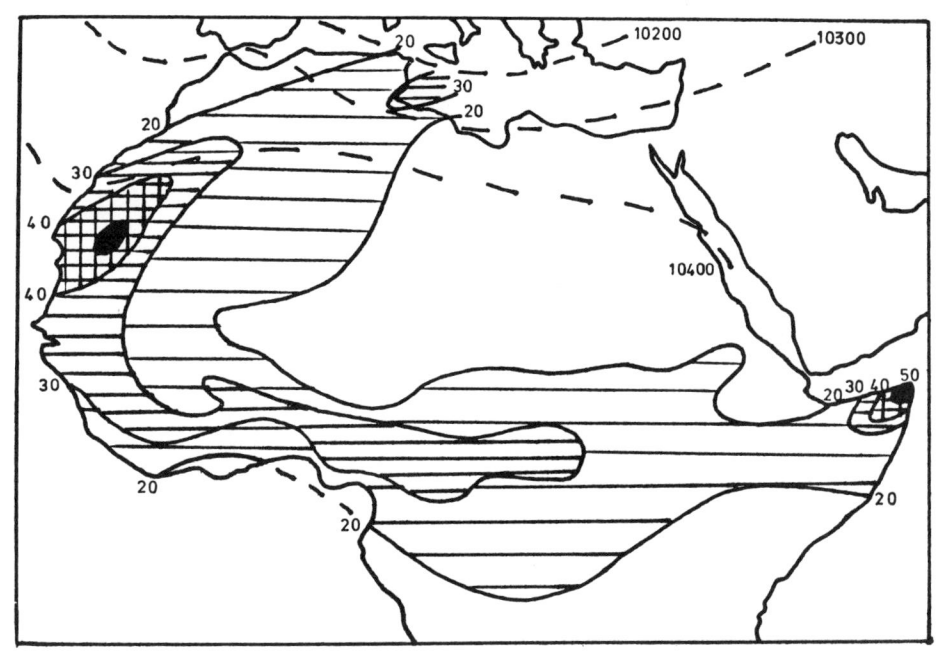

Figure 8.2. Mean September–October rainfall (1931–1960) expressed as a percentage of mean annual rainfall. The dashed lines indicate the mean height, in feet, of the 700 mb surface of constant pressure for the period 8–12 October. A close link between tropical and mid-latitude climates is shown in West Africa.

centuries have been stable. There certainly have been recurring droughts, but the generally accepted view is that the recent droughts have been no more severe than previous ones and that there is no evidence for longer-term climatic deterioration. This has important implications for development planning, for it is assumed that climatic conditions in the future will be similar to those experienced earlier this century. It is this assumption that forms the basis for determining water availability in development planning and in project design and I shall return to this later.

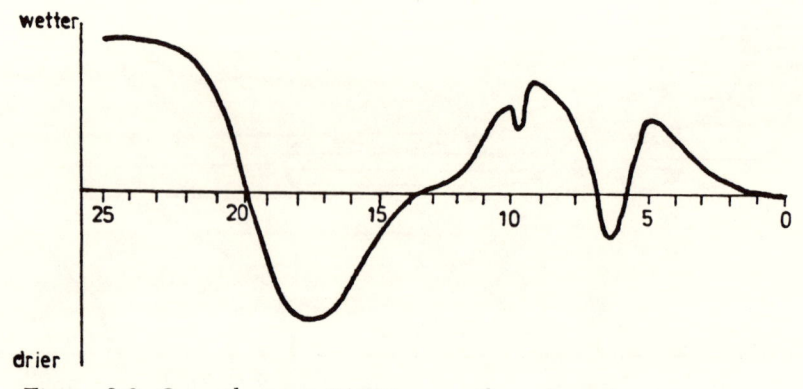

Figure 8.3. Over the past 25,000 years there have been some major climatic shifts. The curve shows the variations in moisture conditions in the zone to the south of the Sahara Desert. Curve from 20,000 BP; from Wickens 1975. Curve prior to 20,000 BP; based on Rognon 1976.

## DESERT LOCUST PLAGUES

While I regard desertification as an important human problem, many of my examples deal with other forms of life that are in greater harmony with the environment and more sensitive to its changes than is man. The sparsity of life in dry lands and the tenuous linkages among the life forms means that small changes can trigger profound effects. The Desert Locust provides an excellent example of a life form in the arid and semiarid areas of the tropics that is sensitive to variations in climate; it can also be an important agent in causing a reduction in vegetation cover and in the process of desertification.

The Desert Locust (*Schistocerca gregaria* Forsk.) has for long been considered one of the world's most serious agricultural pests. The earliest records consist of carvings of locusts on tombs of the Sixth Dynasty (2420–2270 BC) and the eighth plague of Egypt, which is recorded in the book of Exodus (about 1300 BC). In one season in 1954/5 locust damage in Morocco alone was estimated at $12 million. A swarm in Somalia in 1958 measured 400 square miles and contained an estimated forty billion locusts. Because each locust consumes the equivalent of its own body weight in food each day, such a swarm would be capable of eating 80,000 tons of food a day. Given a choice of food locusts are selective, but in areas of sparse vegetation they will devour anything that is green.

The Desert Locust can invade a total area of eleven million square miles, which is twenty percent of the world's land surface and includes the whole or part of sixty-five countries. Figure 8.4 shows the geographical distribution of the Desert Locust.

The level of infestation of locusts varies tremendously from year to year. During quiet spells, which are called recessions, there are only scattered low-density populations and these are restricted to the more arid regions (Fig. 8.1). In other years more than fifty countries are infested by many swarms and such periods are called plagues. Figure 8.5 shows the year-by-year fluctuations since 1860 in the number of countries invaded by swarms. In the earlier years international efforts to control the Desert Locust were not coordinated and the reporting network was not well developed. The dashed lines represent a reconstruction of the probable levels of infestation. It is clear that there is no regular periodicity in the fluctuation between plagues. Despite minor outbreaks in the late 1960s and late 1970s, there has not been a major Desert Locust plague for twenty years, and this is unique in the 120-year historical record of locust plagues. This has provoked the view among locust control experts that man now has the Desert Locust under control. My view is different: it is that the level of infestation by Desert Locust swarms is related to climatic conditions in the semiarid breeding areas and that for the past

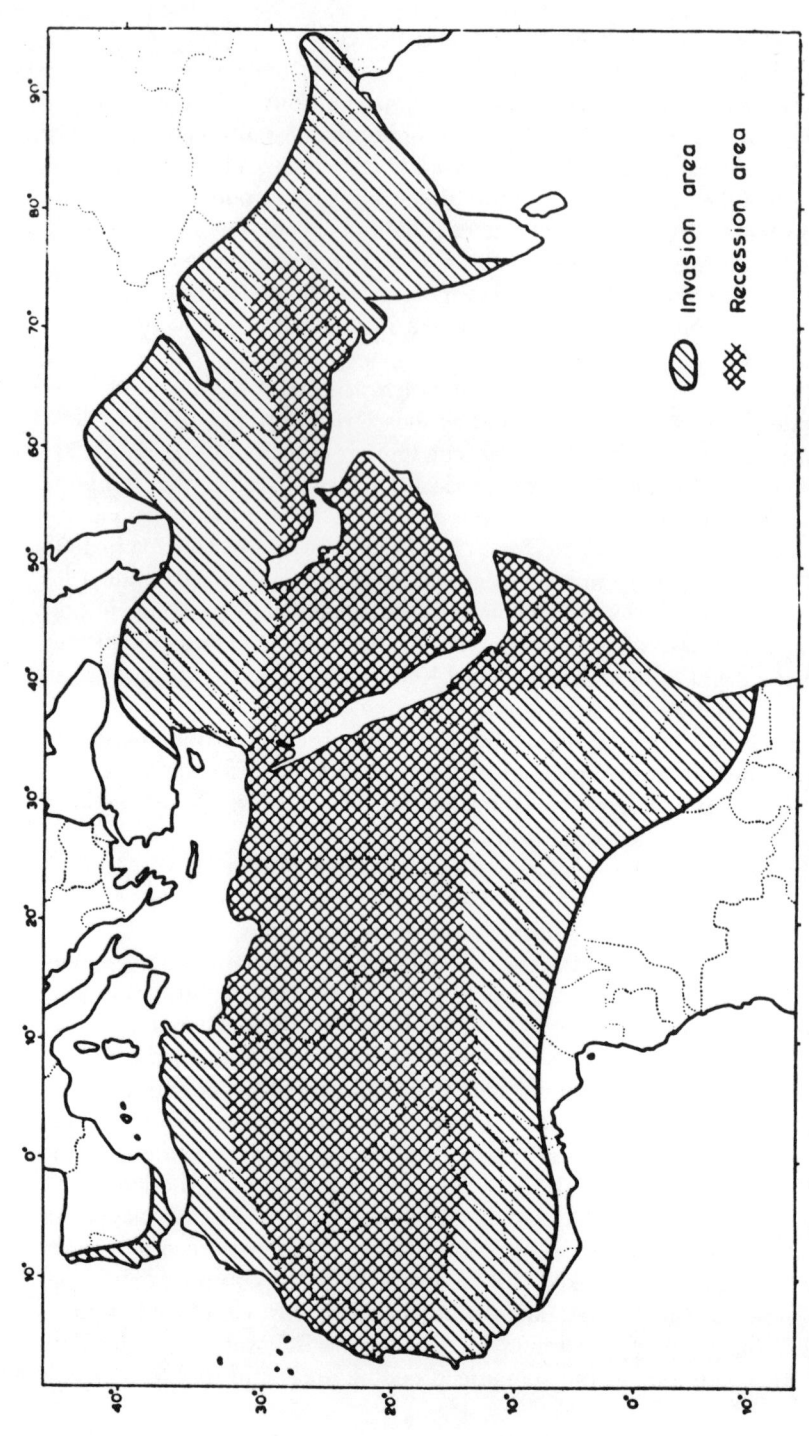

Figure 8.4. The distribution of the Desert Locust. This map shows the maximum area liable to invasion during plagues and the smaller area where the locusts have been found during recessions; from Hemming 1968.

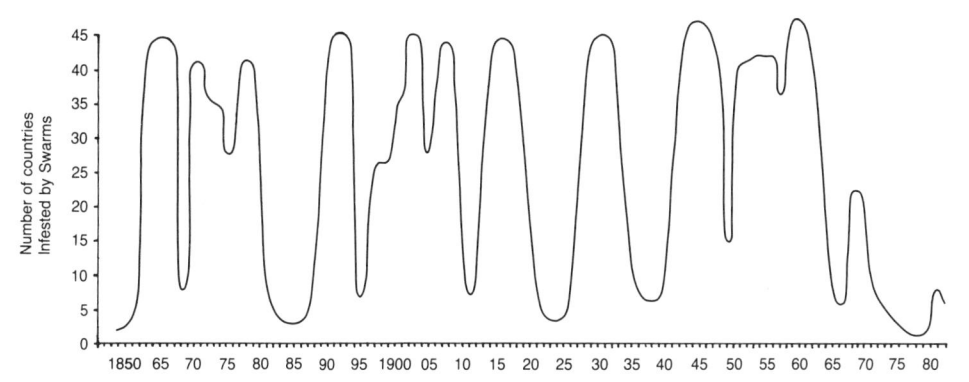

Figure 8.5. Historical record of plagues of the Desert Locust (1860–1980); 1860–1972 from Waloff 1973.

twenty years these conditions have been unfavorable for the build-up and maintenance of a major plague. During this period, it is undeniable that some control operations have been successful, but I do not believe that these operations significantly changed the natural course of events. I shall attempt to substantiate this view, and to do this we must first look at the climatic factors that are of significance in the population dynamics of the Desert Locust.

For successful incubation of the eggs, which are deposited about 4 inches below the surface of the soil, there must be moisture available in the soil—equivalent to about an inch of rainfall. So the first requirement is that there must be good rains in areas that are usually quite dry.

Once the eggs have hatched and the hoppers have progressed to the fledgling stage, they require an air temperature of at least 70°F for flight. This is the second critical climatic constraint. Temperature also acts as a limiting factor in locust development in another way. The incubating period, that is the length of time it takes for the eggs to complete their development, varies greatly from ten to seventy days, depending on the temperature. In North Africa in winter and spring, for example, incubation is greatly retarded, whereas in the summer breeding areas the process is accelerated. If conditions are suitable, three or more generations of locusts can be produced in a year.

The Desert Locust is highly mobile and is transported downwind; hence wind-field patterns are also important in understanding the population dynamics of the species. It is the capacity of the Desert Locust to migrate over thousands of miles that is one of its most important characteristics. This is the reason for the necessity for international cooperation and coordination in research and in control operations. The downwind migration of Desert Locust swarms results in their movement toward and subsequent concentration in areas where low-level winds converge and rain consequently falls. Adult locusts, therefore, are continually arriving in just those areas where the soil is moist and the vegetation green; these being essential requirements for successful breeding and maturation.

As I described earlier, in Africa and southwest Asia the major weather phenomena are seasonal; therefore the major migration and breeding patterns are also seasonal. The to-and-fro movement of meteorological systems during the year results in a circulatory pattern of migration. For example, swarms produced in western Africa south of the Sahara in summer migrate northwards and breed in North Africa the following spring and give rise to new swarms, which then return southwards to the summer breeding grounds.

For the build-up of a plague successful breeding over successive generations is required (Waloff, 1973). As breeding during recession periods is restricted largely to those areas in which the mean annual rainfall is less than 200 mm, it is reasonable to hypothesize that there must be unusually good rains over large areas for a rapid increase in numbers. A few examples will help pull together some of the points I have been making.

I mentioned that winter rainfall in North Africa and the Middle East is associated with disturbances in the mid-latitude westerlies. Figure 8.6 shows seasonal rainfall from 1951–52 to 1969–70 at three widely separated stations in this zone: Beirut in the Lebanon; Riyadh in Saudi Arabia; and Atar in Mauritania. Although mean seasonal rainfall at these stations is about 900, 90 and 25 mm respectively, it is apparent from Figure 8.6 that there are large departures from these mean values at each station, but also that there is a high degree of correlation between the stations. It seems obvious that there must be very large-scale mechanisms controlling the variations in rainfall right across this zone. As the build-up of a locust plague requires successful breeding by successive generations and each generation of locusts can be transported thousands of miles, the fact that good rains do in fact occur over large areas in the same years does provide some evidence for the existence of the necessary favorable environmental conditions.

In order to improve the knowledge of the relationships between locust plague dynamics and rainfall conditions in the breeding areas, I constructed a plague-rainfall model (Fig. 8.7). My method was to determine the average number of countries infested by swarms in each year of each plague from 1904 to 1966, starting with the first year of build-up of each plague. The model shows an average of four countries infested by swarms

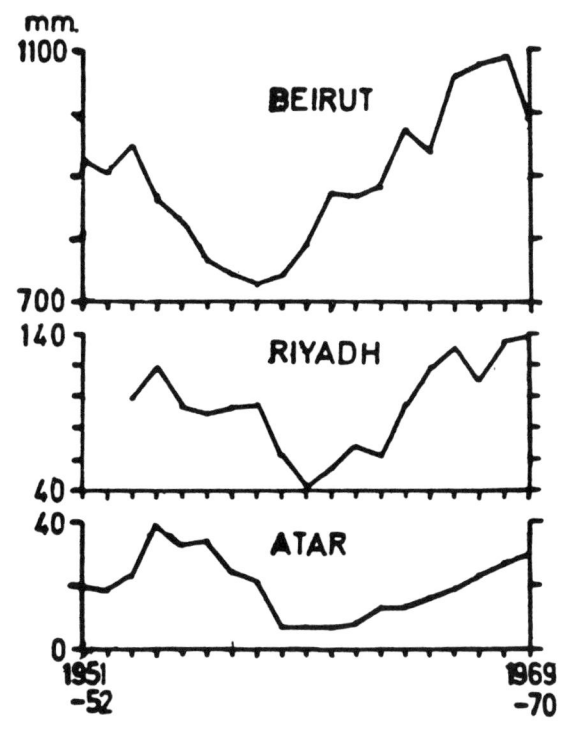

Figure 8.6. Five-year running means of seasonal rainfall (October–May) in millimeters at Beirut (Lebanon), Riyadh (Saudi Arabia), and Atar (Mauritania); from Winstanley 1973.

in the first year, building up to an average of thirty-eight countries in the fifth year and declining to four in the ninth year.

The next step was to determine the rainfall levels in the breeding areas in these years. For each year I calculated the mean percentage of normal (1931–60) seasonal rainfall for stations in the summer breeding areas and a similar figure for stations in the winter–spring breeding areas. I then plotted these regionally averaged rainfall figures on the same diagram showing the locust infestation levels.

It is evident from Figure 8.7 that there are large variations in the level of regionally averaged rainfall during the life span of the average plague. Winter–spring rainfall varies from as much as 25 percent above normal to 30 percent below normal. Rainfall in the summer breeding areas varies from 17 percent above normal to 21 percent below normal. From this model it appears that the buildup of a locust plague is associated with

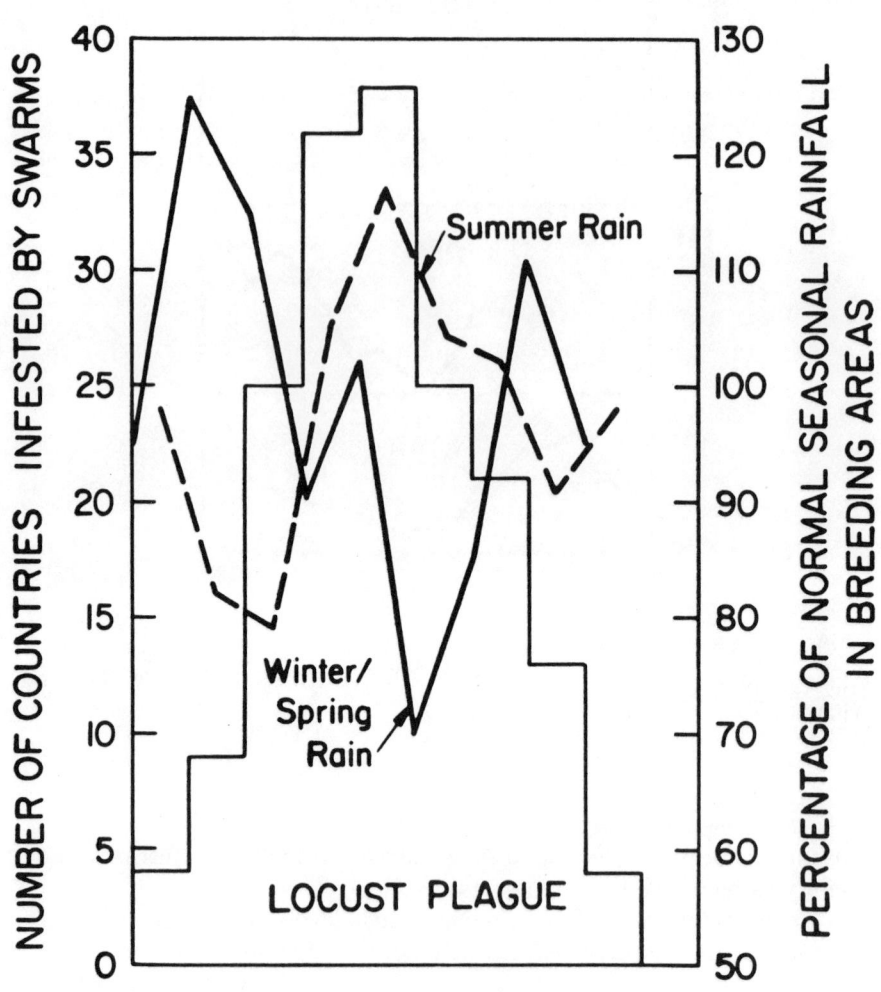

Figure 8.7. Model of infestation levels during a Desert Locust plague in relation to seasonal rainfall in breeding areas; for explanation, see text.

widespread heavy rainfall in the winter–spring breeding areas and that a plague reaches its greatest proportions in association with heavy rainfall in the summer breeding areas. It seems that a plague declines when winter–spring rainfall is much below normal and summer rainfall also declines.

What are important are the relationships between seasonal rainfall conditions in different parts of the extensive breeding zone: rainfall in some parts is dependent specifically upon meteorological conditions in the mid-latitude westerlies, in other parts upon conditions in the tropics, and still others upon interactions between the two. It seems that the population level of the Desert Locust is dependent upon rainfall conditions in widely separated, but complementary, breeding areas in the arid and semiarid tropics and sub-tropics. There is no one "outbreak" area in which swarms are formed. It is these variations in rainfall that are very important in determining overall levels of biological productivity in the same areas.

This is only a tentative model, for it is difficult to obtain historical rainfall data for many of the arid and semiarid breeding areas, and the number of stations used in the analysis is not constant during each plague. However, plague dynamics are not well understood and these preliminary results do warrant further investigation and research. I believe that we will not be able to reasonably determine whether man has the Desert Locust under control until we know more about the natural factors associated with upsurge and declines of plagues.

I mentioned earlier that rainfall in these regions is associated with air circulation patterns, and that these are important in transporting the locusts from one breeding area to the next. A brief description of a cyclonic storm that developed over North Africa in September 1969 provides a good illustration of the significance to the Desert Locust of one type of synoptic system. At 1200 GMT on 23 September 1969, the storm was near its peak (Winstanley, 1970). The storm subsequently moved westward, which is highly unusual, and produced about five inches of rain in Malta on the twenty-third and five inches in Biskra on the twenty-eighth. Total September rainfall at Biskra amounted to almost twelve inches, as against the average figure of less than one inch.

It is the warm southerly winds ahead of such depressions that frequently transport locusts northward from their summer breeding areas in West Africa to their winter–spring breeding areas in North Africa. Behind the cold front temperatures drop quickly from over 100°F to about 75°F and locust flight is greatly restricted.

This storm was associated with a slow-moving disturbance—known as a cut-off low—at a height of about 18,000 feet in the atmosphere and a band of rain extended northwards from the tropics into the Mediterranean area. It was this rain over Mauritania and the Spanish Sahara, and similar rains during subsequent weeks, that permitted the successful breeding of the Desert Locust in these areas.

Another example illustrates the complexity of meteorological conditions in another part of this extensive arid zone, in the Red Sea area. For many years it was known that locusts breed on the winter–spring rains that occur along the Red Sea coastal plains of Saudi Arabia, fly across the Red Sea, breed again on spring–summer rains in Ethiopia or Sudan and from there disperse throughout West, East, Central and North Africa. What was puzzling was how the locusts were able to fly across the Red Sea, when the winds reported at the synoptic stations on the Red Sea coast were consistently blowing in either a southerly or northerly direction. To solve this problem, a field operation was mounted to study the behavior of locusts in relation to meteorological conditions. This involved the establishment, under difficult conditions, of a network of pilot-balloon stations and thermohygrographs, and the use of a mobile low-level radiosonde and a light aircraft fitted with Doppler radar to measure winds.

What we discovered was a complex wind structure on the Red Sea coastal plain in which local katabatic, anabatic, sea-breeze and land-breeze circulations interacted with the synoptic scale wind field, which along the Red Sea is characterized by northerlies and southerlies separated by a strong low-level convergence zone. What we determined was that locusts, which breed on highly variable winter–spring rains along the southern Red Sea coastal plain, move northwards with the synoptic-scale, orographically channeled southerly winds. From here they can be transported westwards across the Red Sea either on the easterly winds associated with the upper-level return flows of the sea-breeze and anabatic circulations between about 6,000 and 11,000 feet, or with strong synoptic easterlies which spread across from central Arabia behind southward-moving cold fronts.

In this case, too, rains in the Red Sea area are associated with the spread of moist air northwards from the tropics as it feeds into disturbances in the mid-latitude westerlies. After successful breeding, the complex wind-field patterns allow the locusts to be transported across a wide sea from one continent to another. One agent in the process of environmental degradation is thus exported.

Over the last decade per capita food production in sub-Sahara Africa has declined by 10 percent or more. Population in the region is expected to double in only twenty-five years and the occurrence of a major Desert Locust plague, or plagues, in the future could have serious implications for food supply and could exacerbate the problems of environmental degradation. Population levels of the Desert Locust are strongly determined by climatic conditions and the Desert Locust continues to be a major threat to human welfare.

## PALAEARCTIC BIRD MIGRANTS

Some species of birds also migrate seasonally over thousands of miles. The Whitethroat *(Sylvia communis)* is one species that breeds in Western Europe in spring, migrates to the zone along the southern fringe of the Sahara Desert in the fall, spends winter there and returns northward the following spring.

In Britain annual fluctuations in bird populations are monitored by the Common Bird Census of the British Trust for Ornithology. It is known that the Whitethroat left Britain and Western Europe in normal numbers in the fall of 1968, but the Common Bird Census taken in 1969 showed that the population level had declined by about 77 percent (Winstanley, Spencer and Williamson, 1974). Similar population reductions were recorded throughout Western and Central Europe. Tens of millions of Whitethroats were lost. Furthermore, since the 1969 collapse, the Whitethroat has shown no sign of recovery.

The conclusion of our research was that the cause of the rapid decrease in the number of Whitethroats in Europe was high mortality in their wintering quarters between about $12°-18°N$ in West Africa, where a reduction in rainfall upset the ecological balance. In the summer of 1968 seasonal rainfall in this region averaged 25 percent below normal and rainfall still has not reverted to previous higher levels. Although species can adapt to gradual environmental changes, it seems that rapid and sustained changes can alter population levels drastically. The Whitethroat, too, thus appears as a link in ecological changes brought about at times of low rainfall. Again, what is illustrated here is that climate-induced ecological changes in the semiarid areas of Africa can also have repercussions in distant regions. It is the migratory nature of insects and birds that provides the link between the regions.

In the case of the Whitethroat it appears that it was a victim of the same climatic factors that contribute to the process of desertification, rather than itself being an active agent in the process. It is an example of a reduced level of biological productivity during drought periods.

## FISHERIES ALONG THE SOUTHERN EDGE OF THE SAHARA

Some fish, too, migrate seasonally, although in the zone with which we are concerned the distances involved are not great. As unusual as it might sound, fishing is an important activity in the semiarid zone along the southern fringe of the Sahara. Fish is an important source of protein and of export revenue. Inland fishermen, as well as nomads and settled agriculturalists, are dependent upon the rains and the amount of water in the lakes and rivers.

In 1968 the total production of freshwater fish in Mauritania, Mali, Senegal, Niger, Chad and Upper Volta was about a quarter of a million tons. From 1968 to 1973, however, rainfall decreased and severe droughts occurred: the discharge of the River Niger at Koulikoro, for example, decreased from 672 cu.ft.sec.$^{-1}$ to 106 cu.ft.sec.$^{-1}$; and the area of Lake Chad was reduced from 9,000 square miles to 3,300 square miles (Winstanley, 1975).

It was the virtual disappearance of the annual floods on the Senegal, Niger and Chari Rivers and extremely low water levels during the dry season that seriously disrupted the biology of the fish, and particularly their reproductive cycle. Normally, during the rising floodwaters in summer the fish spread by lateral migration over the floodplains and reproduce in the braided channels. As the floods recede there is a return migration to the main river and other permanent water bodies. In general, fish growth is positively correlated with the intensity of the flooding and poor growth results from severe drawdown conditions. Fluctuations in catch from year to year can thus be related to differences in flood intensity in previous years.

During the severe drought years the main breeding grounds of many species either simply disappeared, or the immersion period was too short to permit successful reproduction and growth. As the headwaters of these rivers are in the humid areas further south, it is obvious that rainfall must have been below normal in these regions also. The result was a 50 to 80 percent reduction in the fish catch on these rivers. There was also a two to threefold increase in the price of fish. However, this did not compensate for the lower catch and fishermen's income and export revenue declined. In the case of Mali, there was a 45 percent drop in the exported value of fish from 1969 to 1973.

The effect on Lake Chad fisheries, however, was quite different. Although the area of the lake and possibly the total fish population decreased, the shrinkage of the water body permitted intensive exploitation of fish stocks and from 1969 to 1973 there was a fourfold increase in the catch on the northern lake and nearly a threefold increase on the southern lake. But this higher catch was of little benefit to people in the Sahelian countries most severely affected by drought, as about 80 percent of the fish produced on the lake is consumed further south in Nigeria. Clearly, future rainfall conditions and knowledge of these conditions will be important factors in determining the rational exploitation and management of biological resources in tropical Africa.

As with the Whitethroat, this is another example of reduced biological productivity during drought periods.

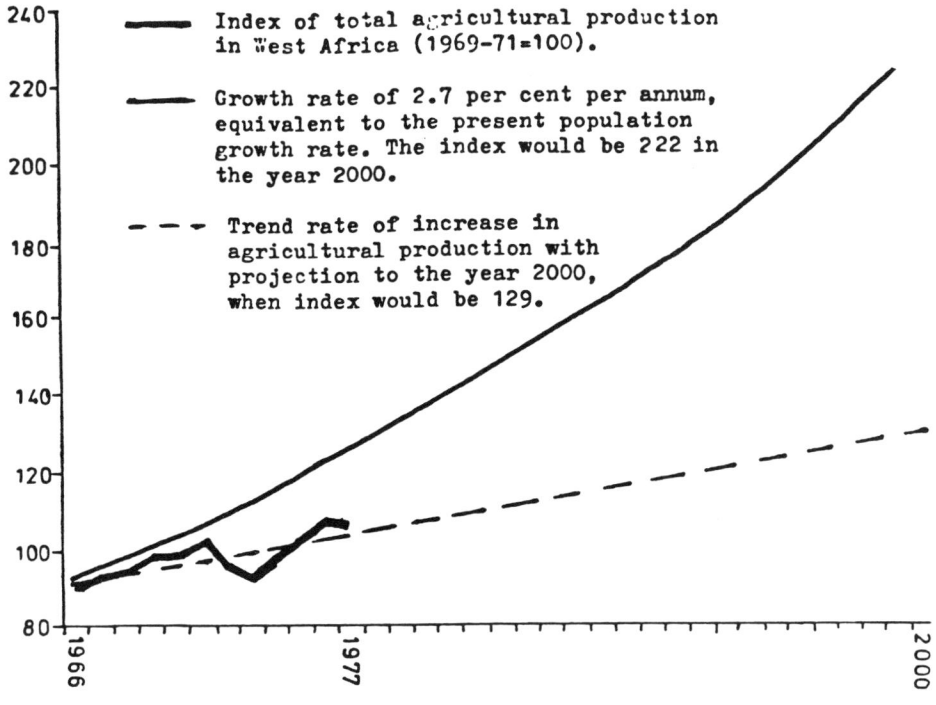

Figure 8.8. Annual agricultural production in West Africa (1966–1977).

## DROUGHT AND AGRICULTURE

Irrigation can offset the effects of low rainfall, but only a small percentage of the land in tropical Africa is irrigated. Food and agricultural production, therefore, is highly dependent upon the rains which, as I have shown, are highly variable. Rather than deal with specific crops or countries, I have produced a regional index of total agricultural production (food and cash crops) in seventeen countries in West Africa (Fig. 8.8) and these include the whole range of ecological conditions from semiarid to tropical rain forest. From Figure 8.8 it is apparent that the rate of increase in agricultural production during the 1970s failed to keep pace with the

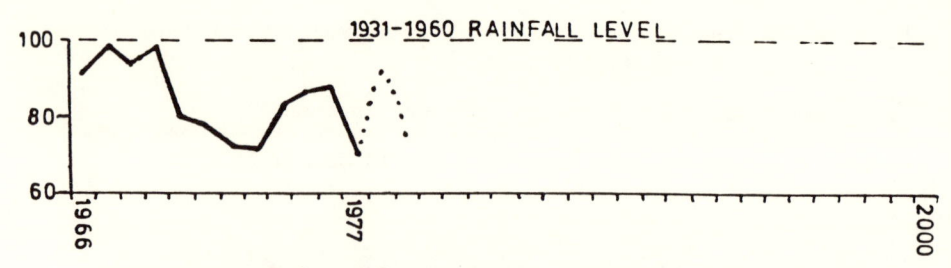

Figure 8.9. Annual rainfall in West Africa (1931–1960 = 100) using data from sixty-four stations in eleven countries.

population growth rate. Consequently there was a decrease in per capita food production in many countries, contributing to widespread starvation in the Sahelian countries in 1972 and 1973 and necessitating much higher food imports for many countries.

In Figure 8.9 I have produced a regional index of mean annual rainfall for the period 1966 to 1979. From a comparison between Figures 8.8 and 8.9, it is obvious that persistently below-normal rainfall has been a major factor in the slow and fluctuating increase in agricultural production; even from 1978 to the present, rainfall has not recovered to the 1931–60 levels.

Although maybe another 10 percent, or so, of the land in West Africa could be irrigated to reduce the threat of drought, it is extremely costly to develop major irrigation projects. Particularly in the Sahelian countries, thousands of wells have been dug in an attempt to increase water supply and combat desertification. However, well digging often has tended to exacerbate the problems of environmental degradation and desertification. In any event, most agricultural production in tropical Africa will continue to be directly dependent on the rains.

## CLIMATIC CHANGE

I am now in a position to return to some of the statements I made earlier concerning the consensus on the stability of climates in this part of the world. The consensus that emerged in the mid-seventies was that the decrease in rainfall from the late 1960s to 1973 was merely a short-term phenomenon. The rains were expected to revert to higher levels. It is clear from Figure 8.9 that this has not happened. There have now been sixteen consecutive years when the regional rainfall index for these countries has been below the 1931–60 "normal" level. If rainfall is regarded as basically a random variable, then six consecutive years with below-normal rainfall can be expected to occur on average about once every sixty or seventy years. However, the statistical odds against the occurrence of ten to sixteen consecutive years with below-normal rainfall are astronomical and can hardly be considered to be within a reasonably expected frequency under stable climatic conditions. It is this type of change in the frequency of extreme climatic events that suggests a change in climate.

As a final consideration, attention needs to be given to the evidence I have of longer-term deterioration in climatic conditions over large parts of tropical Africa. I should like to stress that we do not have a climate prediction capability and that the probability of further climatic change is unknown. Nevertheless, longer-term climatic deterioration has not previously been identified and the subject is controversial. I suggest that we cannot ignore the possibility of further climatic deterioration, that this would have serious consequences for development in the region and that there is a need to evaluate this evidence and to assess its significance.

By analyzing the few available rainfall records back to the 1850s and gleaning quantitative climatic information from the diaries and reports of the early explorers, I have been able to reconstruct climatic conditions over large areas of tropical Africa for the past 125 years. What emerges are two distinctive patterns of climatic change. In those areas that are characterized by a single rainfall maximum in summer (which includes much of the humid areas of West Africa that are source regions for the major rivers, as well as the semiarid regions bordering the southern Sahara and extending into Ethiopia) there is statistical evidence, significant at the 95 percent level of confidence, of a linear trend towards lower rainfall, amounting to a decrease of between 25 and 40 percent over this period. There is considerable variability about this linear decrease, but the recent droughts are seen to be the most severe on record. As would be expected, a similar historical reconstruction of river flow in tropical Africa also shows a linear trend and this amounts to a decrease of about 50 percent since the 1850s.

The other pattern of climatic change has occurred in areas with a quite different climatic régime and the change is of opposite sign, that is, there is evidence of a longer-term trend towards higher rainfall. In the relatively small areas centered around Accra in southern Ghana, Luanda in Angola, and in the border country around northern Kenya, western Somalia and southern Ethiopia, the positive linear trend shows an increase in rainfall and river flow of some 50 to 60 percent from the 1860s to the 1960s. These three regions are characterized by a bimodal seasonal rainfall distribution with peaks in April–June and September–November in contrast to the single summer maximum in the region characterized by a decrease in rainfall.

What appears to have been happening is that the tropical rains in the northern summer have become increasingly restricted in their northward penetration, thus producing less rainfall in the regions with a maximum in July–August and a greater accumulation of rainfall in those regions with maxima in spring and fall. These climate changes, although of opposite sign, form a coherent whole in explaining the historical evolution of climates in tropical Africa.

By comparing the rainfall levels shown in Figure 8.9 with the summer rainfall levels shown in Figure 8.7 to be associated with the locust plague model, it can be seen that climatic conditions since the termination of the last major plague in the early sixties have been very different from the conditions typically associated with plagues. The model in Figure 8.7 shows that major locust infestations have been associated with rainfall in the summer breeding areas some 5 to 17 percent above normal. Since the 1960s summer rainfall in West Africa has been 2 to 29 percent below normal. While the region covered by these data does not include the whole of the locust breeding areas, it does represent an important part. As stated earlier, my view is that more analysis of changes in natural environmental conditions and their relationships to locust populations is required before we can say with any degree of confidence that man has the Desert Locust under control.

Furthermore, the cyclonic storm and heavy rains that occurred over North Africa in September 1969 and which were important for locust breeding, can also be viewed in a broader perspective. The band of cloud and moisture that extended across the Sahara Desert emanated from West Africa where, as we have now seen from an analysis of the historical climate record, rainfall in spring and fall in the late 1960s was the heaviest for at least 100 years. Heavy rains in the Mediterranean area, therefore, resulted from a combination of unusual meteorological conditions in both the mid-latitude westerlies and in the Tropics.

Assessment of the significance of this evidence of longer-term climatic change is important in many areas of development planning, including water resource projects, agricultural planning, the management of inland fisheries and in formulating plans to combat desertification. In determining future water availability, the general practice is to assume constant mean rainfall and then to calculate expected frequencies of extreme events. Should the trend toward lower rainfall continue in the areas with a summer rainfall maximum, then there will clearly be far less water available in the future than is generally anticipated.

In the regions where rainfall had been increasing for at least a century up to the 1960s, rainfall in the 1970s was far lower than would have been expected from a continuation of the historical trends. There is a possibility, that is difficult to quantify, that the tropical rains in Africa have now become so restricted in their range of seasonal migration that in future lower rainfall might also be expected in those regions that until the 1960s had experienced a trend towards higher rainfall.

I can give a practical example to illustrate the potential significance of this point. In the early 1970s it was realized that by the end of the decade the hydro-plant at Akasombo on the River Volta in Ghana would be operating at full potential and new energy sources would be required. The main options were between oil-fired thermal plants, utilizing imported oil, and a second hydro-plant downstream from Akasombo. To determine the economic feasibility of building a second hydro-plant, an estimate of water availability to the year 2000 was required. Data on the discharge of the River Volta, available since 1929, showed that the lowest twenty-year discharge value was 41,580 cu.ft.sec$^{-1}$ and it appeared that there would be sufficient water available to justify building a second hydro-plant. It has subsequently been built at Kpongo. From 1972 to 1978 (n = 7), however, the average discharge of the Volta was only 28,000 cu.ft.sec$^{-1}$, compared with the previous lowest seven-year value of 35,400 cu.ft.sec$^{-1}$. For the average discharge from 1972 to the end of the century to reach the historical value of 45,800 cu.ft.sec$^{-1}$, the discharge over the period 1979 to 2000 will have to average about 51,000 cu.ft.sec$^{-1}$.

The point is that thirty to seventy years of historical records of rainfall and river flow in tropical Africa are not an adequate basis on which to determine future water availability. Rainfall from now to the year 2000 may indeed be high and result in a twenty-year mean discharge not significantly different from the long-term average value. However, in view of the evidence of longer-term changes in rainfall discussed previously, I suggest that we should not be too optimistic about a return to higher rainfall. I suggest that the evidence for these historical patterns of climatic change, and the possibility of their continuation, be evaluated in feasibility studies for all major water resource projects in tropical Africa. While the use of water in the major rivers can be important in irrigation development and in combating the effects of drought, it is important to remember that the amount of water available in these rivers is determined by the very same patterns of rainfall variability with which the droughts are associated. Variations in climate determine total water availability.

## CONCLUSIONS

I hope I have shown that the level of rainfall is of fundamental importance in determining the level of biological productivity and ecological conditions in Africa. As agriculture is the most important sector of the economy in many countries and agricultural productivity is closely dependent upon rainfall conditions, climatic factors also become important exogenous variables in economic growth and development. Some 75 percent of the economically active population in tropical Africa are directly dependent upon agriculture for their livelihood, as against less than 4 percent in the United States, and agricultural products contribute up to 90 percent of export revenues. It is precisely because the agricultural sector is so dominant that variations in rainfall have such great impacts on these societies and economies. In the U.S., on the other hand, severe drought such as occurred in 1980 has a large impact in dollar value, but this represents only a small percentage of the gross national product of the country. This is because the economy is so diversified and the agricultural sector, which is the most sensitive to climatic variations, is not dominant. In sub-Sahara Africa, population is expected to double in only twenty-five years and it is inevitable that pressure on resources will increase. Even if the rains were to return to "normal," the process of environmental degradation and desertification would be difficult to control. If the rains do not return to normal, the problems will be compounded.

I submit that understanding the nature of climatic variations is important in studying the process of desertification and in formulating appropriate plans of action. However, there are also other causes of desertification and climatic variations also have far wider significance and greater impacts than merely in the area of desertification. What we are talking about in general are interactions between man and the variable environment in which he lives. The greater the understanding of these complex linkages and of the nature and causes of environmental change, the greater will be the opportunity for implementing successful development strategies that are designed to exploit climatic resources and yet also take into account the risks inherent in the variable nature of climate and the uncertainties associated with imperfect knowledge.

## REFERENCES

Bunting, A. H., Dennett, M. D., Elston, J., and Milford, J. R. (1976) Rainfall Trends in the West Africa Sahel, *Quarterly Journal of the Royal Meteorological Society*, 102, 59–64.

Gerster, G. (1961) *Sahara: Desert of Destiny*, Coward–McCann, 302 pp.

Glantz, M. H. (ed.) (1977) *Desertification: Environmental Degradation in and around Arid Lands*, Westview Press, Boulder, Colorado, 346 pp.

Hare, F. K. (1977) Connections between Climate and Desertification, *Environmental Conservation*, 4, No. 2, 81–90.

Hare, F. K., Kates, R. W., and Warren, A. (1977) The Making of Deserts: Climate, Ecology and Society, *Economic Geography*, 53, 332–346.

Hemming, C. F. (1968) *The Locust Menace*, Anti-Locust Research Center, London, 31 pp.

Kidson, J. (1977) African Rainfall and its Relation to the Upper Air Circulation, *Quarterly Journal of the Royal Meteorological Society*, 103, 441–456.

Le Houérou, H. N. (1977) The Nature and Causes of Desertification, in *Desertification* (Glantz, 1977), Westview Press, pp. 17–38.

Lamb, H. H. (1972) *Climate: Present, Past and Future*, Vol. I, Methuen, 613 pp.

Mason, B. J. (1976) Towards the Understanding and Prediction of Climate Variations, *Quarterly Journal of the Royal Meteorological Society*, 102, 473–498.

Meadows, D. H., et al. (1972) *The Limits to Growth*, Universe Books, 205 pp.

Rapp, A. (1974) *A Review of Desertization in Africa—Water, Vegetation and Man*, Secretariat for International Ecology, Stockholm, SIES Report No. 1, 77 pp.

Roche, M. (1973) Note sur la Secheresse Actuelle en Afrique de l'Ouest, Report of the 1973 Symposium on Drought in Africa (eds., D. Dalby and R. J. Harrison Church), Center for African Studies, University of London, 53–61.

Rognon, P. (1976) Essai d'Interpretation des Variations Climatiques au Sahara depuis 40,000 ans, *Rev. Geogr. Phys. Géol. Dyn.*, 18, 251–282.

United Nations (1977) *Desertification: Its Causes and Consequences*, Pergamon, 448 pp.

United Nations (1978) *United Nations Conference on Desertification: Round-Up, Plan of Action and Resolutions*, U.N., 43 pp.

Waloff, Z. (1973) Some Temporal Characteristics of Desert Locust Plagues, Draft Report, Center for Overseas Pest Research, London, 36 pp.

Wickens, G. E. (1975) Changes in the Climate and Vegetation of the Sudan 20,000 B.P., *Boissiera*, 24, 43–65.

Winstanley, D. (1970) The North African Flood Disaster, September 1969, *Weather*, 25, No. 9, 390–403.

Winstanley, D. (1973) Recent Rainfall Trends in Africa, the Middle East and India, *Nature*, 243, No. 5407, 464–465.

Winstanley, D., Spencer, R., and Williamson, K. (1974) Where have all the Whitethroats gone? *Bird Study*, 21, No. 1, 1–14.

Winstanley, D. (1975) *Fisheries along the Southern Edge of the Sahara*, Unpublished report, Environment Canada, 1975, 13 pp.

W.M.O. (1966) *International Meteorological Vocabulary*, W.M.O., T.P. 91.

# 9

# ANOTHER LOOK AT THE CONCEPT OF DESERTIFICATION

Michel M. Verstraete

National Center for Atmospheric Research
Boulder, Colorado

Desertification is, etymologically speaking, the making of desert conditions. Many individuals and organizations have been involved with this concept, which has received a number of interpretations over the years, especially during the last decade. Now that we have some perspective on this issue, it is appropriate to have a closer look at the emergence and evolution of this concept, particularly in view of the central controversy that emerged concerning the causes of desertification.

## EMERGENCE OF DESERTIFICATION AS AN ISSUE

The concern about environmental degradation in arid and semiarid regions has been recurrent throughout history. Without going back to ancient times, one can point to documents that show a preoccupation in the first few decades of this century, such as the "Interim Report of the South African Drought Investigation Commission, April 1922" (reproduced in Glantz, 1977), or the works of Stebbing (1935, 1938, quoted in Glantz, 1977b) in Africa, not to mention the large literature available on the Dust Bowl that affected much of the United States in the thirties (Lockeretz, 1978).

But the word *desertification* itself was apparently introduced by Aubreville (1949). As a forester, he was observing the progressive replacement of tropical and subtropical forests in Africa by savannas, a process he called savannization. He identified both fire and deforestation by local populations as the main perturbing factors that allowed more arid conditions to set in, and used the term desertification to designate extreme cases of savannization, characterized by severe soil erosion, changes in the physical and chemical properties of the soils, and invasion of more xeric plant species.

Although Aubreville's book must have been, and probably still is an important contribution to the field of tropical forestry, the original meaning of the word desertification, and in particular its application to any ecosystem, however humid, was not generally accepted: ten years later, Le Houerou (1959) introduced the word desertization to emphasize the role of human activity in arid and semiarid regions bordering actual deserts.

Neither word was really popular, though, as evidenced by the fact that no dictionary included either of them until very recently. Meanwhile, scientific research on the problems of these regions continued, in particular under the auspices of the United Nations Educational, Scientific and Cultural Organization (UNESCO).

It was not until the late sixties and early seventies that the word desertification became widely used, in a different context. For a series of consecutive years in that period, the monsoon rains that bring the essential water to the Sudano-Sahelian region of Africa were once again grossly insufficient (severe droughts did occur before, most notably around 1913 and in the 1940s). Although the severity of the drought depended very much on latitude, annual rainfall amounts decreased dramatically in many parts of Africa north of the Equator (Nicholson, 1981).

Interestingly enough, the drought and its associated sufferings were not covered in the mass media until the newsworthiness of this issue had been firmly established, even though a number of technical reports from various national and international agencies were available and reported severe and degrading conditions in this part of Africa (Morentz, 1980). And thereafter, the extent and gravity of the problem may have been grossly exaggerated (Simon, 1980), or incorrectly analysed (Lappe and Collins, 1977). Furthermore, the profound origin of the economic, social, and political disruptions that plagued the Sahelian countries, in particular the "famine" situations, was variously interpreted either as being the consequence of the drought (Brown, 1981), or as the result of perturbations in the world markets and international relations, as well as the local social and economic structures (Garcia, 1981).

According to many authors, the governmental and public attention given to desertification is generally attributed to the social, political, economic, or environmental implications of the drought that affected much of West Africa from 1968 to 1973 (Glantz, 1977a, or Biswas, 1978). How this drought eventually led to a concern about desertification remains somewhat obscure, although several elements can be identified.

First, the drought in the Sahel was believed to have ended in 1975 or 1976 (Winstanley, 1976, or Newell et al., 1976), while the degradation was seen as continuing. This perception that the degradation was chronic while the drought lasted only a few years may have prompted the need for a wider concept such as desertification.

It is important to realize that the actual situation is rather more complex because annual precipitation levels started to decrease in the early sixties (Hare, 1977), and the drought may have been much longer than usually assumed. On the other hand, these same precipitation levels never returned to those common in the fifties, which were exceptionally high (Winstanley, 1973), so that it is not quite clear whether the drought in the Sahel ever ended or not.

This point is important because the same argument of a short-lived drought versus longer term degradation has been used later to "prove" that the drought was not a primary cause of desertification, but merely an aggravating factor. There is little doubt that drought is not the only factor in desertification, but its importance cannot be discounted on the basis of such an incorrect perception either.

Another argument that is sometimes made implicitly for using a concept wider than drought is that the degradation seemed more extensive than that associated with similar precipitation deficits at other times or in other parts of the world. Some other factors than drought must therefore have been at work.

Whether or not other factors are involved may be difficult to establish, however, because the climatic conditions are never quite comparable; for example, the 1913 drought in the Sahel was more severe but less widespread than the 1972 one. Moreover, the observed differences in the impacts of such "comparable" climatic perturbations might very well result from inherent differences in vulnerability or resilience of the concerned societies to a given climatic perturbation.

Also, the late sixties and early seventies were characterized, in Europe and the United States, by an increasing awareness and concern about environmental problems, as evidenced by the holding of the Stockholm Conference on the Human Environment (1972), or the publication of the Report of the Club of Rome on "The Limits to Growth." This interest in environmental issues may have helped us to view the problems of the Sahel from a broader ecological perspective, rather than just as the consequences of drought.

In any case, the scale of the problem and the complexity of its consequences prompted the United Nations General Assembly (GA) to address the problem (Warren, 1978). In addition to creating a special office within its structure (now known as the United Nations Sudano-Sahelian Office, UNSO) to organize the recovery from the drought, the GA also decided to convene a world conference on desertification, which was held in Nairobi in 1977. Numerous documents and reports were prepared for this conference, including a World Map of Desertification and a number of case studies (Verstraete, 1983).

Perhaps the boldest step taken by this conference was the adoption of a Plan of Action to Combat Desertification (PACD), whose major objective was to stop (as opposed to recover from) desertification by the year 2,000. The United Nations Environment Programme (UNEP) was assigned the role of overseeing the implementation of this PACD through its specially created Desertification Branch and UNSO, which continues to care for most of the Sahelian countries and a few others.

The United Nations Conference on Desertification (UNCOD) was meant to be a technical conference (UNEP, 1977), but it became politicized because it was quickly recognized that this issue was not independent of the more general problems of international relations, economic development and other global issues.

For example, some of the detailed analyses commissioned for the UNCOD showed the importance of social, political, and economic factors in the degradation of the environment (Warren et al., 1977, or Kates et al., 1977, for example). Even the long-term consequences of colonialism (Renault-Benmiloud, 1974) or the effects of international conflicts (see in particular the Resolutions of the UNCOD: United Nations, 1978, p. 38–41) were perceived by some as important reasons for the catastrophe. This evolution may also have forced a more global view of the situation, calling in turn for a much broader concept than drought to describe it.

Finally, it became apparent that the very large sums of money (at least US $400 million per year for twenty years, according to the United Nations, 1978) which were estimated to be necessary to stop further desertification would have to come from the developed, or the oil and mineral-rich countries, or both. What started as an environmental problem in drought-stricken countries of West Africa became an element of the North-South dialogue on development.

## THE DEFINITIONS OF DESERTIFICATION

The concept of desertification received a number of interpretations since the term was first introduced in 1949. In fact, if there is one thing most authors will agree upon, it is to recognize that there is no general agreement on the meaning, nature, and extent of desertification.

A few quotations of published definitions will suffice to make the point:

(1) "Desertification is the impoverishment of arid, semi-arid, and

some subhumid ecosystems by the impact of man's activities. [. . .] Desertification is the result of land abuse." (Garduno, 1977). [Emphasis on human land use].

(2) "Natural deserts are widespread over the surface of the earth. Their extent fluctuated in the Quaternary period but exhibited a general inclination to increase. This is the process of natural desertification of former meadows, prairies, steppes, and alluvial plains." (Kovda, 1980). [Emphasis on geologic time scale phenomena].

(3) "Desertization has been defined as the extension of typical desert landscapes and landforms to areas where they did not occur in the recent past. [. . .] The word desertification has been—and still is—used by many authors to describe degradation of various types and forms of vegetation, including the subhumid and humid forest areas, which have nothing to do with deserts either physically or biologically." (Le Houerou, 1977). [Emphasis on landforms and vegetation].

(4) "Desertification is the diminution or destruction of the biological potential of the land, and can lead ultimately to desert-like conditions. It is an aspect of the widespread deterioration of ecosystems, and has diminished or destroyed the biological potential, i.e. plant and animal production, for multiple use purposes at a time when increased productivity is needed to support growing populations in quest of development." (United Nations, 1978). [Emphasis on economical impacts].

Part of the confusion surrounding the term desertification may come from the fact that other words have been proposed over the years to either replace or overlap with the original one, although the introduction of alternative words may well be a response to the confusion itself.

First, there are expressions like desert encroachment, or intensification of desertlike conditions, which really mean desertification. Other authors seem to prefer different words, like desertization (Le Houerou, 1976), aridization (Kovda, 1980), aridification (MacLeod et al., 1977), xerotisation (Kovda, 1980), sahelisation, or even crypto-desertification (used in the national case study presented by Zaire at the United Nations Conference on Desertification). UNEP also organized a conference on de-desertization in Iran, in 1975.

In addition to these variations in emphasis, there are also very strong divergences about the courses of actions that should be taken. According to the Secretariat of the UNCOD (United Nations, 1977), "Desertification can be halted and ravaged land reclaimed in terms of what is known now.

All that remains is the political will and determination to do it." This may be contrasted with the views of El-Baz who is quoted as saying that most desertification is part of a drying trend that has probably been going on for about 6,000 years, and that it is extremely important not to throw money into trying to reverse an inevitable natural process (Holden, 1979).

Clearly, this concept is being used by different people in different contexts to mean different things. In fact, one could expect that a pastoralist's view of this phenomenon is only remotely connected to that of a minister in charge of economic development. (The former has to survive in this environment!) But even among scientists the meaning given to desertification is often very much dependent on the author's discipline and objectives.

As a result, the literature (not only scientific) contains probably as many "definitions" of desertification as there are authors willing to deal with the subject. This confusion has often been openly expressed; for example, Carder (1981) termed desertification "a muddled concept," Winstanley (1983), earlier in this volume, claims that the "use [of the word desertification] has probably created more problems than it has helped to solve," and El-Baz (1983), also in this volume, even suggests that the word is unnecessary and should not be used at all!

## BEHIND THE CONFUSION, AN EMERGING CONCEPT?

The main points of dispute may, however, be classified into a number of categories, such as:

> Where is desertification taking place: in deserts (Meckelein, 1980), in arid and semiarid regions, as is usually assumed, or even in more humid regions (Aubreville, 1949)?

> How fast is desertification progressing: on geological time scales (El-Baz, 1983), or on the time scale of decades, as implied by the UN Plan of Action to Combat Desertification?

> How can desertification be assessed and measured, and what are the relevant indicators to monitor (Reining, 1978)?

> What are the main factors of desertification, and do these include such processes as waterlogging and salinization, locust plagues, urbanization and industrialization, war, and so forth?

> What are the solutions to desertification: resettling people, technical fixes and technological transfer, legislation and taxation, external aid

from richer countries, or better international relations, to name but a few?

But, by far, the two most controversial disputes are whether desertification is due mainly to human misuse of the natural resources or to climatic variability (or changes), and whether desertification is a reversible or irreversible process. These issues will now be discussed at some length.

Certainly, the opinion that desertification is primarily (if not exclusively) man-made is very common, especially since the UNCOD, and some authors even include it as part of their definition (Garduno, 1977, quoted above). There is little hard evidence on the actual "causes" of desertification (Warren et al., 1977), but there are reasons to believe that some human activities such as agriculture, wood cutting, or even some forms of tourism may have a negative impact on fragile ecosystems.

However, one cannot neglect the evidence that slow climatic changes do modify the location and extent of "natural" deserts. Indeed, abundant evidence exists both from archeology and paleogeomorphology of rather wetter periods in the past. But even if such a climatic shift toward drier conditions is taking place, it must yet be proven that it could explain the accelerated degradation observed over periods of decades.

There are also various nonobjective (and often nonexplicit) reasons for claiming that desertification must be man-made. In particular, if climate were the major cause of desertification, very little could be done about it (except for forecasting climatic fluctuations and trying to minimize their impact), since it is not (yet?) possible to modify intentionally the climate on a regional scale. On the other hand, if desertification results primarily from the impact of individuals and societies on the environment, then some action could be taken to correct the problem and avoid further degradation, although the question of responsibilities must then be addressed.

These questions ought to be approached from an open, if not objective, point of view. This has not really been done, however, perhaps due to the difficulties of designing and implementing interdisciplinary research programs on the appropriate scale, but perhaps also because the implications of the results of such studies are feared. For instance, the mission of the United Nations (and all the Plans of Action to combat desertification, for that matter) should be completely reoriented if desertification were an irreversible natural process.

Of course, what I am saying now is that ideological positions or economic considerations may interfere with the definition of desertification. There is nothing wrong with this: as a matter of fact, most definitions depend heavily on the perception one has of the concept and also the likely use one is going to make of it. But it is important to recognize these preconceptions, in particular to be aware of the limitations of the definition chosen.

How, then, can we approach the problem of desertification? Clearly, the suggestion by El-Baz (1983) to avoid using the term does not help very much. After all, there are other concepts, such as drought, climate, or desert that also suffer from the lack of unique, widely accepted definitions. In fact, what concepts, except perhaps for some purely mathematical ones, actually enjoy the privilege of being indisputably well defined? And who would suggest to forbid the use of the words "climate" or "drought" because the terms are not properly defined?

Furthermore, most important definitions are dynamic; that is, they evolve in time. The very difficulties one experiences with the use of the word desertification may be a necessary prelude to the creation of a new paradigm and the establishment of this issue as a scientific field of its own (see Kuhn, 1970, for a thorough discussion of the emergence of new ideas in science).

It could even be argued that a key word is as necessary to a potentially emerging field of science as a flag is to a newly formed nation: it symbolizes the independence and originality (the existence, one is tempted to say) of the new field. In fact, the battle around the word desertification might be a battle for the establishment of desertification as an acceptable independent field of research (see Odum, 1977, for a very enlightening discussion of the emergence of ecology as an acceptable field of research).

It is too early to say whether this will indeed be the case: a new paradigm must be developed first as a focusing and catalyzing concept. But the publication of one or more specialized journals on desertification in the future might be taken as a possible signal of such a development.

To summarize, the definition of desertification is very much a question of personal perception. And, to a large extent, the disagreements between different authors result from a different choice of definition. The views expressed in this book are no exception to this. In fact, a definition is always, by nature, a conventional starting point: no value may be attached to it and no definition may be claimed to be better than any other, per se. A definition is not true or false: it is a given starting point.

This being so, many different definitions of desertification have been proposed, and it may well be that some of them might be more useful than others for limited groups of users, in specific situations or for particular purposes. Furthermore, the concept of desertification has evolved in time, and will probably continue to do so, as a result of changing perceptions of our environment, progress in various related scientific fields, and so forth. In short, it may not be possible or even desirable to design a unique definition of desertification.

Having shown that the concept of desertification is difficult to handle, and why there are objective as well as nonobjective reasons for the multiplicity of definitions, it remains to give some indications on where to go in the future. This will be achieved in two stages, first by indicating what elements should be included in any definition of desertification in order to make it clear and accurate, and then by raising a few more points in connection with some of the controversies mentioned earlier.

## INGREDIENTS OF A WORKING DEFINITION

Before proceeding further, we note the uselessness of defining desertification, directly or indirectly, in terms of deserts as geographical entities, since this term has also received a number of interpretations from various disciplines. But it is interesting to note that the first meaning of the verb "to desert," in English as well as in French, is "to leave behind," "to go away from." The term desertification might therefore, linguistically, refer to the action of abandoning.

This interpretation is interesting in two respects: first, it clearly represents the deteriorating living conditions of those people actually suffering from desertification (they often have to be moved elsewhere); and, second, the historical evolution of the concept, while following a completely different path, seems to have converged recently (in the post–United Nations Conference on Desertification era) toward such a sociological interpretation (see Mabbutt, 1980, for further discussion of this topic).

Even though it is not feasible to design a definition of desertification that would fit all users and usages, it is possible to identify some of the elements that should be included in any definition to make it clear and unambiguous. In fact, a clear-cut position on each of the disputed points mentioned above would provide a good starting point.

A first important element is the location and spatial extent of the regions considered to be affected by this phenomenon: for example, should it include or exclude deserts themselves, arid, semiarid or subhumid zones, or even other regions. Of course, this is meaningful only if the location and extent of these regions is itself clearly specified, or can be specified with specific indicators.

Another obvious element to include is the period and time scale of interest (when it occurs, and for how long), since some authors use the term for designating the creation of deserts on geological time scales, while others use it exclusively to refer to degradation processes on the time scale of some ten to fifty years.

Equally important is the indication of the exact nature of the concept. While some authors consider desertification to be the root cause of the social, economic, political or ecological problem, others view it as the ultimate consequence or end result of the degradation (as shown graphically by Lamprey, 1978), and yet others, such as the United Nations, refer to it as the process of ecological degradation itself.

And, of course, a working definition should specify whether the main focus is on overgrazing, wood cutting and deforestation, soil erosion, salinization, or any other such factor. It would further clarify the discussion if any factors excluded from the definition were also explicitly mentioned.

The question of reversibility or irreversibility (natural or man-made) should be addressed explicitly, since this has very important consequences on how the problem is approached and solved.

In addition to these characteristics, some other elements of information may help assess the nature and limitations of a particular definition of desertification. For example, specifying the intended user and uses of it will help in understanding the reasons behind the particular choices being made. No less important, at least in the case of a definition to be used as a basis for action, is the target population: again, an official concerned by the progressive deterioration of the economic potential of a region will not address exactly the same problem as an aid organization concerned with the fate of the local population.

The point of all this discussion is that the definition of a concept such as desertification should be tailored to the particular needs of each potential user. It is unreasonable to assume that one can design, promote or even impose a universal definition, because of the divergent opinions and interests of the potential users. But the lack of uniformity should be compensated by very detailed accounts of what is really meant by desertification in each case.

## FURTHER THOUGHTS ON THE DISPUTED POINTS

Due to lack of space, it will not be possible to treat in detail each of the five points mentioned in the earlier section on an emerging concept, but it may be useful to throw out a few ideas, show possible research avenues, and point to the shortcomings of some of the approaches undertaken in the past. Some of the following remarks may seem provocative: they are intended to be so, the objective being to stimulate further discussion.

The question of reversibility or irreversibility has attracted considerable attention. Some authors insist that the term desertification should be restricted to irreversibly damaged situations, to distinguish them from the (presumably) temporary and recoverable ones created by drought. Others will not accept such a restriction, on the grounds that the word should be applicable for designating situations in which something can still be done to alleviate the effects or correct the evolution.

While reversibility is rather well defined as a concept in thermodynamics, its meaning in the present context is less than obvious. In particular, it is not always clear whether this term refers to

> the return to earlier conditions under the influence of natural processes or due to human intervention (and then, how far back);
>
> the recovery of the previous productivity or simply the ability to stop further degradation (reversibility in the trend); or
>
> the economic feasibility of the recovery, as opposed to its theoretical feasibility.

What is often meant by irreversibility is the fact that a particular environment has been degraded to such an extent that it is not economically recoverable, for all practical purposes, on a time scale of a human generation. A given situation may therefore be reversible in some countries and not in others, depending on the available resources, both financial and technological.

This question cannot be discussed meaningfully without a detailed consideration of the processes involved, however. If vegetation has been affected to such an extent that seeds are lacking, it may be possible to set up reseeding projects, and this is actually done in some cases to increase the ratio of palatable species. But there is no way to replace the soil that has been blown away by wind erosion, or to remove most of the salt of salinized agricultural fields.

This discussion of the processes involved shows again the importance of time scales: while plant species can respond to external fluctuations in a matter of days or weeks, the soil properties take much longer to change significantly, with the possible exception of severe cases of soil erosion (Rapp, 1975). With the human component responding on approximately the same time scale as the vegetation (because of the nature of pastoralism and agriculture), it is clear that soil transformations will be responsible for most of the problems of irreversibility.

The nature and some of the reasons of the society versus climate controversy (as an explanation for desertification) have been given above. It should also be pointed out that the discussion is often based on research results from very limited perspectives: for example, much of the climatic impact research so far has been devoted to either the study of long-term variations of past climates (Nicholson and Flohn, 1980, for instance), or to the question, raised by Otterman (1974, 1976) and Charney (1975), of the impact of a change of surface albedo on the local or regional precipitation levels. The importance of these effects has yet to be fully established (Kedar, 1976, Hare, 1977, Idso, 1977, Sagan et al., 1979), but this should not be done at the expense of research in other areas (Verstraete, 1981).

One way to approach the climate versus society problem is to construct "thought" experiments, or, in modern language, to design representative models of the reality and run them under controlled conditions and constraints.

For example, one might wonder whether this planet would suffer from desertification in the absence of man, everything else being the same. The first answer coming to mind might be negative, yet even a cursory study of population dynamics reveals that the population levels in a multispecies environment tend to fluctuate considerably in time, even under moderate environmental forcings. It is therefore conceivable that episodes of overgrazing by wild ungulates would also occur in such a system (as can be observed in National Parks), and that the combination of these events with "natural" droughts would generate episodes of accelerated environmental degradation.

One could also inquire as to what would be the situation if humans had to live under a strictly constant climate, repeating itself exactly from season to season and from year to year. In this case, the climatic factor seems to have vanished completely, and any desertification would have to be attributable unambiguously to man. Yet, it should be noted that since this constant climate would provide no opportunities for natural recovery, any abuse in the exploitation of the resources would translate in a degradation that could only be compensated by further human intervention (irrigation, fertilizers, and so forth).

This consequence implies an important and often overlooked point, namely that climate variability means both "bad" and "good" episodes. Indeed, if the "bad" environmental events are causing trouble, the "good" events not only allow recovery but also promote qualitative jumps forward in growth and development. In fact, the exceptionally good rainfall periods of the fifties and early sixties in the Sahel may have encouraged the growth of the livestock beyond the long-term carrying capacity (Winstanley, 1973).

Of course, a more realistic case study would consider the joint effects of climate variability and human activities on the environment. Now, if this variable climate were perfectly unpredictable, it is probable that, irrespective of the skills, techniques, and technologies developed, desertification would occur sometimes at some places, just because of the fundamental inability to design efficient policies to match the level of exploitation of the natural resources to their intrinsic variability.

In other words, the relative impacts of man and climate on the environment cannot be easily separated or assessed in absolute terms. They are dependent on the nature and intensity of the imposed perturbation, as well as on the sensitivity of the environment to that particular kind of perturbation. And this sensitivity is of course a function, inter alia, of the local climate and of its variability. This brings one back to the very important concepts of equilibrium, stability, and resilience of an ecosystem (Noy-Meir, 1974), or of vulnerability and susceptibility of societies (Timmerman, 1981) to mild or severe external fluctuations.

## CONCLUDING REMARKS

The Earth was once lifeless, and yet living creatures did manage to appear (under the then prevailing conditions) and colonize the whole planet. So on this time scale at least, previous experience tends to show that living organisms can conquer desert areas.

On the other hand, living species have also gone through difficult periods during critical epochs of the Earth's geological history. For example, entire groups of animals, including five orders of reptiles, disappeared at the end of the Cretaceous period (Budyko, 1974): compared to the life span of these creatures, this was a slow but irreversible disappearance. And what if desertification were our present perception of a similar "natural" evolution of this planet? Are we today's dinosaurs?

The "opposition" between society and climate may have been a grossly oversold issue. In many cases, desertification probably results from land uses that are inappropriate in nature, extent, intensity, or timing, considering the past and present climatic and environmental conditions, and their intrinsic variability.

Unfortunately, such a debate also tends to mask some other important questions: for example, which segments of the population are going to suffer from desertification. Clearly, the usually more fragile environment supporting the "lowest" social classes living in poor economic conditions will be more prone to desertification, while the wealthier classes often own not only the most productive resources, but also the financial means to develop them and to cope with degradation if necessary. To put it another way, particular social groups may have few alternatives to survive, given the economic constraints, but to desertify.

What we view, then, as the crucial question facing the atmospheric scientists, and all other nature-oriented scientists as well, is how to develop the knowledge that will be necessary to assess the situation, predict its likely evolution, warn of the probable consequences of human land uses and projects, or alleviate the effects of already ongoing degradation: in short, provide the scientific background on which to base ecologically sound policies and strategies to develop the entire society in a long-term and sustainable way.

This is obviously a very complex process, and since it is going to affect the standards of living, as well as the structure of the society and of the economy, both in the "developed" world and in "developing" countries, an interaction is required between the entire scientific community and the political forces to define the best course of action (Spooner, 1981).

## ACKNOWLEDGMENTS

During the short period available to write this paper, I have benefited from the help and comments of a number of colleagues. Jean Pascal van Ypersele read through my preliminary notes and made significant suggestions as to the structure and content of the paper. Nuzhet Dalfes and Sharon Nicholson made very constructive comments on the first draft. Diana Liverman then helped me to turn the second draft into a presentable paper, both by raising new issues, improving the language, and providing further references. Finally, William Kellogg, Linda Mearns, and Robert Dickinson helped me in polishing up the paper to its present form. Many thanks again to all of them.

## REFERENCES

Aubreville, A. (1949) *Climats, Forets et Desertification de l'Afrique Tropicale*. Societe d'Editions Geographiques, Maritimes et Coloniales, Paris.

Biswas, Margaret R. (1978) U.N. Conference on Desertification, in *Retrospect, Environmental Conservation*, Vol. 5, No. 4, pp. 247–262.

Brown, Lester R. (1981) "World Population Growth, Soil Erosion, and Food Security," *Science*, Vol. 214, pp. 995–1002.

Budyko, M. I. (1974) *Climate and Life*. Academic Press.

Carder, D. J. (1981) "Desertification in Australia—A Muddled Concept," *Search*, Vol. 12, No. 7, pp. 217–221.

Charney, Jule (1975) "Dynamics of Deserts and Droughts in the Sahel," in *The Physical Basis of Climate and Climate Modelling*, GARP Publications Series, No. 16, WMO, Geneva, pp. 171–176.

El-Baz, Farouk (1983) "A Geological Perspective of the Desert." Chapter 7 in this volume.

Garcia, Rolando V. (1981) *Drought and Man: The 1972 Case History, Volume 1: Nature Pleads Not Guilty*. Pergamon Press.

Garduno, Manuel Anaya (1977) "Technology and Desertification," in *Desertification: its Causes and Consequences*, edited by the Secretariat of the UNCOD, Pergamon Press, pp. 319–448.

Glantz, Michael H., ed. (1977) *Desertification: Environmental Degradation in and around Arid Lands*. Westview Press.

Glantz, Michael H. (1977a) "The U.N. and Desertification: Dealing with a Global Problem," in *Desertification: Environmental Degradation in and around Arid Lands*, ed. M. Glantz, Westview Press, pp. 1–15.

——— (1977b) "Climate and Weather Modification in and around Arid Lands in Africa," in *Desertification: Environmental Degradation in and around Arid Lands*, ed. M. Glantz, Westview Press, pp. 307–337.

Hare, F. Kenneth (1977) "Climate and Desertification," in *Desertification: its Causes and Consequences*, edited by the Secretariat of the UNCOD, Pergamon Press, pp. 63–167.

Holden, Constance (1979) "Egyptian Geologist Champions Desert Research," *Science*, Vol. 205, pp. 1357–1360.

Idso, S. B. (1977) "A Note on Some Recently Proposed Mechanisms of Genesis of Deserts," *Quarterly Journal of the Royal Meteorological Society*, Vol. 103, pp. 369–370.

Kates, Robert W., Douglas L. Johnson and Kirsten Johnson Haring (1977) "Population, Society and Desertification," in *Desertification: its Causes and Consequences*, edited by the Secretariat of the UNCOD, Pergamon Press, pp. 261–317.

Kedar, Ervin Y. (1976) "No Desertification Mechanism," *Science*, Vol. 194, pp. 747–748.

Kovda, Victor A. (1980) *Land Aridization and Drought Control*. Westview Press.

Kuhn, Thomas S. (1970) *The Structure of Scientific Revolutions*. Second Edition, University of Chicago Press.

Lamprey, Hugh (1978) "The Integrated Project on Arid Lands (IPAL)," *Nature and Resources*, Vol. XIV, No. 4, p. 2.

Lappe, Frances Moore, and Joseph Collins (1977) *Food First, Beyond the Myth of Scarcity*. Houghton Mifflin.

Le Houerou, H. N. (1959) *Recherches Ecologiques et Floristiques sur la Vegetation de la Tunisie Meridionale*. Alger, Institut de Recherches Sahariennes de l'Universite.

——— (1976) "Etudes Regionales et Propositions de Developpement: 3. Tunisie," in *Peut-on arreter l'extension des deserts? Une etude plus particulierement axee sur l'Afrique*, ed. A. Rapp, H. N. Le Houerou and B. Lundholm, Ecological Bulletins, No. 24, pp. 133–141.

——— (1977) "The Nature and Causes of Desertization," in *Desertification: Environmental Degradation in and around Arid Lands*, ed. M. Glantz, Westview Press, pp. 17–38.

Lockeretz, William (1978) "The Lessons of the Dust Bowl," *American Scientist*, Vol. 66, No. 5, pp. 560–569.

Mabbutt, J. A. (1980) *Desertification in Australia*. Water Research Foundation of Australia Report No. 54.

MacLeod, N. H., J. S. Schubert and P. Anaejionu (1977) "Report on the Skylab 4 African Drought and Arid Lands Experiment, Chapter 10" in *Skylab Explores the Earth*, NASA Publication SP-380, pp. 263–286.

Meckelein, Wolfgang, ed. (1980) *Desertification in Extremely Arid Environments*. Stuttgarter Geographische Studien, Band 95.

Morentz, James W. (1980) "Communication in the Sahel Drought: Comparing the Mass Media with Other Channels of International Communication," in *Disasters and the Mass Media*, National Academy of Sciences.

Newell, Reginald, Minoru Tanaka, and Bijoy Misra (1976) "Climate and Food Workshop: A Report," *Bulletin of the American Meteorological Society*, Vol. 57, No. 2, p. 192–198.

Nicholson, Sharon E., and Herman Flohn (1980) "African Environmental and Climatic Changes and the General Atmospheric Circulation in Late Pleistocene and Holocene," *Climatic Change*, Vol. 2, pp. 313–348.

Nicholson, Sharon E. (1981) "Rainfall and Atmospheric Circulation during Drought Periods and Wetter Years in West Africa," *Monthly Weather Review*, Vol. 109, pp. 2191–2208.

Noy-Meir, I. (1974) *Stability in Arid Ecosystems and the Effects of Man on It*. Proceedings of the First International Congress of Ecology, The Hague, Netherlands, September

8–14, 1974, Centre for Agricultural Publishing and Documentation, Wageningen, pp. 220–225.

Odum, Eugene P. (1977) "The Emergence of Ecology as a New Integrative Discipline," *Science*, Vol. 195, pp. 1289–1293.

Otterman, Joseph (1974) "Baring High-Albedo Soils by Overgrazing: A Hypothesized Desertification Mechanism," *Science*, Vol. 186, pp. 531–533.

——— (1976) "Reply to Kedar (1976)," *Science*, Vol. 194, pp. 748–749.

Rapp, Anders (1975) "Soil Erosion and Sedimentation in Tanzania and Lesotho," *Ambio*, Vol. 4, No. 4, pp. 154–163.

Reining, Priscilla (1978) *Handbook on Desertification Indicators based on the Science Associations' Nairobi Seminar on Desertification*. American Association for the Advancement of Science.

Renault-Benmiloud, Michele (1980) *Pastoralisme, Domination Coloniale et Desertification de la Steppe Algerienne, Production Pastorale et Societe*. Bulletin de l'Equipe Ecologie et Anthropologie des Societes Pastorales, Supplement a MSH-Informations, No. 6, pp. 12–20.

Sagan, Carl, Owen B. Toon, and James B. Pollack (1979) "Anthropogenic Albedo Changes and the Earth's Climate," *Science*, Vol. 206, pp. 1363–1368.

Simon, Julian L. (1980) "Resources, Population, Environment: An Oversupply of False Bad News," *Science*, Vol. 208, pp. 1431–1437.

Spooner, Brian (1981) "The Significance of Desertification," in *Global Aspects of Food Production*, ed. M. S. Swaminathan and S. K. Sinha, Academic Press.

Stebbing, E. P. (1935) "The Encroaching Sahara," *Geographical Journal*, Vol. 86, No. 5, pp. 509–510.

——— (1938) "The Man-made Desert in Africa," *Journal of the Royal African Society*, Supplement, Vol. 37, No. 146, January, p. 13.

Timmerman, Peter (1981) *Vulnerability, Resilience and the Collapse of Society: A Review of Models and Possible Climatic Applications*. Environmental Monograph No. 1, Institute for Environmental Studies, University of Toronto.

United Nations (1977) *Desertification: Its Causes and Consequences*. Compiled and edited by the Secretariat of the United Nations Conference on Desertification, Nairobi, Pergamon Press.

——— (1978) *United Nations Conference on Desertification, Round-Up, Plan of Action and Resolutions*. New York.

Verstraete, Michel M. (1981) "Some Impacts of Desertification Processes on the Local and Regional Climate," in *Climatic Variations and Variability: Facts and Theories*, ed. A. Berger, D. Reidel.

——— (1983) *The United Nations Organization and the Issue of Desertification*. Proceedings of the Workshop on the Physics of Desertification held at the International Centre for Theoretical Physics in Trieste, Italy, November 1980.

Warren, Andrew, and Judith K. Maizels (1977) "Ecological Change and Desertification," in *Desertification: its Causes and Consequences*, edited by the Secretariat of the UNCOD, Pergamon Press, pp. 169–260.

Warren, Andrew (1978) *Conference Reports: United Nations Desertification Conference*, *Disasters*, Vol. 2, No. 1, pp. 27–28.

Winstanley, Derek (1973) "Rainfall Patterns and General Atmospheric Circulation," *Nature*, Vol. 245, pp. 190–194.

——— (1976) "Climatic Changes and the Future of the Sahel," in *The Politics of Natural Disaster: The Case of the Sahel Drought*, ed. M. Glantz, Praeger Publishers, pp. 189–213.

——— (1983) "Desertification: A Climatological Perspective." Chapter 8 in this volume.